D0948777

Front Page Economics

Front Page Economics

GERALD D. SUTTLES
WITH MARK D. JACOBS

THE UNIVERSITY OF CHICAGO PRESS   CHICAGO AND LONDON

GERALD SUTTLES is best known for his urban studies while at the University of Chicago. During the many years he was there he helped train a number of graduate students in ethnographic methods. Many of those students are now among the best-known sociologists. Suttles is now retired as an adjunct professor at Indiana University.

The University of Chicago Press, Chicago 60637
The University of Chicago Press, Ltd., London
© 2010 by The University of Chicago
All rights reserved. Published 2010
Printed in the United States of America
20 19 18 17 16 15 14 13 12 11 10   1 2 3 4 5

ISBN-13: 978-0-226-78198-3 (cloth)
ISBN-10: 0-226-78198-4 (cloth)

Library of Congress Cataloging-in-Publication Data

Suttles, Gerald D.
    Front page economics / Gerald D. Suttles ; with Mark D. Jacobs.
        p.   cm.
    Includes bibliographical references and index.
    ISBN-13: 978-0-226-78198-3 (cloth : alk. paper)
    ISBN-10: 0-226-78198-4 (cloth : alk. paper)   1. Financial crises—Press coverage.
2. Business cycles—Press coverage.   3. Economics—Public opinion.   4. Economics—
Sociological aspects.   5. Mass media and public opinion.   6. Stock Market Crash,
1987—Press coverage.   7. Stock Market Crash, 1929—Press coverage.   8. Global
Financial Crisis, 2008–2009—Press coverage.   I. Jacobs, Mark D., 1947-   II. Title.
    HB3722.S888 2010
    330.973—dc22

                                                                        2009038348

♾ The paper used in this publication meets the minimum requirements of the American National Standard for Information Sciences—Permanence of Paper for Printed Library Materials, ANSI Z39.48-1992.

Contents

Foreword by Mark D. Jacobs   vii

Acknowledgments   xvii

PART I.   **The Social Construction of the Economy: 1929 and 1987**

CHAPTER 1.   The Daily Press and Our Collective Conscience   3

CHAPTER 2.   The Grounding of the Economy   16

PART II.   **The Daily Dramatism of Economic News**

CHAPTER 3.   The News as Figurative Narratives   45

CHAPTER 4.   Personae and Their Purposes   72

CHAPTER 5.   Wordscapes and Toonland   88

PART III.   **The Telling of the Great Crashes**

CHAPTER 6.   The Annual Business Cycle and Its Promoters   115

CHAPTER 7.   The Voice of the People   136

CHAPTER 8.   Congress and the Courts Have Their Say   153

PART IV.   **The Transformation of Ideology**

CHAPTER 9.   Normalizing the Economy: Popular Ideology and Social Regulation   187

Methodological Appendix   197

Notes   211

Works Cited   229

Index   241

Foreword

Four decades ago, in his classic work *The Social Order of the Slum*, Gerald Suttles revealed how residents of Chicago's Addams neighborhood navigated the dangerous uncertainties of their local streets by forming cognitive maps of their defended communities within the broader context of the surrounding city. The press contributed to the problems of social control in that neighborhood by emphasizing its dangers.

In *Front Page Economics*, Suttles turns his attention from urban sociology to economic sociology. How, during the crises of 1929 and 1987, did people navigate the dangerous uncertainties of the marketplace? The press contributed to these problems, too, but by downplaying the dangers rather than by emphasizing them. Once again, confronting situations of "limited liability," individuals took recourse in the formation of cognitive maps—this time in the form of economic *wordscapes* within their broader societal contexts, rather than urban landscapes.

In the intervening decades, Suttles's methodological approach has retained its power to redirect fields of inquiry. Suttles rethinks the nature of problems from the ground up, by painstakingly assembling elementary bits of evidence and fitting them into larger patterns of meaning, ambiguity, and social action. In *The Social Order of the Slum*, those bits of evidence consist of pedestrian paths, places for gossip, terms of slang, styles of clothing, and inventive arrangements for sharing the central playing field throughout the temporal cycle. In *Front Page Economics*, they consist of the temporal cycle of article frequencies, the personae of the reporters, images of political cartoons, the characters, storylines, and the changing discourse of newspaper articles. Suttles literally spent years in the musty microfiche room of the Chicago Public Library, plumbing the language of decades of daily newspaper coverage.

In the earlier book, Suttles recast the very research problems of urban ethnography. Before Suttles, scholars had debated whether the subcultures of urban youth gangs were oppositional or integrative. As Suttles demonstrated, they were, rather, *provincial*; to the denizens of the Addams area, central societal values were primarily irrelevant to the challenges of their daily lives. How can social control be locally grounded in particularistic rather than universalistic standards of conduct? In his hard-nosed focus on the empirical evidence, Suttles solved the core ethnographic challenge of achieving empathy with his subjects without romanticizing them, and in so doing vastly expanded our conception of social control.

In the current book, Suttles recasts our very conception of economics. Economic life too, of course, poses challenges of social control. Suttles observes that the business press routinely assumes a role of crowd control, reassuring a nervous public in the face of bad economic news. This book subverts the accepted notion that scandals are manufactured by the sensationalism of the press; in most cases, as Suttles suggests, the press normalizes rather than sensationalizes misconduct. Above all, however, this book demonstrates that economic *science* is hardly scientific. The core metaphors of economic discourse are changeable in subliminal ways. What do we even mean when we speak of *the economy*?

In retrospect, *The Social Order of the Slum* was a landmark not only of urban sociology but of the sociology of culture as well. The term *sociology of culture* hardly existed when that book appeared; it was not until 1987 that the American Sociological Association approved the establishment of a Culture section. Although Clifford Geertz had started publishing the essays that came to mark the "cultural turn" in sociology (and other disciplines) as early as the 1960s, it was not until 1973—five years after Suttles's book—that Geertz's *The Interpretation of Cultures* appeared. Before then, "culture" was treated largely as a matter of the societal values and norms at the heart of the various grand and middle-range functionalisms that dominated the discipline. Yet the conclusion of *The Social Order of the Slum* anticipates by some two decades cultural sociology's "discovery" of cognition as analytically prior to morality. In Suttles's formulation, "the subcultural commonalities of the Addams area consist primarily of a selective search for private information rather than the invention of normative ideals" (1968, 232). Despite the momentous theoretical implications of this claim, Suttles presents it (in characteristically understated fashion) as simply an empirical finding.

Front Page Economics also stakes new directions in the sociology of culture. Economic collapse destroys established understandings and expectations, creating what Geertz calls a need "to render otherwise incomprehensible social situations meaningful, to so construe them as to make it possible to act purposefully within them." In other words, the uncertainty produced by economic collapse calls out the search for "maps of problematic social reality and matrices for the creation of collective conscience" (1973, 220).

Geertz's words could serve as well—on a general level—as a guide for Suttles's inquiries. But because Suttles's work is more methodical than Geertz's, it achieves a programmatic value often missing from studies of culture. Suttles reconstructs maps of problematic social reality by tracking metaphors, narratives, and *dramatisms* through his exhaustive review of news coverage. He brings to life the operation of Kenneth Burke's pentad—act, actor, agency, scene, purpose—in the day-to-day life of business. He traces the mutual embeddedness of the related discourses of professional economists, reporters, businesspersons, politicians, prosecutors, and the public at large.

But in economic life as well as in urban street life, the first question Suttles has us ask is "where are we?" This must precede any discussion of economic relations or business ethics. And it demonstrates the uncanny *timeliness* of Suttles's work. This manuscript was completed well before the Great Stock Market Crash of 2008. It was intended primarily as a reflection on studying social cognition. Yet it turns out to have great practical relevance as an intellectual portal to exploration of the current global economic crisis. I will try to demonstrate this briefly in the following pages by extending Suttles's line of inquiry from 1929 and 1987 to 2008.

Missing the Signs of Economic Collapse

As early as 2003, the legendary investor Warren Buffett had issued apocalyptic warnings that derivatives were "financial weapons of mass destruction." In the summer of 2004, former U.S. Fed chairman Paul Volcker claimed that "there's a 75 percent chance of a financial crisis in the next five years." In prose drafted in late 2007, when the Dow was at an all-time high, the financier George Soros asserted that "we are in the midst of the worst financial crisis since the 1930s" (2008). All these prophecies were widely reported in the press. Although many if not most business reporters on cable television operated as shills for Wall Street, priming the stock market and housing bubbles with their boosterism, the corps of business reporters in the *New York Times* and other serious newspapers soberly assessed the perilous state of the economy for years before the great crash of 2008.

Why, then, did the recent global stock market crash come as such a surprise? The widely proffered explanation, that some mix of greed, folly, and corruption was secretly operating on Wall Street on an unprecedented scale, is at best only partial. The claim is in a certain sense comforting, since it implicitly exculpates the wider public from failures of commonsense prudence. Yet the history of greed, folly, and corruption on Wall Street is a long one. And given that famous investors and the business pages of leading newspapers had long warned of the specific financial risks that have now come to pass, there had to be a form of denial at work, constituted in part by a loss of collective memory. Although the events of 2008 recapitulate in essential respects those of 1929 and 1987, why even to this day have financial actors and wider publics repressed the memories of those earlier great crashes?

Culture and Cognition

One reason has to do with the culture of scandal, as part of a larger form of social disorganization that I have called (at the suggestion of Gerry Suttles) the "no-fault society." The three dimensions of the no-fault society—constrictive individualism, blurring of "public" and "private," and laxity of the rule of law—encourage practices of contentious evasion by parties with shared responsibilities of all sorts, making it difficult to enforce (or even conceive) accountability for failure (Jacobs 1990). I have applied this perspective to explain the relative lack of scandal surrounding the U.S. savings and loan crisis that surfaced in the late 1980s. For the most part, societal reactions only normalize patterns of underlying corruption. Full-blown scandals erupt only from dramas of cover-up and revelation that eventuate in the discovery of "smoking guns." What we remember are those dramas, rather than the states of ongoing corruption. "The hollowing out of our collective memory of scandal shapes the dramatization of subsequent scandals. . . . Scandals that become sensationalized . . . divert attention from those that do not, and trivialize subsequent scandals that do" (Jacobs 2005, 378).

Another reason is that new situations are unrecognizable as repetitions of older ones. The "facts" of the still-unfolding financial crisis echo those of past crises: market bubbles leading to credit squeezes; absurdly leveraged risk; regulators missing in action; foreclosures, bankruptcies, and failures; bank runs; "bear rallies"; suspicions of short-sellers; bailouts; banks "too big to fail"; privatizing profits while socializing risks. But the *form* of factual accounts always emerges from the *ground* of figuration. And in perhaps the most fundamental respect—the very conception of what an economy is—the figurative ground shifted architectonically from 1929 to 1987 to 2008.

Thus Wall Street, Main Street, and Capitol Hill missed the clear warnings in large part for reasons of culture and cognition. Cognitive frames are made of mnemonic stuff and provide the stuff of memory. Just as our economy and ecology create the limiting conditions for our culture (as Marshall Sahlins [1976] has convincingly argued), our culture provides the very categories for understanding—and remembering—our economic and ecological choices. Culture may be conceived as the medium of lived experience through which we conduct our everyday life (economic and otherwise). As Suttles demonstrates, we can capture the texture of that medium by making explicit the figurational basis of the language of economics, and the dramatistic forms of the economic narratives we construe. In this way, apparently abstruse types of literary analysis have urgent practical economic significance.

Lagged Shifts in the Figurative Ground

In comparing newspaper coverage and more general public understanding of the two greatest crashes of the last century (in 1929 and 1987), Suttles discovers that the modern usage of the word *economy* (as a system of production, consumption, and exchange) did not even exist in 1929. Indeed, according to his revealing linguistic research, *economy* did not assume its modern usage until John Maynard Keynes introduced it in 1934. (It is relevant to my larger argument that within two years of coining that usage, Keynes also found it necessary to issue a warning—which went largely ignored—against running the economy as a "casino.") Discursively then, the 1929 crash was a matter not of the "economy," but only of "the business." The social landscape of business was conceived according to the metaphor of nature—a sphere of activity naturally occurring and naturally self-correcting. By contrast, by 1987, the social landscape of the economy was conceived largely according to the metaphor of a machine, amenable to social engineering. But it was a compound metaphor: perhaps as a vestige of the earlier metaphor grounded in the figuration of nature, the economy was also conceived to be "sick," in need of therapeutic intervention.

In an effort to extend Suttles's analysis, I have used a series of Lexis-Nexis searches to trace the frequency and usage of various keywords in the *New York Times*'s financial reportage of recent years. Replicating his method of tracing figuration and dramatisms in this coverage helps us understand the cognitive frameworks contributing to today's crisis. Since the crisis became evident, the figurative grounding of the economy has been shifting yet again. But as William Ogburn's old theory of cultural lag would suggest, the process of adapting this conceptualization remains lagged. Like the proverbial military strategists, financial analysts always seem to be preparing to address the last crisis.

In 1987, the economy was viewed as if it were a "marvelous machine," although a "sick" one. Those images would have made better sense of the 1929 crisis than the ones available at the time. But by 1987, the "machine" was no longer "marvelous": a significant portion of economic activity was taking the form of "cash for trash," "daisy-chain land flips," and "busting out" banks. The combination of unlawful risk-taking, collective embezzlement, and cover-up suggested that a more apt image of the economy was that of the casino (Calavita and Pontrell 1999). One of the best accounts of the transformation of the economy over the past quarter century was given by the deconstructionist art critic Mark Taylor: "By the 1980s, the combination of deregulation and privatization as well as new technologies, financial instruments, and markets had turned Wall Street into a casino" (2004, 174).

A Casino Economy?

The term *casino economy* never gained much currency in the United States, despite the relevance it has had to this day. *Business Week* published the cover story "The Casino Society" in September 1985, leading with an epigram from Keynes: "When the capital development of a country becomes a byproduct of the activities of a casino, the job is likely to be ill-done." Michael Lewis used the phrase in his best-selling exposé *Liar's Poker* (1989); the criminologists Kitty Calavita and Henry Pontell used it during the 1990s in a series of scholarly articles and books about the savings and loan crisis. But the phrase doesn't appear in the news pages of the *New York Times* until 2009, except in articles reporting anger in the United Kingdom, France, and Germany over the importation of irresponsible U.S.-style financial speculation. The *Los Angeles Times*, as reported by Calavita and Pontell, quoted (on October 26, 1989) a Nobel Prize–winning French sociologist, Maurice Allais, using the term to refer to the pursuit of windfall profits from speculative wagers rather than from the production and sales of goods and services.

Suttles's comparison of the investigations and prosecutions of wrongdoing in 1929 and 1987 suggests one reason why the casino metaphor never made it into the civic consciousness. The widely publicized Pecora hearings exposed the collusion of politicians and bankers in the reckless speculation and looting that preceded the Great Depression. The skillfully elicited revelations spun a convincing—and memorable—dramatism of a "web of influence" that exposed the systemic nature of the corruption and led to legislative reform. This dramatism emerged, however, before the economy could even be conceived as a system. By contrast, the hearings and trials of the late 1980s focused on exposing the wrongdoing of particular individuals, diverting attention from the systemic character of the financial corruption.

Spreading Virally through the Shadow Banking System

Although the image never gained widespread traction, the casino economy has over the past quarter century further attenuated sound economic practice, to the point of creating what Mark Taylor calls the "spectral economy." Wall Street investment banks exploited downturns in the academic marketplace to recruit PhD mathematicians and physicists ("quants") to produce computer-designed financial instruments so abstract and abstruse that they could not be fully explained discursively. Until they started to unwind, these derivatives, collateralized debt obligations, credit default swaps, and other undecipherable instruments seemed to generate unheard-of profits—even though economic exchanges had lost their materiality and the money exchanged electronically had become an empty signifier. As I write this, the Obama bank bailout plan has been delayed because the best political, financial, and economic experts cannot even agree on a method to start valuing the "toxic assets" on the books of financial institutions around the world that represent the fallout of this spectral economy. Again, the deconstructionist Taylor provided the clearest economic explanation of what was to come:

> With the fever of speculation spreading, new products and the investment strategies with which they were traded created a crisis in which more and more financial assets rested on a dwindling collateral base. As derivatives became more abstract and the mathematical formulas for the trading programs more complex, markets began to lose contact with anything resembling the real economy. To any rational investor, it should have been clear that markets were becoming a precarious Ponzi scheme. Contrary to expectation, products originally developed to manage risk increased market volatility and thus intensified the very uncertainty investors were trying to avoid. (2004, 8)

The "shadow" or "stealth" banking, financial, and credit systems consist of the complex of unregulated, secretive institutions—including divisions of certain investment banks, hedge funds, private equity funds, insurance companies, special purpose vehicles, offshore banks, and the like— that have engaged in intangible financial speculation rather than genuine investment. Yet it is only since 2008 that the *New York Times* has called the shadow economy by name, even though those institutions have been recklessly leveraging risk for decades. The spectral economy has been hiding in plain sight.

The vicissitudes of the applying a *virus* metaphor to the economy provide yet another example of cultural lag in comprehending the full dimensions of economic transformation. A LexisNexis search of the *New York Times* confirms Suttles's claim that in the 1980s, economic problems were figuratively represented as a form of "illness." Thus, addressing the nation about economic worries in October 1982, Ronald Reagan said, "Inflation is like a virus in the economic bloodstream, sometimes dormant and sometimes active, but leaving the patient weaker after each attack." In those days, the metaphor of the virus was reassuring, since viruses were routine and passing. A few months after Reagan's speech, for example, the vice president of American Express attempted to calm jitters about a relatively large stock market decline by declaring that the market had "only a 24-hour virus."

But since the 1980s, certain viruses have become deadly, and the metaphorical uses of that term have assumed apocalyptic connotations. The most frequent use of *virus* in the pages of the *New York Times* occurred in connection with AIDS. There were also frequent uses connected to SARS and the avian flu. Articles warned not only of the global spread of these viruses themselves but also of their economic impacts. The late 1980s saw the emergence of the "computer virus"; by the late 1990s the information technology departments of large corporations around the globe were working in full crisis mode to mitigate the catastrophe anticipated from the "millennium virus." After 9/11, there were widespread fears of cyberattacks in the form of computer viruses. By 2008, the metaphorical "virus" said to be affecting the economy had been transmuted from something routine, contained, and passing into a virulent lethal pandemic. And the word *virus* had developed a new association with the instability of computer systems.

This new figuration is evident in the heart of a summative analysis by Gretchen Morgenson, the *New York Times*'s chief investigative financial reporter, on September 28, 2008:

> Although America's housing collapse is often cited as having caused the crisis, the system was vulnerable because of intricate financial contracts known as credit derivatives, which insure debt holders against default. They are fashioned privately and beyond the ken of regulators—sometimes even beyond the understanding of executives peddling them.
>
> Originally intended to diminish risk and spread prosperity, these inventions instead magnified the impact of bad mortgages like the ones that felled Bear Stearns and Lehman and now threaten the entire economy.
>
> In the case of A.I.G., the *virus* exploded from a freewheeling little 377-person unit in London, and flourished in a climate of opulent pay, lax oversight, and blind faith in financial risk models. It nearly decimated one of the world's most admired companies, a seemingly sturdy insurer with a trillion-dollar balance sheet, 116,000 employees and operations in 130 countries. [italics added]

The title of this article captures Morgenson's image of the economy: "a web of risk."

The Economy as Information System

The set of metaphors that newspapers are starting to use in describing the present crisis indicate the most recent shift in the figurative ground of conceiving the economy. The economy is something that *crashes* when credit *freezes*, as the virtual or *shadow* banking system is disabled by a *virus* spreading in real time along the pathways of global *networks*. The economy is metaphorically becoming an information system. Its core is being transformed into the vulnerable, digital infrastructure of the global trading network. Of course the economy remains a compound metaphor, retaining vestiges of previous usages. When we speak of the "business cycle," we are alluding to its grounding in the figuration of nature; when we speak of "jump-starting" the economy, we are alluding to the figuration of the machine. It was not until the present crisis that we started thinking of the economy primarily as a computer network. Although the press covered the contrarian warnings of Buffett, Volcker, and Soros, among others, the warnings could not gain public traction because not just their substance but also their mnemonic frames were too dissonant from the emergent practice. We could not see the impending malfunctions in part because we were looking for problems of a natural or mechanical sort. We feel as helpless in the face of this economic crisis as when our computer starts emitting inscrutable error messages, or when we lose Internet access, or when we can't get the system to reboot. What we need to start watching out for is not so much cyberattacks or fatal system errors as the spread of online gambling by speculators posing as institutional investors, playing by their own house rules.

Mark D. Jacobs
April 2009

Acknowledgments

This book began one day at the University of Chicago when Morris Janowitz came into my office, plopped a manuscript down on my desk and said, "Here, you are probably the only one interested in this. Read it and work with him." Morris knew his health was rapidly declining and that he might not last through another dissertation, especially one as original as Mark Jacobs's, eventually published as *Screwing the System and Making It Work*. It was a fascinating study of how social workers explain their failures and yet go on to the next case. What they said to themselves and others, however, was a narrative story that more nearly resembled a piece of literature than something they might have learned during their training as social workers. Jacobs turned to literary critics, especially Northrop Frye, to reveal how their stories conformed to a narrative form that restored order and necessity to their failures.

Like Morris, I saw in this approach a methodology that would go well beyond content analysis and ad hoc coding systems in the study of texts and speech. The approach was not entirely new. I had encountered it in the work of my teachers Joe Gusfield and Bernie Farber, and I am indebted to both, especially Joe, who gave a close reading to the first draft of *Front Page Economics*. Michael Schudson also read that draft and provided many helpful suggestions.

Having moved to Indiana University, I have had the good fortune to meet Doug Maynard, who let me sit in on his class on conversation analysis. David Nord also graciously allowed me to sit in on his journalism course. Nord's work figures prominently in this study, and I am indebted to his knowledge of how journalists are themselves aware of the role of figurative language in their work.

Since first reading *Screwing the System and Making It Work* I have learned a lot more from Mark Jacobs. He provided a critical review of two separate drafts of *Front Page Economics*, and practically every page has been improved by his reviews. I would have made him coauthor, but he refused.

My wife, Kirsten Gronbjerg, also read the early drafts and made many suggestions that improved the study. Her patience with my unfriendly relation to computers also comes close to sainthood. I would like also to thank Doug Mitchell, who has shepherded this manuscript through its many reviews at the University of Chicago Press. Those who know Doug or the University of Chicago Press will also know how important he has been to guiding authors and reviewers in the publication of works of sociology. He has held us to a standard that we can be proud of. Finally, the drawings in book are not my own but those of the young, talented artist Mike Mannery.

PART I

The Social Construction
of the Economy: 1929 and 1987

CHAPTER ONE

The Daily Press and Our Collective Conscience

The genre of journalism is almost by definition incoherent. It is a daily sampling of a rushing flow of occurrences and observations, which has no beginning and no end. Readers must find (create, actually) coherence through connection, interpolation, and inference (Nord 2001, 74).

The elementary definition of metaphor (and metonym) from which we should work is the predication of a sign-image upon an inchoate subject. The first mission of metaphor is to provide identity for such subjects (Fernandez 1986, 31). We are, indeed, "time binders" concerned to find the kind of identity and activity that will concretize the inchoate, fill the frame in which we find ourselves, and bind the past and the future together (ibid., 45).

How do readers and journalists create coherence from this rushing flow of occurrences? How is it that they rescue the specious present from the appearance of accident and remake it into necessity? How do they weigh these occurrences and measure the emotional impact aimed at their readers? Do readers and journalists simply go their separate way, one reading and the other writing? Or, are they assisted by a kind of shared word magic that remakes the news into a recognizable, plausible and, perhaps, a reassuring story?

This book explores these questions by reviewing in some detail the rhetoric used in the *Chicago Tribune*'s news on the American economy in 1929 and 1987. Many readers will recognize 1929 as the year of the great stock market crash. Many will have forgotten the 1987 crash. The 1929 crash was the big one in our collective memory while the 1987 one is quite forgettable. Yet, there are strong similarities between them.

Why do they remain so different in our collective memory? What kind of news accompanied each and how did it contribute to this difference in our collective memory? What can it tell us about how editors, journalists, and their informants regulated reader response in two extended periods of crisis?

The choice of the *Tribune* is largely a personal one. I once knew some of its journalists and have been reading the *Tribune* for the last forty years. But it could be justified on other grounds. In 1929, the *Tribune* had the largest circulation of any paper in the country, and it was still among the top newspapers in circulation in 1987. For balance (a word from the journalist's lexicon), I have made extensive comparisons with the *New York Times*. Both papers were proprietary in 1929 and by 1987 they still took a clearer stand on the economy and polity than the noncommittal language of, say, the Associated Press. If "mainstream" journalists had any kind of word magic, a wide sample should be found in the 1929 and 1987 *Times* and *Tribune*. (See the Methodological Appendix for further details.)

Nineteen twenty-nine and 1987 are also apt choices because there was a lot of economic news in both years and journalists got a workout with whatever word magic they had. In both years widespread alarm was feared and journalists were openly called upon to help manage public reaction. Thus, each year provides a rich sample of the journalists' rhetorical skills and their responsibilities in good times, really great times, and very, very bad times.

Another thing that makes the periods interesting is that the discipline of economics underwent a revolution after 1929 and the newspapers followed with a revolution in reporting that change. In 1929 the economy had belonged to the businessman, and he (all of them were "he's") was the journalist's informant and fellow linguist. By the 1940s, however, the discipline of economics provided a new informant, primarily the bank or brokerage economist who pushed aside the businessman's rhetoric. The rhetoric that followed, however, was neither that of academic economics nor one devised only by journalists.

Of course, this change in rhetoric did not occupy the entire period between 1929 and 1987; it was completely over by 1940. But the story of how this change occurred step by step and became standardized would be incomplete without a comparison of the rhetorics and their broader implications by 1987. The business world of 1929 was conceived as a work of nature, regulated by its own invisible parts. By the 1940s it was a man-made engine that raised the unsettling questions of who owns it, who runs it, who repairs it, and who sacrifices for it in return. During each crisis, however, rhetorical resources were called upon to legitimate prior and subsequent economic arrangements while normalizing novel responses to the crisis. To foreshadow some of the rhetorical problems presented by these crises the chapter following this one focuses on the rhetorical problems that were posed by the fundamental change following the 1929 crisis and what I call the "grounding of the economy" as a man-made reality by the late 1930s.

While this book focuses primarily on journalistic rhetoric it follows a sequence of steps that progressively trace this rhetoric through each market crash, the advice of the experts and presidents, and the readers' responses to each crisis of confidence. I then turn to the scandals and legislation that followed each crash, our collective memory of each crash, and, finally, how the rhetoric of popular economics is embedded in our collective memory.

This order of inquiry may seem to wander at times but it really tries to stitch together a series of findings that are treated separately in synchronic media studies. It is, then, a *natural history* of two big news stories and the journalists', experts', politicians', and readers' changing rhetorical resources in managing each crisis.

Ideology and Rhetoric

In 1929 and 1987, journalists, experts, presidents, and readers were drawn into the newspapers in strikingly different ways. But in both years they were very similar in adopting a persuasive rhetoric rather than merely a technical or descriptive vocabulary. I should pause here, however, to say that I do not consider rhetoric, ideology, or political persuasion as mere deception. Some kind of worldview, Weltanschauung, or Cosmopolis that goes beyond established knowledge seems to be essential in times of uncertainty and ambiguity. Even at their best the social sciences can provide only a rough weighting of future alternatives. Nor can any of them do more than learn from the past. They can make projections but not predictions. When we step into the future, then, persuasion and conviction depend upon a rhetoric that brings together morality and reasoned argument into a language that can reach a general audience.

Thus, as economic reasoning is brought into the media it must be adapted to this rhetoric and made a part of a larger worldview. It is not surprising, then, that a capitalist press includes a favorable place for capitalism in this wider worldview. That is not at issue here. Our principal concern is to show how this is done and what some of its consequences were in our popular but durable collective memory.

At the present time there is a tendency of some economists and their fans to make economic reasoning the sole basis for social policy, or what George Soros calls "market fundamentalism," the idea that all decisions are best settled in the marketplace.[1] But even those who advocate this point of view lace their language in a wider rhetoric that recommends itself to the general reader. Otherwise their work is safely stored in technical journals. It is their wider, more sharable rhetoric that is being sought out here.

Slumps, Market Breaks, Crashes, and Market Failures

The stock market crash of 1929[2] is written of as a full-scale crisis of capitalism followed by a new industrial contract—the New Deal—between labor and capital. In what is often described as the worst crisis since the Civil War, it was followed by equally significant changes in discourse and political policy (Burk 1988). The crash in 1987, however, is told primarily as a brief market break overcome by that "Maestro," Alan Greenspan (Woodward 2000). (This was also the official diagnosis by the SEC.) Afterward, we had only to respond to Ronald Reagan's continuing invitation to "come home America."

Reagan's restoration was probably the high point of the rhetorical consensus that had been worked out during and following the 1940s. Despite his popularity among neoconservatives, Reagan's hero was FDR and the New Deal era in post–World War II (the 1950s) was the home he (and perhaps those who voted for him) beckoned us to. Certainly that is indicated by this study of the *Chicago Tribune*. But Reagan's restoration has not lasted and the rhetorical consensus reached in the 1940s and 1950s may be entering a period of contest as we come face to face with globalization. Globalization got its benign newsworthy start in the Reagan years but has been followed by much criticism (Fiss and Hirsch 2005). Globalization stands in direct conflict with the social contract and rhetoric worked out during the Roosevelt, Truman, and Eisenhower years. With globalization the industrial contract ("workplace socialism" it was called at its best) ends. Labor and capital have no fixed location and the nation becomes a legal rather than a moral community. Patriotism becomes empty rhetoric. That is quite a moral and conceptual leap to be spliced onto a rhetoric of understandings and reassurance in which the nation, community, and the economy were almost coterminous. Yet, even the critics of current globalization are in favor of it in principle if not in practice (James 2001; Soros 1998; and Stiglitz 2002). Still, in our latest skimming of the Tribune's coverage of the economy, the newspaper continues the vocabulary of previous decades although obvious news releases toy with an alternative rhetoric more nearly attuned to globalization (see Fiss and Hirsch 2005, 43) and neoconservatism. This book documents the continuity or this rhetoric and the challenge of changing realities that question its continuity.

Frame Analysis

My principal task here is to lay down a method that can reveal the rhetoric that accompanied the great crashes and contributed to the response to and remembrance of each. What we need, then, is a metalanguage—a language about language—that summarizes and makes plain which parts of these ideologies surfaced in 1929 and 1987 and hints at what might be surfacing now.

In recent years such a metalanguage has begun to surface. It is called "frame analysis," and an extended version of it is the primary methodology of this study. Frame analysis is an approach that has brought sociologists, communication researchers, and linguists together in the study of the mass media and social movements. As you might expect it has taken a somewhat different direction in each discipline.

If you trace back the footnotes to frame analysis, however, they usually converge on Erving Goffman's *Frame Analysis*. Goffman traces the concept back to William James, Gregory Bateson, and Ludwig Wittgenstein (Goffman 1974, 6–7). Goffman was primarily concerned with the "multiple realities" problem, or the question, "Why am I in this social reality and why should I bother to stay in it?" For Goffman, social worlds were scripted and had only a tenuous hold on willful individuals. The general idea was that there is no "Ur" vocabulary that refers definitely to a "real social reality" but only multiple linguistic opportunities of reaching a consensus on a referential *frame* within which we can "play like" we have found reality. Such social realities might be like play but they have real consequences.

Increasingly, sociologists have searched among vocabularies to understand why some of them capture people and move them to action while others leave them cold. In conversation analysis, for example, the focus is upon the local face-to-face interaction order. Douglas Maynard's study of diabetic and AIDS victims is an interesting example, for while he focuses on patient-doctor interaction he shows how some of their "trial runs" become elaborated and standardized into more widely shared "frames" (although he never mentions the term) in subsequent practice. He closes the study with an epilogue ("How to Tell the [good/bad] News") that seeks to script doctor-patient experimentation and take it out of the local interaction order and into social practice (Maynard 2003, 247–53). The "trial runs" become a shared social reality, departures from which might come to be seen as wrong or deviant.

A variation on this approach is Karl Weick's sensemaking studies of executive decision making under heavy organizational constraints. Executives are not free agents but must reach a final agreement. A good example is Mitchell Abolafia's study of decision making at the Federal Reserve, where the members must reach decisions that are weighty and widely publicized (1988 and 2005). Abolafia concludes that the "policy makers prefer to weave complex narratives that are used retrospectively and prospectively . . . to create a richer, more pertinent narrative" [from scattered data]. "As such this constant re-framing is a rational response to the situation, presumably more rational than applying models [alone] that aren't trusted" (Nee and Swedberg 1993, 224). Under very different but equally uncertain circumstances Ann Swidler describes a somewhat similar but more eclectic "cultural tool box" of frames that we draw on to meet the everyday uncertainties of love (Swidler 1986).

A contrast to these temporary or episodic cultural frames is the dramatic reframing that goes on in social movements where a widespread denial of previous frames opens the way to a new "imaginary society" (Snow et al. 1986). Here the old frame provides only a kind of negative counterexample to promote an original vision.[3]

All of these examples capture frames only in the midst of their transition. What I am interested in, however, are mass media frames that last for decades without much change and that remain in popular history even after new frames have replaced the old ones. When such frames change, do they become equally durable or only transient? Michael

Schudson suggests an answer in his study of social memory. He writes that "a cultural object [like a social frame] is more powerful [persistent or memorable] the more it is *within reach*, the more it is *rhetorically effective*, the more it *resonates* with existing opinions and structures . . . the more thoroughly it is retained in institutions, and the highly resolved it is toward *action*" (1989, 179, italics in original).

What I aim to do here is to provide a methodology that will take the steps spelled out by Schudson in charting the long duration of journalist frames and also reveal some of the changes that lead to a dramatic change in those frames. All the while, I want to show how reporters made coherent and memorable news of the American economy in two times of crisis.

Media Studies and Frame Analysis

Communication scholars have already employed frame analysis in a number of studies of media rhetoric. (For example, see Bennett and Entman 2001; Entmen 2004; Ettema and Whitney 1994). Entman (2004, 4–6) sees these studies as falling into two camps. The "hegemonic" camp argues that given journalists' vows of objectivity, balance, and nonpartisanship they can only pass on what competing politicians say. Entman, however, sees himself as belonging to an "indexing" camp that, "contrary to the hegemony view . . . believe that when elites disagree about foreign policy, media reflect the discord in ways that may affect . . . policy." Entman goes further to develop a "cascade model" in which successive disagreements between political news releases open up the reporters' opportunities to reframe the news less in terms of prior claims than as political strategies that are more or less empty of genuine efforts to fulfill political promises. The study is a convincing deconstruction of political frames and how reporters may reveal and shift the balance between contending politicians and, thus, effect public policy.

Media studies often focus on this cat-and-mouse game between politicians and reporters who mold rhetorical frames aimed to arouse or sooth readers. The studies are fascinating but their methodology is a rather opportunist singling out of concepts and phrases that might have emotional impact or resonate with other concepts that may have persuasive value. I find the selection of terms persuasive but difficult to replicate or defend against alternatives.

I find George Lakoff's studies of figurative language and the role of figurative language in the construction of frames more convincing and defensible. Lakoff has written two books (1996 and 2004) on the subject, the most recent of which takes on the task of how to frame political campaigns that are in keeping with American democratic values. For Lakoff, a psychologist and a linguist, frames are unconscious mental structures that allow us to understand things like the economy that are beyond immediate experience. They have a foundation in what he calls a "source domain" schooled in actual individual experiences of the object world.[4] It is these residual experiences that are extended by figurative language to a world beyond experience. It is a virtual world, but still one *grounded in experience* and made real by analogy.

If you think about it, almost everything you read in the newspapers or watch on TV requires an imagination that goes beyond personal experience. Understanding them, according to Lakoff, is possible only by some kind of linguistic extension of the lived experience. Frames, then, are the verbal templates of these lived experiences that, in turn, are extended to all sorts of other things beyond experience. These extensions not only recreate a kind of understanding but also arouse some of the emotional content that remains in the original, unconscious *source domain*. More than that, they share in the "reality" of the original experience. Essentially, then, Lakoff's approach is a revival of John Locke's "ideas of sense" theory of mind.

The way to make these extensions of the domain is by figurative language that is warranted by "real experience." Or, to put it in more detail, figurative language consists of the extension of grounded experiences and their verbal templates by means of metaphor, metonym, and personification. Frames are very complex extensions that elaborate a coherent and consistent analogy built around a "master metaphor" that is enlarged by placing it in a plausible context that includes personae and metonyms.[5] Frames, then, are not just an arbitrary grab bag of suggestive words used figuratively, but a highly systemized and elaborated gestalten that evoke some of the familiarity and emotions that originate in the real world of direct experience.

Of all these media studies, my use of frame analysis most nearly resembles that of Lakoff. I argue that by figurative language we can change one textual or verbal social reality into another. I also argue that metaphors are combined with personification and metonyms to create a complex frame rather than a few concepts that might fulfill Schudson's requirements for a cultural object to remain in use and arouse emotional and cognitive conviction. Like Lakoff, my primary data are textual rather than the speech, music, or body language that have been so important in sociological studies of social movements.[6] But like other sociologists, I am interested in dramatic changes in frames as well as their construction and durability.

In two important ways, however, this study makes very different assumptions from those of Lakoff. Lakoff believes a grounded or foundational vocabulary arises from experience that is shareable because something is "out there" to be shared. These experiences (the "source domain") provide the experiential base and vocabulary from which figurative extensions originate to convey their sense of reality and to convey the emotional force of their origin.

If one follows the history of words, however, they wander all over the place from being what appears to be the "source" to being "figurative" and subsequently source again. Think of the word *nucleus*, which at one time or another has been used to refer to the shell of a small nut, a wall of parchment, the fringe of a metropolis, the center of an atom, and families consisting only of parents and children.[7] Which is the lived experience or the extension? For a long time the nucleus of an atom was entirely a hypothetical entity among most physicists, but can they now "experience" it in cyclotrons?[8] Is it only now that the word *nuclear* is grounded?

It seems to me that many words—not all, of course—have a popular provenance; that is, a history of usage that widely acknowledges their prior or contemporary conventional use as "current" in the sense that it draws no obvious contrast or comparison when applied to "its" subject. When used in this way it is not funny, ironic, unusual, a new insight, or a neologism. The use has behind it some claim of authority or "ownership." Initially at least, figurative language is used to create that contrast between established use and a novel use. It must seem ironic, funny, draw a new resemblance, provide a simplification, or reveal a new perspective (Burke 1943, 503–17; see also Fernandez's Archimedean point, 1986, 73–99). In this capacity, the term also draws upon previous authority. Often this popular provenance seems to include some group or institution whose use is attributed to priority or authority over its use. "They know what it really means," it is said. The dictionary may be used to defend this use, but it is only one line of defense among claimants.

A word has to be extended from some "origin," then, to yet another subject before we consider it sufficiently "figurative" to throw new light on a subject—to draw contrast, likeness and insight, irony or outrage, humor or pathos. In time metaphors may lose this capacity to draw contrast if they are used routinely. When they lose this provenance, it is a "dead metaphor."[9] The new subject becomes its provenance. It now "belongs" to its new users (sometimes including its older ones) and carries less and less of its previous connotation, although it may linger for decades as being the less obvious of "literal uses." Most of the metaphors identified in this study are near death; it is only when they are surrounded by their complementary metonyms and personae that they strike us as figurative language and bring into mind the contrast with other "more literal" usage. The entire ensemble of tropes establishes the boundaries of what I will call a "frame" or, following Kenneth Burke, a "dramatism" (1945, xv–xxiii).

Figurative extensions may also be quite unstable. This is most obvious in the case of words borrowed from the demimonde, teenage slang, or regional and ethnic dialects. Each of these sources has a certain *truth-making* authority that lends itself especially to irony. They may be thought to speak from privileged experience or without guile and pretense, or they may be warranted by in-group craft practice and talk. Or again, without inhibition. Languages borrowed from these sources can fall out of use rapidly because they are dropped by prior users or lose their ability to bring a novel, ironic, or persuasive light on an old subject.[10] They are short-lived fads and their extension may be equally short-lived.

But there is a distinct body of language that is much more closely guarded by some institutions. I do not mean only the dictionary, although it often documents the judgment of these institutions. More important are the people and institutions that make up the dictionary; most notably the Church, the Polity, the Law, and the Academy. Each of these institutions and their practitioners (politicians, the clergy, judges, lawyers, scientists, engineers, tradesmen, executives, and such) go to a great deal of trouble to *ground* their language with formalisms. The church, the law, and the polity do it primarily through the examination of prior cases and appeals to constitutional documents with a known history of interpretation. The academy and especially the sciences often go further to give their concepts an explicit operational meaning by some technique of objectification in as required by P. T. Bridgeman's conception of objectivity. Various people in these institutions defend their language. I mention the church, state, and science because they are powerful enough to defend their words with formal procedures that "prove" they are "right." Words borrowed from the demimonde, teenage slang, and regional and ethnic dialects are less defensible, easily borrowed, and relatively quick to lose their authority, or their claim to a privileged perspective. Undoubtedly, we draw upon them to describe alternative social worlds especially when they connote some of the authority or attraction of their source.

What I mean by *grounding*, then, is this kind of formalization and/or measurement and subsequent defense of word usage, not individual experience. Terms identified this way have a particular attraction because they carry with them the authority of a more-or-less powerful and knowledgeable provenance. Since a technical vocabulary is grounded in this way, it also tends to be stable so that extensions and contrasts are also more lasting and retain some of their borrowed authority as well as some ability to throw a favorable light on other subjects. This becomes important when ideologues, politicians, journalists, and pundits seek to find words that are within reach, powerful, rhetorically effective, resonate with existing opinions and structures, more thoroughly retained in institutions, and more highly resolved toward action—Schudson's recipe for a frame that is "powerful," persistent, and memorable.

From Frames to Dramatisms

A promising methodological approach to the identification and interpretation of frames is suggested by Kenneth Burke's concept of a "dramatism" (1945, x–xvi). A literary critic, it was Burke's contention that any social philosophy, theory, ideology or, indeed, any extended social argument (he called them "casuistries"[11]) can be condensed and rendered into a narrative story. This can be done, he contended, by using the vocabulary and grammar of the argument or theory itself.

Such an analysis would include what Burke called his five "generating principals," which, taken together, would form a dramatism, that is, a story. The approach is explicitly dramaturgical and the "principles" are taken to be sufficient to transform an extended argument into a condensed literary form: a package of meaning with interdependent parts[12] that can be grasped and remembered as a whole. Once you know the "principles" of a casuistry, you can grasp the whole in the same way you might grasp a short story.

1. The first of these principles is an agent or what we might call an actor although Burke's and my agents are not necessarily human.
2. Second, there would be the act or what stage directors call, "the action," or, as it turns out, a narrative.
3. Third, a dramatism would include the purposes of the agent (or agents).
4. Fourth, there would be the means or implements used by the agent; something that Burke called agency, which is not to be confused with current use to indicate an opening for choice in social control.
5. Finally, all of this was to be mounted on a stage, completing what is called Burke's "pentad."

Burke, like Goffman, is obviously drawing upon the stage as an analogue to all our representations of life, that is, all our "multiple realities." What Burke calls a dramatism is just a step ahead of what became the dramatistic approach in sociology. Indeed, early practitioners of that approach, like C. Wright Mills, Erving Goffman, and Howard Becker, acknowledge their debt to Burke.[13] In his own work, however, Burke dwelled exclusively upon the written text as I do also. What he saw in the written word was one of life's governing forms, a way of regulating conduct rather than just description, analysis, speculation, or fiction. Dramatisms were a way of defining social reality.

Burke's work is full of insightful examples that superimpose one or more of his generating principles upon some philosophical or literary discourse.[14] But at no point does he fully deploy all his generating principles on a single body of text. His analysis is subtle and suggestive but never a sustained deconstruction of a historical, philosophical, or literary manuscript. He displays an encyclopedic knowledge of literature as if the reader had read everything he had read. My use of his pentad is plodding and simpleminded. Undoubtedly he would be outraged by it.

But if you look closely at Burke's abbreviated examples, almost invariably they single out some figurative terms as the diagnostic evidence to assign one or another of his generating principles to a line of argument or fiction. Although Burke provides no discussion of his usage of tropes, he does include a list of "four master tropes," metaphor, metonym, synecdoche, and irony.[15] It is as if the reader should have known all along that it is figurative language that turns one social reality into another.

In applying Burke's dramatisms to a study of news coverage of the American economy some adjustments must be made. In newsprint Burke's agents turn out to be a collection of *personae* who not only provide the action but also embody the moral dimensions of the dramatism. The act itself, of course, is a stream of action that forms a *narrative*, which belongs to a recognizable literary *genre*. In the newspaper Burke's *stage* includes a "setting," as it would in theater performances, only in the newspaper it must be a "wordstage," or as I call it, a "wordscape." As in the theater, the implements that give the agents their agency are inseparable from this wordscape. In my wordscapes there are always decorative and identifying elements that suggest a setting rather than just a platform with the essential implements.

When Burke's dramatistic approach is applied to news on the economy what the reader ends up with is not an obvious ideology but a story or rather a daily episode in a story. It is a story that has characters, action, the implements they use, and a stage (or wordscape) on which the action takes place. The reader receives this dramatism one "scene" (news article) at a time so the moral or ideological content is fragmented and implicit. Readers may look for the moral or ideology but it is only when the dramatism is revealed in its entirety that it becomes obvious. In 1929 readers were dolled out an ideological version of Marshallian economics. As the crash worsened, that dramatism came under trial. It was to be replaced by quite a different dramatism, one that was an ideological extension of Keynesian economics. But each of these ideological extensions becomes obvious only if we deconstruct a large number of articles and rearrange their vocabulary to fit Burke's dramatism.

The next chapter covers the period following the 1929 crash when the first of these dramatisms came under trial and the New Deal followers of Keynes began to fashion a new dramatism. The next four chapters provide a detailed comparison of the 1929 dramatism and the one that followed it, taking in turn their narratives, their personae and purposes, and their wordscapes and their implements. With that in hand, we turn to how the dramatisms were visualized in cartoons, how they still figure in our collective memory and how readers responded to news on each crash. Stay with me.

CHAPTER TWO

The Grounding of the Economy

Prosperity is no idle expression. —Herbert Hoover, Campaign Address, 1928

In the period following the 1929 stock market crash, economics underwent a revolution that was to be followed by a revolution in news reporting. In 1929 one could recognize in news reporting a rough, implicit version of Marshallian economics turned into faith and ideology. What we now call the economy was made up of independent parts brought together by the natural forces of supply and demand. Only after the failure of much optimism did this ideology come into question. The alternative that came into view was a much more unified conception of the economy in which government might play a strong regulatory role. One reason for this reconceptualization was the construction of the National Accounts, which for the first time gave a timely and holistic account of national wealth. The other was Keynesian economics, which gave specification to the possibilities of economic regulation. The forthcoming war, in turn, gave urgency to this reconceptualization and opened up a much wider range of intervention into the economy. What had been an eclectic collection of different economic institutions became a collective possession in which shares were debated as a matter of social design rather than only individual striving and ownership.

Following this revolution, there would also be a revolution in how economic news was reported. This chapter focuses only on this reconceptualization of the fragmented 1929 world of business into a unified national economy by 1940. A comparison of the language the newspapers used to capture and make coherent these constructions follows in the next three chapters.

* * *

In 1929 there was no economy. There was business, of course, but that was often contrasted to finance or commerce. Shipping and traction (rail freight at that time) were usually listed separately and farming was almost always treated separately. What we now call the business sections of the *Tribune* and the *New York Times* reflected this fragmentation of economic activity. The first full Finance and Commerce page in the *Tribune* made the separation of finance and commerce especially plain by placing them as titles at opposite sides to head the page. Subsequent pages might vary with headings like Commodities, Real Estate, or Curb Exchange. The *New York Times* was more systematic. In its most elaborated form it started with the heading Financial and Business in a single box on the left side of the first full page and went on to Commodities, Business Opportunities, Stock Exchange, Out of Town Exchanges, Foreign-Exchange Rates, Bond Sales, Bid and Quotations, and Real Estate as subsequent headings. After the Financial and Business page the order might vary some, and there could be omissions or two or three topics to a page. Although there were several consecutive pages devoted to money making, sometimes the sports and racetrack results just trailed off into late stock quotations before the first full page of Financial, Commercial, and Business news.

The contemporary reader would have soon realized that this was not a hierarchical typology that moved from the general to the specific or even an aggregate that made up some well defined whole. One was presented with a series of more or less independent activities that were about making money. Some of these activities were more than independent of one another; they were thought to be in a winner-takes-all contest.[1] In the *Tribune* the stock market was especially suspect since it diverted money from "legitimate lines of business." Farming was usually said to "follow its own trend" while the agricultural spokesmen claimed to be the victims of business and the commodity exchange. Retail, construction, and industry might compete in the same way. This was, after all, the heyday of institutional economics and Wesley C. Mitchell, its premier practitioner, would be sought out for council after the crash.[2] According to the *Tribune*'s "Scrutator" the business of America was "sound throughout" but, he went on, mining was badly "overmanned." Agriculture was worse. It was commonly assumed that the great advantage of "institutions" (corporations[3]) was the capacity to regulate "overproduction" and

"overmanning." That was exactly why Alexander Legge wanted to orga-
nize farmers the way he had organized International Harvester. Left un-
constrained, overproduction and ruinous price competition were thought
to be inevitable and what caused the business cycle. It was as if they had
read Marx and wanted to defeat him by legalizing cartels.

This sort of thinking gave shape to the most immediate remedies adopted by both Hoover and Roosevelt to end the depression. Much of
Hoover's effort went into meetings (what the press called "Pow Wows")
with separate economic units (for example, banking, industry, construction, shipping, and state governors) to encourage them to restrain
"overproduction" and price competition.[4] Hoover was unsuccessful
but Roosevelt required much the same thing with the National Industrial Recovery Act. The NIRA, however, included provisions to restrict
production and to eliminate monopolies, which made it appear contradictory to most observers. When it was ruled unconstitutional in 1935,
both the *Times* and the *Tribune* had turned against it, but for opposing
reasons.

The Natural Business Cycle

This kind of thinking was quite congenial to the prevailing institutional
school of political economy, and it gave a particular cast to interpretations of the crash. As Alexander D. Noyes put it on New Year's Day,
1930, in the *New York Times*:[5] "The stock market's collapse was reaction from an orgy of reckless speculation. No such excesses have been
practiced by trade and industry. . . . In contrast with the complete financial illusion which had prevailed on the stock market . . . there had been
sober study of the realities in general industry." Noyes goes on to find
other independent signs of encouragement: "the expenditure of more
than $2,000,000,000 on constructive industry. . . . Nothing can stop in-
dustrial expansion with such yearly increases in population and individual wealth as the United States presents. . . . The indomitable spirit of
confidence in . . . American prosperity. . . . The position of overshadow-
ing economic power in world finance won by the United States."

Secretary of Commerce Robert Lamont along with Treasurer Andrew Mellon followed much the same line of argument, only in greater
detail, by finding encouragement separately in manufacturing, mineral
production, domestic trade, foreign commerce, public utilities, and new

construction contracts in that order. "Following the security liquidation [the bankruptcy of stock investors and their lenders] in October and November," Lamont told readers on the outset of 1930, "interest rates were at the lowest levels in 18 months." Presumably everything was in place for another go at Hoover prosperity.

In saying this Lamont was probably only doing what he had advised Hoover to do in November. When the president held his "prosperity pow wows" shortly after the crash, he met on separate days with railroad officials, big industrial leaders, utility men, bankers, and labor leaders. He also sent telegrams to all the state governors, urging them to spend now. The powwows were essentially cheerleader sessions, but they were endorsed by both papers because the main danger was thought to be the spread of panic from the stock market to "essential" business, commerce, and industry. Editorials recognized that installment buying might have spread "liquidation," but both newspapers gave it their best effort. The slump, they wrote, was confined to the stock market and prosperity was just around the corner.

This fragmentation of what we now call the economy was combined with a "naturalistic" theory of business cycles.[6] A version of it was published in the *Times* on New Year's Day, 1930.[7] I quote it almost intact:

The Cycle of Prosperity

Before the war, every great Wall Street Panic was made a basis for measuring the cycle of prosperity. The general tradition was that a "full cycle" occupied something like 20 years—as from 1873 to 1893—but with 2 short cycles intervening, each with its alternate boom and crisis. Thus after the peace of 1893 and the subsequent readjustment came the boom period of 1899–1901 and the reaction culminating in the "little panic" of 1903; next another boom until the panic of 1907.

The report of the President's Committee on Economic Changes makes a somewhat different pre-war calculation. Measuring not from the panic itself but from the end of the subsequent liquidation, and using what pre-war economists called the "short-cycle," calculation by Professor W. C. Mitchell makes the average length of the cycle in the three pre-war decades three years and four months. Since the war it finds the cycle shortened. Writing in 1928, the report reckons one such period since May, 1919 to October, 1921 or 29 months; a second from October, 1921 to August, 1924 or 34 months; and a third from August, 1924 to December, 1927, or 41 months—the last having about the pre-war duration. The cycle which began in the last month of 1927 would not on this basis of reckoning, be terminated until the liquidation now in process is completed. Its duration thus far has been just two years.

The old fashioned plan of reckoning from panic to panic would doubtless have made the first post-war cycle last from December of 1920 to October of 1929 or nearly the duration of the traditional "short cycle" of pre-war days. That would not compare closely with the 14 years of the "full-cycle" from 1893 to 1907, or the twenty years from 1873 to 1893 or the intervals from 1857 to 1878 and 1837 to 1857. But we do not yet know whether this present episode is or is not an old-time "major crisis."

The general idea was that once debtors and inventories were cleaned out and lenders were left with some money in their hands, interest rates would fall and investment and consumption would resume until prosperity, overconfidence, and overproduction led to another orgy of reckless speculation only to end in a "panic year" followed by a longer period of liquidation and overproduction. Recovery occurred when all the economic institutions were sufficiently liquidated and moving in the same direction. As with locusts, there were little and big panics and full and short cycles in the business world. The latter's length depended on the liquidation process as well as the period of mounting prosperity and the scale of the panic. Judging from the above calculations the liquidation had another year or two to run before signs of recovery were assured. The tendency to narrow attention down to liquidation inflicted by the stock market was consistent with an institutional interpretation of Marshallian economics dressed up in a naturalized rhetoric.[8]

This seems to have been the general view in the *Tribune* and *Times* for the next five years, although others were betting on a natural or normal recovery at the start of each year. In March of 1930 columnist Fred Harvey (the *Tribune*'s chief reporter on the stock market) found stocks at a new peak, and throughout most of 1931 and part of 1932 he looked on the positive side of the stock market. As the market worsened, he disappeared from the *Tribune* and the stock market reports lost his cheering voice. The *Tribune*, however, did recruit two prominent businessmen, George Reynolds from Continental Bank and Frank Wetmore from First National, to provide more solemn assurances on each New Year's Day from 1930 through 1932. In 1930 Reynolds assured readers that 1929 was a perfectly normal year, while Wetmore allowed that the "deflation taken by itself has had and will have relatively little influence on business." The *Times* featured numerous bankers and "utility heads" who gave similar cheer on that New Year's Day.

By the end of 1930, however, it was recognized that a "depression" might be afoot in the "after-panic year" of 1931. Still, it was said that "experience teaches that at some time in the second year after a great financial panic, reactionary influences will have spent their forces" (A. Noyes in the *Times* but also published in the *Tribune*). George Reynolds in the *Tribune* congratulated the present generation on having seen "what a genuine depression is like" but also reminded them that a "slump cures itself." The *Times* reported that an upturn in business was seen in all the Federal Reserve districts. There was "Cheering Forecasts in Central Europe" by Austrian bankers. The persistence of the depression into 1932, however, led Irving Fisher to say (in the *Tribune*) that the scramble to get out of debt had so deflated the dollar that remaining debts were larger in real value than all the previous ones.[9] He recommended moderate inflation in the future; "reflation," he called it.

This sort of damning of the old year and looking to the new one with fresh promise continued throughout most of the 1930s. It spread almost immediately to gigantic downtown New Year's Eve celebrations gleefully reported in both Chicago and New York. The *Tribune* reported that up to half a million people congregated in the Loop to bid a "regretless farewell" to the old year (1931) and to welcome the new one. The reporters especially delighted in the massive violation of the Volstead Act by "hip nippers." The "dry agents" were on duty but utterly helpless before generous "revelers" openly sharing libations and showering kisses on whoever's wife was handy. Each year they "made whoopee" into the wee hours, and after the repeal of the Volstead Act both the quality and quantity of drink were said to have improved. Since everyone was calling for less pessimism, reporters and citizens joined these pep rallies, and each celebration was said to be larger than the previous one. They were reported to be remarkably trouble free, and even the police were said to have enjoyed them.

But as the years wore on, there were noticeable signs of strain at keeping up a cheering front. Fred Harvey and "Cotton" Mather,[10] two of the more optimistic reporters, were gone. Hoover was reduced to pleading for people to buy "at home." Only the 5 and 10 cent stores prospered. Even the National Conference Board blamed the banks for not extending "adequate credit accommodations to industry and trade as a whole." Despite the "flowing bowl" and "revelers filling the night" on New Year's Eve in 1932, whoever reported on the stock market wrote that there was

only "an ill concealed sigh of relief . . . [A]s some of the philosophers of
the trading posts said, it's only the turn of a calendar sheet after all."
Even John Maynard Keynes's 1933 open letter in the *Times* to President
Roosevelt gave the NIRA low marks and likened proposed increases
in the money supply to "trying to put on flesh by letting out the belt."
Keynes's endorsement of still more public works, however, brought forward a trio of economic newsmakers in the *Times*—Irving Fisher, Wilford King, and "Professor" Moley—who remonstrated that all that could
be done had been done.

The theory of the natural business cycle had strong staying power. As
late as 1935 signs of economic recovery were taken by the *Times* to have
"confirmed the view of the more conservative school of economists who,
all along, refused to see anything unexampled in the depression.[11] . . . It
was predicted that it would be overcome by the same recuperative forces
which worked successfully in the past. . . . It was a mere recurrence on a
magnified scale of past major depressions." When still stronger signs of
recovery showed up in early 1936, the coverage of the *Tribune* turned ju-
bilant. "The country was recovering despite the New Deal," argued Arthur Sears Henning; indeed, it was the "erasure of the NIRA" six months
earlier that had cleared the way by freeing business "from New Deal regimentation and other radical innovations."

The *Tribune*, however, continued to sour on national economic management throughout the remainder of the 1930s. Its reporters had enabled readers to enjoy the ostentation, rum running, and wild speculation of the 1920s even as they condemned them. It made for great
comedy. In the early 1930s they also did their best to cheer business on.
As things improved by 1935, however, the popularity of the New Deal
was hard to swallow. A 1936 rise in the income tax was a "Roosevelt
tax." By 1937, the president was said to "possess a dictator's power . . . to
change the price of gold . . . and do other things that would profoundly
affect stock and commodity prices and other features of the country's
economy."[12] The 1937 recession was judged a "depression" and the paper
applauded when there were some signs of division in New Deal ranks
over Roosevelt's "malefactors of great wealth" speech and, again in 1939,
when Vice President Garner was rumored to be in revolt. Throughout
the depression the *Tribune* referred to the unemployed as "idle workers."[13] Coverage of the stock market shrank so that by 1940 only the Associated Press's account was published on most days. On one occasion it
consisted of three one-sentence paragraphs.

The *Times* also showed signs of austerity; bylines became much rarer and articles began to look like they were written by a committee. However, there was little of the schadenfreude that crept into the *Tribune*. Like the *Tribune*, the *Times* still occasionally carried the reviews of economists Colonel Leonard Ayres, Lionel Edie, and David Friday, who were promising a "natural" recovery well into the 1930s. In neither the *Times* nor the *Tribune* was there ever a declared end to the depression or a renewed conception of the business cycle. Instead, news making in both papers was overtaken by new events and new ideas. One of those ideas was that of the economy.

Constructing the Economy

How does an inclusive term like *the economy* become fixed in the mass media as if everyone knows what it means? If you looked in the dictionary in 1929 it was treated as a synonym for "thrift," sometimes with a narrower application to money management alone. Occasionally it was also used in the phrase "to practice economy," where the objective was not thrift alone but good budgetary management as might be implied in the Greek *oikonomia* (domestic stewardship) from which it is derived. The *New York Times Index*, however, simply referred the reader to "thrift."[14] At the time, economy as "thrift" was a fairly large entry (for example, there was an Economy League and an Economy Grocery Store chain), but nothing under it suggested "the structure of economic life in a country or area" that enters Webster's dictionary between 1957 and 1961 (between the second and third editions).[15] The Nobelist Charles Schultz at the University of Chicago assured me that the concept was occasionally used by 1929. But it was not newspaper language. The *Reader's Guide to Periodical Literature* continues to refer the reader to "thrift" until 1965. Much earlier, in 1944, however, the *Guide* does reference a scholarly journal article[16] that uses the term in Webster's 1957 sense. By the early 1950s the *Guide* also documents its entry into popular literature. And, by 1967, Kucera and Francis find that Webster's usage ranks among the top 1,500 *common nouns* in a sample of one million words.[17]

The concept is so important—I will try to support this as I go along—that I thought it worth the ordeal of trying to trace its appearance through the years 1930 to 1987 in the *Tribune* and the *New York Times*. Since I was interested not only in its occurrence but also to whom it was attributed, who used it, and the context in which it did rhetorical service, I selected one copy[18] each year from both papers and searched the front page and entire business section for all articles that might plausibly use the concept.[19] I focused on articles that concerned broad national economic issues, especially those on macroeconomic[20] policy, and also on those that simply reflected on economic trends or contextualized microeconomic events in a larger setting. I always included the stock market report for that day because I wanted to know when the stock market was taken to track the economy rather than compete with "legitimate lines of business."

Since I knew that the New Year's Day editions of the papers carried forecasts on the forthcoming year and reflections on the past one, I examined them as well from 1930 to 1940. In the early 1930s these forecasts were quite elaborate, especially in the *New York Times*, which included reports from several European capitals; all the Federal Reserve districts; the prophecies of politicians, businessmen, and economists; and the wisdom of senior reporters such as Alexander Noyes. This extensive reporting on New Year's Day slacked off about 1938, and I discontinued looking at *every* New Year's issue by 1940 and examined one only every three or four years.

I also read all the *Times*'s coverage of the American Economic Association from 1929 to 1940. Finally, I followed up a number of stories in other editions if they seemed at all promising or intriguing.[21] The one-a-year sample produced 655 articles, about eleven each year, 61 percent of them from the *Times*. The New Year's Day and opportunistic samples added another 230 articles distributed in almost exactly the same ratio between the two papers but concentrated (85 percent) in the years before 1949, which I came to take as the end of the "formative" period in which the term *economy* became conventionalized in *its use and users* much as it was in 1987.

Drift and Ambiguity: 1930–36

Economic as a modifier was in wide use in 1930 and 1931 as you can see in the sentences and phrases listed below.

1930: (1) The year of 1929 will be *recorded in American economic annals* as productive of the greatest paradox in history. —O. A. Mather in *Tribune* +

1930: (2) Since the great world war *we have gone through several economic erup-*

tions and none of them destroyed *general prosperity* for more than a short
time. —George M. Reynolds, Chairman, Continental Bank in *Tribune* +

1930: (3) Incomplete phrases: German *economic* history; *economic* situation; a
continuance of *prosperity and progress*; an *economics of stewardship*.

1931: (4) [(Secretary) Lamont] expressed the belief that "*the inherent strength
of our economic structure will enable our country* to lead the world in a vigorous recovery from the present depression as we have done in the past."
—Secretary of Commerce Lamont in *Times* +

1931: (5) It may seem trite and of cold comfort to reiterate that fundamental conditions generally are sound despite the fact that *parts of the economic structure of this country and the world are out of joint*. —O. A. Mather, *Tribune* +
Italics added. * = random sample; + = additional samples

They are by no means exhaustive of my sample for those years. Most
of the uses to which *economic* was put would be entirely familiar today. But, despite a search through several additional issues of each paper in these years, I found no evidence of the use of *economy* as an inclusive noun meaning something other than "thrift" or "public budgeting."
What came closest was "our economic structure" (see 1931), but that implied something particular to American economic activities (free enterprise) or a specific institutional structure (for example, "trustification")
rather than the *whole* of economic activity. It was very rare.

Another possible candidate was prosperity, which was sometimes
treated as an almost palpable (see sentence no. 2 in 1930) state of economic affairs. At best, however, it was a phase in the business cycle.
Hoover chided people for any other use of the concept.

It was in 1932, three years later, that I encountered the first usage of
economy as an inclusive noun by Secretary of Commerce Robert P. Lamont (see below).

1932: (6) Most of our domestic difficulties could have been corrected prior to
this time had it not been for the destructive effect on *our own economy*[22]
of a series of *financial crises* abroad. —Secretary of Commerce Lamont in
Times + and *Tribune* +

Clearly the worldwide economic crisis required of Lamont a term that
would be inclusive of all American economic activities so as to sharply
juxtapose them to all other foreign economic activities. "Our economy"
does that. As you read on, the news release confirms this reading. The fi-

nancial crisis in Central Europe has "created apprehension and fear" in the United States and led to "numerous bank failures" and lowered optimism all around. Hoover has tried to mend things with a moratorium on foreign debts but "the favorable effects of these agreements . . . were vitiated by lack of cooperation in Europe." ("France," the *Tribune* reporter confided.)

Would Lamont's readers have understood him in this way? Some with economic training probably would. But "economy" (as in the headline "Hoover persistent for economy," that is, a balanced budget) still had the wider use as budgetary stewardship, and many readers might have taken it that way. Either use, however, would do rhetorical service for Lamont.

Almost certainly 1932 readers would have read budgetary stewardship into a 1932 statement below by Alfred P. Sloan, president of General Motors.

1932: (7) It is hard to conceive how any substantial foundation can be built for a *more effective national economy* until we adjust ourselves in harmony with our present national position. . . . [W]e have done practically nothing with respect to the *important question of governmental expenditures* which are exacting an impossible burden on constructive enterprise. —A. P. Sloan in *Times* +

Sloan speaks of "a more effective national economy" and, one sentence later, of "governmental expenditures" and the burden of taxation on business firms. Of course, we can never know exactly what Lamont or Sloan had in mind, but both precede "economy" with qualifiers ("our" and "national"). These qualifiers or others like them (for example, "the U.S. economy") are used consistently as if to alert the reader to a distinctive American form of "free enterprise."[23] Eventually, this practice would decline in favor of "our or the economy" as Webster's definition was established.[24]

My inclination was to attribute the more modern usage to Lamont but not to Sloan in 1932. However, an extensive search of articles covering Lamont's remaining year as secretary of commerce never quoted him as using the word again. It is not until 1935 during one of his New Year's addresses that Sloan unambiguously used "the economy" in Webster's sense (see below, no. 16).

For the next four years, however, this sort of ambiguity would still accompany the use of "economy" while references to "business," "commerce," "finance," and the like continued as the most general references. An illustration of this occurs in a 1933 article (below) where "govern-

mental economy" and "balancing the budget" are listed separately but
could mean the same thing.

1933: (8) Democratic leaders . . . looking for guidance in the pressing problems
now before them, involving *governmental economy, balancing the budget,* a
beer tax and farm relief, will confer next Thursday night with President Elect
Roosevelt. *Tribune* +

Indeed, the remainder of the article is concerned entirely with expenditures and revenue. John Maynard Keynes was quoted occasionally in the
newspapers and until 1934 speaks only of "the economic system" (see
below).

1933: (9) In the *economic system* of the modern world, output is primarily produced for sale;[25] and the volume of output depends on the amount of purchasing power. —J. M. Keynes in his open *Times* letter to President Roosevelt +

Very rarely others use this phrase. It becomes widespread only after
1945 when it is used primarily to contrast different kinds of economic
systems, especially that of the United States and the USSR.
    Nonetheless, in 1934, it is Keynes who provides us with our first unam-
biguous usage that is close to Webster's in the third and later editions.

1934: (10) If we take the average of the pre-boom years 1923–25 as 100, the sche-
matic picture, which I see in my own mind, of the rate of progress of the
American economy toward normal, after smoothing out the excessive rise
and subsequent fall in the middle of 1933, is, very broadly, as follows . . . [a table estimating current national income indexed to 1923–25]. —J. M. Keynes
in a letter to the *New York Times*

Keynes is at pains to explain that the index of industrial production is in-
adequate but uses it as a proxy for all monetized goods and services. For
him the American economy is that inclusive entity that produces this total product. Keynes here is very near the measurements that would give
"the economy" its subsequent reality and almost invariably reported as a
single, monetized entity in our National Income and Product Accounts.
From 1933 to the late 1940s, from the depression to World War II and
European recovery, events would drive a statistical project to give "the
economy" this substantive and newsworthy existence.[26] But this did not

occur before some other variations in usage contributed further ambiguity to the "economy." The remaining three sentences from 1934 illustrate three shadings of this ambiguity. The first (no. 11) seems to hark back to the idea of household economy, and there is nothing else in the article to dissuade this interpretation.

1934: (11) [I]t was disclosed that the population of these areas were living on a *deficit economy* and were no longer able to meet their own taxes and other expenditures. —Paraphrase of John Ferris of the TVA at a joint session of the American Statistical Association (ASA) and the American Economic Association (AEA) in the *Times* +

The notion of a "planned economy" was also initially a source of ambiguity. It was introduced by sponsors of the New Deal, and the sentence below comes from an inaugural meeting of the American Economic Congress where General Hugh Johnson laid forth the aims of the National Recovery Act (NRA).[27]

1934: (12) "Industry must devote itself to the organization of a permanent system which will allow for a *planned economy to prevent the disastrous alternating periods of expansion and depression* which have beset American business and industry since its inception." —General Hugh S. Johnson, head of NRA, speaking before the first American Economic Congress. *Times* +

The use of the phrase by the New Dealers brought forth both perplexity and venom from Herbert Hoover (see below). He went on to characterize the planned economy as "catchwords [that] cloak incarnate passion for power . . .

1935: (13) Two years ago the phrase more frequently used was "*Planned Economy*." But as that has become so obviously "*Planned Extravagance*," it has been less used . . . Even "*National Planning*" is threatened with ejection by a still newer glittering phrase, "*the Third Economy*." —Herbert Hoover in *Tribune* +

. . . an attempt of a collegiate oligarchy to sanctify by a phrase a muddle of uncoordinated and reckless adventures in government—flavored with unctuous claims to monopoly in devotion to their fellow man."

   Two other uses of the word in 1934 (14 and 15 below) were as ambiguous as those in 1933. The first because there is no article before "world economy" and the second because I thought "world economic" might be a misprint for "world economy." Both may have suffered from translation.

1934: (14) Convinced that monetary stability is an essential condition to the return of economic normality, the undersigned governments believe that by insuring the stability of their currencies they will contribute to the restoration of *world economy.* —Proclamation of 7 gold bloc nations reported in the *Tribune.**

1934: (15) The instability of most currencies . . . [is] an important unfavorable element which should not be lost sight of nor should . . . [its] depressing influence . . . on general *world economics* be overlooked. —Reporter Fernand Maronis, correspondent to the *Times* +

Notwithstanding Hoover's tirade against the very concept of an economy, the controversy over it seemed to work toward some clarification among other newsmakers by 1935. Alfred P. Sloan was no more pleased with a planned economy than Hoover (no. 16), but he was beginning to use the concept.

1935: (16) Today the magic possibilities of industrial regimentation and the so-called *planned* economy no longer cast the spell of yesterday. —A. P. Sloan Jr. in *Times* +

Still he contrasted it strongly to "the present system of free enterprise" as one might use the phrase "national economic structure." He defends free enterprise because it "would create demand, extend consumption and increase employment," while he thought the NRA's planned economy would do just the reverse.[28] But he did identify the economy with its product.

Toward Standardization, 1936–40: The National Income and Product Accounts Enter the News

Two weeks after Hoover's speech, Robert Nathan, one of Simon Kuznets's students, made a news release on his latest findings on national income. By way of paraphrase, the release included the clearest definition of the economy that I would encounter in the entire period of 1929 to 1987 (no. 17).

1935: (17) Of these two lines, *net income paid out* represents the amount paid to individuals by business from resources for their productive services. *Net income produced* represents the value of all commodities produced or services rendered after depreciation of capital equipment and depletion of raw materials or more briefly, *the net product of the national economy.* —The *Times* paraphrase of Robert Nathan, Chief Economist, Income Division, Department of Commerce +

The economy was that which produces the net national product.[29] Nathan and Kuznets had been working on these accounts ever since 1932 when the U.S. Senate had passed a resolution requesting the secretary of commerce "to report . . . estimates of the total national income of the United States for each of the calendar years of 1929, '30 and '31" (quoted in Perlman 1983, 138–39). Kuznets and Nathan extended the estimates to 1932, and "interest in *National Income 1929–32* was substantial. Within about 8 months after it was printed, almost 4,500 copies had been sold. This was almost 800 more than sales of the *Statistical Abstract* for that year. Press coverage of the report was also generally good" (Duncan and Shelton 1978, 79).

The national economy was now a single, measurable *household.* No longer a conglomeration of institutions that shaded off into individual households and subsistence farms, or a distinctive economic structure, it had crisp boundaries coterminous with the nation itself. Although the secretary of commerce did not encourage continued publication, Robert Martin, who had worked with Nathan, was able to publish updated estimates in the *Survey of Current Business* (*SCB*). When Nathan returned, the accounts were expanded and soon extended to 1935. By 1937, *monthly* updates would become available in the *SCB* and, "a flood of requests from businessmen made it apparent that the purchasing power uses were the most frequent" (Duncan and Shelton 1978, 81).[30] As the economy became a measurable thing, references to it would become more standardized.

Keynes's *General Theory of Employment, Interest, and Money* was published in 1936. When I began this search for the origins of the economy, I thought this would surely be the linguistic watershed from which all else would flow. Indeed, after beginning the study I came across an article by Mike Emmison (1985, 139–55) making roughly this argument in his dating of the concept in the *New Statesman*, the *New York Times*, *Time Magazine*, and *The Economist*. He reports no specific references to Keynes, and the British pattern may have followed much the same pattern as in the United States because British economists were actually the first to attempt a measurement of the national product. Their efforts, like those in the United States, originated as an effort to allocate production for a nation at war.

Neither Keynes nor *The General Theory* drew attention from the *Times* and *Tribune*. *The General Theory* passed unnoticed in the popular press,[31] and references to Keynes's work were to either a popular article, "How to Avoid a Slump" (1937)[32] or *The Economic Consequences of the Peace* (1920), neither of which uses the concept. Keynes was quite newsworthy over much of the 1930–40 decade, but coverage of him and his work reached its lowest point in the middle three years. Keynes rarely uses the concept economy in his writings, and the 1934 quote above is the only instance I could find in all the *Times* articles that cited or paraphrased his work before 1940.

What was more apparent from the secondary literature was a relatively small number of economists working at the interface between their discipline and the immediate problems of national fiscal management in England and the United States. In England, "James Meade and Richard Stone were compiling for Churchill's war cabinet an accounts system that would reveal any possible slack areas that could be filled with orders for war material" (Perlman 1983, 142). Kuznets and Nathan began the U.S. accounts system in response to congressional alarm over the depression; Nathan consolidated the system for publication in the popular *Survey of Current Business* only to have the project enlarged by the 1937–38 recession (ibid., 140–41) and then swallowed up by the War Production Board trying to accomplish the same thing as the British started with.[33]

One gets some sense of the urgency of these changes of government responsibility in the quotations of economists and newsmen during this period. Both the quotes below are from meetings of the 1936 American Economic Association.

1936: (18) Picturing the problems of war and peace . . . as a contest between autarchian tendencies . . . in *the economies of* dictatorial nations and the forces making for a return to *the freer economy* based upon international cooperation," Professors Marcus Nadier and Arthur Feiler . . . "hailed the leadership assumed by the United States." —*Times* coverage of the 1936 AEA meetings. +

1936: (19) "The . . . success . . . of future monetary management will . . . determine the extent to which . . . private enterprise can continue to operate under *a price economy.*" —Professor Alvin H. Hansen, 1936 AEA meetings reported in the *Times* +

Conferences on the government and the economy began to surface in
the Press.

1937: (20) Students attended the . . . Harvard-Yale-Princeton two day conference
. . . "The *Role of Government in the National Economy.*" —Notification of
the announcement in the *Times* +

A new generation of economists was taking up a more activist role
and "In practice, the government's various roles in the economy were
held to be *sui generis*" by 1937 (Perlman 1983, 141). Still some economists familiar to us from the great bull market continued to look for a
"natural recovery."

1936: (21) The prediction . . . of [continued] *improvement of recovery* . . . was
made by Lionel D. Edie of Edie-Davidson Inc. and David Friday, consulting
economist of Washington who spoke with Mr Ayres (Col. Ayres) at . . . the
Hotel Biltmore. "The great lesson of 1935 has been the *debunking of the idea
that politics controls business recovery.*" *Times* +

None of the three ever changed their tune on this. Nor did the three
ever speak of "the economy" so far as I could tell from the *Times Index*.
Some older politicians also felt that the influence of economists on business was downright alien.

1936: (22) "He [Keynes] said that if only the . . . government would spend
$400,000,000 dollars a month it would *prime the pump* . . . Of course, as a
foreigner, he found ardent followers in this administration, although he had
none in his own government." —Alf Landon in his "Balance the Budget"
speech in the *Tribune* +

By 1937 Washington bureau chief Arthur Sears Henning for the *Tribune*
stepped into the fray and spread the word. A. P. Sloan also found increasing use for it in his New Year's outlook.

1937: (23) [President Roosevelt] possesses a dictator's power . . . to change the price of gold without a moment's notice and to do other things that would profoundly affect stock and commodity prices and other features of the *country's economy.* —A. S. Henning of the *Tribune**

1937: (24) "Now we pass to another problem . . . the problem of injecting into *our national economy* a greater measure of stability. . . . There are . . . important influences to the contrary . . . among them *industrial strife.*" —A. P. Sloan in the *Times**

1938: (25) While certain economic policies are operating toward *unbalancing the national economy,* demanding an accounting sooner or later, the process has not continued long enough to off set *the normal forces of recovery.* —A. P. Sloan in the *Tribune* +

1939: (26) "This [broad recovery] appears to depend more upon political developments here and abroad as *affecting the economy of the various nations* than upon the existing economic possibilities." —A. P. Sloan in the *Times* +

1940: (27) [T]here is relatively little we can do . . . other than seeking . . . intelligent action . . . to cushion the impact of [foreign] events . . . on *our economy* and national welfare. —A. P. Sloan in the *Tribune* +

As the "planned economy" was redefined in the war effort, debate over it faded. Still the *Tribune* would gloat at the demise of the planned economy while also finding use for the concept (no. 31 below).

1938: (28) Wall street thinks that the denunciations of big business by Secretary Ickes and by Asst. Attorney General Jackson are merely part of a campaign to divert attention from the failure of the *erstwhile program of planned economy.* —*Times* +

1939: (29) Calvin B. Hoover of Duke University said that he was convinced that "such experience as we have had is decidedly unfavorable to *total planning by government*" yet . . . "the picture which the opponents of planning often present of the *nature of our existing economy* is fundamentally incorrect." —*Times* +

1939: (30) Officials insisted that *extension of a "planned" national economy was not on the books* and that the studies were designed to assist business by making available information. —*Times* article on study of national income headed by *Richard V. Gilbert, one of the "Spark Plug Boys."* +[34]

1939: (31) One of the nation's wealthiest landlords . . . has developed *a planned economy that works.* —*Tribune* + article praising Metropolitan Life Insurance's tenant farm management of 1,600,000 acres obtained from bankrupt farmers.

Some members of the Roosevelt cabinet found new uses for the concept, and Republican candidates and their supporters began to use the concept (nos. 32–34 below).

1938: (32) He [Cordell Hull] said an *economy of self-sufficiency* is bound to fail in the long run. He did not [explicitly] mention Germany. —*Tribune**

1940: (33) "We must include the raw-materials producer within *our economy*; share with him the fruits of our vast productive market." —Republican vice presidential candidate, Charles McNary in the *Times* +

1940: (34) The count of the ballots tonight . . . will determine whether we are to continue on the course charted by Mr. Roosevelt in foreign policy and in *our domestic economy* or take a different road . . . marked out by Mr. Wilkie. —A. S. Henning in the *Tribune**

After 1949, the word *economy* is used so exclusively to mean all our market-worthy activity that its use to mean thrift or budgetary stewardship had almost disappeared. General references to "business," "commerce," or "industry" were less frequent and were used in a more restricted way.

By the 1950s I seldom had to look beyond the random sample to find at least one example of its usage each year, and I discontinued doing so after the year 1956. Table 2.1 gives the frequency of articles that include

TABLE 2.1. **Percent of Articles With One or More Mentions of "the Economy," 1932–85**

	Random Sample						
	1932	1939	1945	1956	1966	1977	1985
Percent	–	5	16	16	54	37	70
Mentions (N)	0	4	21	17	47	36	39
Articles (N)	93	73	129	108	87	98	56
	Selected Issues*						
Percent	3	10	31	44	discontinued		
Mentions (N)	4	10	21	7			
Articles (N)	136	96	66	16			

* *Tribune* issues that seemed most likely to cover macro economic issues—e.g., New Year's Day, meetings of the AEA, Christmas sales.

at least one mention of the "economy" as an inclusive reference. By 1950 the concept had become hegemonic among experts, government officials, and ordinary readers.[35] The only modifier that usually accompanied it was "our" *economy*.

The Economy as Expert, Official, and Common Knowledge

In 1929 it was common for *Tribune* journalists to write an entire article on commerce, business, and such without any credited authority. In a sample of over five hundred front page articles on business in 1929, 12 percent were asserted in this manner (see fig. 2.1). The most respected authority on business in 1929 was, of course, the businessman. Over a quarter of all credited informants or sources were businessmen or representatives of lobbies for various businesses. Businessmen were not only a prime source of information, a number of them (for example, Henry Ford, Alfred Sloan) were written of as *national heroes* whose success was proof of their foresight. Early in the 1930s they were often asked for their forecasts for business activity, and Alfred Sloan made a practice of it without being asked. His forecasts were routinely published in both the *Tribune* and *Times*.

Another one-third of the sources in the 1929 *Tribune* were congressmen whose primary contribution was information on legislation (for example, the Smoot-Hartly Tariff Bill) that might bear on business or commerce. Many of the congressmen, even the "Demo-Radicals," were treated with some of the respect uniformly bestowed on businessmen. The "Radical Republican" congressmen were traitors, but they could not be neglected for news making. The presidency was treated with grave respect but rarely credited with any direct information. "Silent Cal" lived up to his nickname while congressmen and federal spokesmen took the blunt of open debate over legislative initiatives. Hoover seemed to become more active as economic difficulties wore on but he made no concessions to journalists and progressively appeared as a kind of bully in both the cartoons and the quotations attributed to him.

From 1939, however, a flood of technical literature began to track the national economy. In that year the National Resource Committee published *The Structure of the American Economy*, a report prepared under the direction of Gardner Means. In its pages the American economy achieved not only a formal definition but also a graphic visualization that

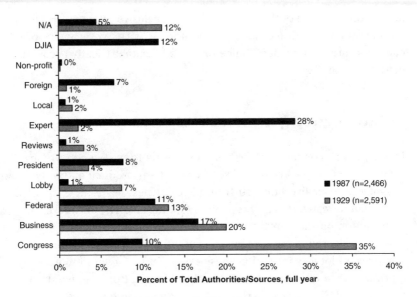

FIGURE 2.1. Type of authorities/sources cited in each year.

showed it as an intricate and intersecting flow of capital, products, services, labor, and government funds. In its maps and graphs, the economy is as tangible as anything else we can find in a book or newspaper. Even earlier, the *Survey of Current Business* was publishing on a monthly basis much that could be found in *The Structure of the American Economy*. Increasingly some of it was routinely reported in the *Tribune* and *Times*. In 1941, Wassily Leontief's *The Structure of the American Economy* was published and the economy would become even more visually available in his input-output analysis. A flood of additional information on the economy was beginning to flow in the form of government reports and following news releases.

Some very able economists had grounded the economy as a unified, measurable "thing" as real as the planet. The journalists now needed another authority than themselves or the businessmen to interpret the flood of information from arcane sources.

By 1987, the big increase is the use of "experts" as sources and informants. Over a quarter of the sources in a sample of 2,466 authorities from 450 articles in the *Tribune* were "experts" (see fig. 2.1). A few of them were academics but the overwhelming majority worked in banks, investment houses, or their own consulting firms. Some were businessmen and women also but were referred to as "experts" or "economists," and they speak a very different language from the businessmen in 1929. Their rhetoric is still current today and attempts to translate something of formal economics into colloquial speech. Some of it is like what you hear from MBAs, but it really seems to be a vocabulary worked out between reporters, readers, and people with various levels of training in economics. The judgments and forecasts of these experts are at the macro or sector level and seldom about only their own firm. Their rhetoric provides an economic "theory" for everyman and is the main concern of the next three chapters.

Of course, not all these authorities in 1987 were "experts" or "economists," and ordinary businessmen and women were still interviewed. Almost always they were asked about their own or similar firms. Although they were only slightly less than the proportion of journalist informants in 1929, there was no one among them who was granted the foresight of an Alfred Sloan or Henry Ford. There were industrial heroes in 1987 (for example, Jack Welch, Michael Milkin) but they were not introduced as "experts" or "economists." They were "Titans," or "Wunderkind."

There is one more important difference in the authorities journalists turned to in each year. In 1987 the proportion of authoritative news coming from the president or the White House had doubled over that in 1929, while the use of congressional informants had shrank to less than a third of what it was. What is most apparent in this change is the increasing importance of international economic news and the "imperial presidency's" responsibility to manage and report on globalization.

Conclusion

In 1929 business, commerce, finance, and transportation ("traction") had belonged to the businessman (usually the owner-businessman) who had the authority to render judgment on them. By the early 1940s the owner-businessmen had taken a back seat to federal appointees, bank economists, stockbrokers and, sometimes, university economists. The front page news was news about the "American economy," something both distinctively American and inclusive of all our economic activities. "Our economy" was written of as if everyone had an entitlement to it as part of the social contract of citizenship itself. It was an entitlement that seemed to gain weight from the threat then posed by the Soviet Union.

But with these entitlements came the measurable prospect of sacrifices by capitalists, labor, the aged, the sick, and any number of other "share holders" who could be singled out and given some measurable role in the collective effort.

This sort of close identity of the economy and the national community comes out clearly in General George Marshall's speech at Harvard University following the end of World War II (see no. 35 below). Our economy had been something worth fighting for and it might require still more sacrifices. The fate of the economy and the national community were coterminous. Ironically, the sacrifices of the Marshall Plan would open the door to globalization and the still deeper question of: who owns the American economy in the global marketplace?

1947: (35) "but it has become obvious during recent months that this visible destruction [in Europe] was probably less serious than the dislocation of the *entire fabric of European economy*. . . . "The feverish preparation for war and
the more feverish maintenance of the war effort engulfed all aspects of *national economies*. . . ." Aside from the demoralizing effect on the world at
large and the possibilities of disturbances arising as a result of the desper-
ation of people. . . . [T]he *consequences to the economy of the United States*
should be apparent to all." . . . [our policy's] purpose should be the *revival
of a working economy* in the world so as to permit the emergence of political and social conditions in which free institutions can exist. —Secretary of
State George Marshall's speech proposing the European Recover Program
(the Marshall Plan) before the 1947 graduating class of Harvard. *Times* +

Appendix 2.1: Background of Early Users of the Concept "Economy"

After researching the year 1935 I never encountered another attempt to define the economy as explicitly as in the paraphrase of Robert Nathan. Implicitly, of course, it was often linked with the entire national product (usually as the GNP). But it was only gradually over the decade that its use extended to almost everyone given a voice on economic subjects. Before 1936 its unambiguous use was confined to economists (for example, Keynes and Nathan), to political leaders (members of FDR's Brain Trust), or celebrity businessmen like Lamont and Sloan.

One very visible member of Roosevelt's Brain Trust was General

Hugh Johnson, a West Pointer who had also picked up a law degree from Berkeley before becoming Bernard Baruch's "economic advisor." Upon joining the New Deal he helped write the National Recovery Act. His training in economics was informal but his position as head of the NRA brought him into heated verbal combat over "the planned economy."[36] Lamont had a degree in engineering (like Hoover, who appointed him secretary of commerce, a position Hoover had occupied) and was a very successful businessman who had served on many corporate boards. Upon his resignation from the Hoover cabinet, it was said that news reporters found him the most open and likeable member of the cabinet.[37] Sloan was probably one of the three most newsworthy spokesmen for the business world during the entire 1930s. Like Henry Ford and Thomas Lamont (of J. P. Morgan),[38] he did not confine his prognostications to his own industry or firm but spoke upon the entire nation's economic condition and quickly came to find a use for the "the economy." He is often credited with inventing the modern corporation and, in particular, its capacity to separate ownership from management and centralized control from decentralized production. Some New Dealers saw in him proof that ownership might not be essential to the economy and sought his approval for their policies. But this was not Sloan's view (Farber 2002).

By 1937 Arthur Sears Henning was drawn into this select group. Henning was head of the *Tribune*'s Washington bureau for thirty-five years and Colonel McCormick's most trusted advisor.[39] He claimed to have known nine presidents personally, gave a weekly "Capital Comments" broadcast on WGN radio, and won the Edward Scott Beck award "for his 1952 series on the American economy" (Unger 1991, 35). After his death, the *Tribune* serialized his memoirs.

Clearly all of these men were at the highest interface among academic economics, the media, and the efforts of government to comprehend and gain some control over the economy. Nathan was directly engaged in the effort to give a systemic description of the economy. Keynes not only lobbied for it in a general way but also "on [his] initiative and advice" (Duncan and Shelton 1978, 84) James Meade and Richard Stone had embarked on a similar objective in England. By the 1936–39 period the debate over a planned economy drew in more professional economists, many of whom are not mentioned above because they did not speak directly of "the economy" but shared news space with those who did.[40] Since it was the practice in this decade to hold the American Economic Association meetings at the same time and place with up to ten other social science association meetings, the debates over economic planning spread across several disciplines in joint sessions, especially those with the American Statistical Association. The "economy" would come to do rhetorical service in all these disciplines.[41]

In the 1941–50 period, those using the concept would spread beyond individuals placed at the academic-media-government interfaces. I no longer had to search the New Year's Eve edition, the articles on the AEA meetings, or track down specific individuals to find an example of its use. Reporters themselves began to use the concept rather than only quote the usage of "experts." In the early part of this period, however, financial editors, like John Forrest at the *Times*, as well as most reporters, continued to preface it by "national" or some other modifier as if to single out American "free enterprise." For example:

1941: (36) Japan now is committed completely to "guns instead of butter" as *a theory of national economy*. A characteristic feature of *totalitarian economy*—reduced standards of living and intensively increased production by heavy and munitions industries. —Reporter Hugh Byas in *Times**

Sometimes the term was attributed to another media or appeared in headlines or in articles with no byline.

1942: (37) This heavy steel activity also means the OPM will make allocations for munitions, steel, heavy rails and other output necessary under a *war economy*. —Attributed to the *Iron Age* by the *Tribune.**

Increasingly, businessmen were quoted as using the term. Some of them had served in federal office during the war and others were spokesmen for trade associations. Some, like Whipple Jacobs, were just favored speakers for quotation.[42] Since the economy was a national possession, supporting it or sacrificing for it became an act of patriotism.

1948: (38) The *European Recovery Plan* will not impose an increased drain on the *American economy* in 1948 declared Harold Boeschenstein, President, Owens-Corning [former administrator of the wartime Controlled Materials Plan]. —*Times**

Use of the term also spread to a wider range of public officials in federal, state, and philanthropic organizations who drew a correspondence between their policies and that of "the economy." Some, like the announcements by Ewan Clague had become routinized press conferences.

1947: (39) Current high prices contain "nothing spectacular" of *an economy wrecking* explosive nature. —Paraphrase of Ewan Clague, director of the bureau of labor statistics, *Tribune**

Adoption of "The economy" was relatively slow in comparison to some more recent vocabulary changes in the *Times Index*. The term *black* for African Americans, for example, comes into the *Index* in 1969, the year after Martin Luther King's assassination. Another year later, President Nixon is quoted as referring to "black people," and the number of entries under "black" quickly outnumbered those under "Negro" until 1977, when the latter was dropped. The term *Hispanic* to refer to Spanish-speaking people came into the *Index* promptly with the 1983 establishment of the National Hispanic Caucus in the Democratic Party, although it did not replace separate, national, or ethnic identities (for example, Mexican or Chicano). *Vagrants*, however, turned into "homeless people" in 1983 promptly after the House Democratic leaders committed themselves to emergency economic assistance for the "homeless."

Most of these vocabulary changes had obvious organizational sponsorship, although *hippies*, which I know was used widely on the streets of Chicago in the early 1960s, had no obvious sponsorship and did not appear in the *Index* until 1967 during the Vietnam war protests. The *yippies*, by contrast, came into the *Index* promptly after the establishment of the Youth International Party in 1968. The *yuppies* come into the *Index* directly after the *yippies* were dropped in 1979. Apparently, consumer generations are simply scheduled to coincide with stylistic promotions. These consumer identities, however, are primarily one-to-one substitutes for previous identities and can hardly be compared to as complete a reconceptualization as that achieved by "the economy," blacks, African Americans, or Hispanics.

PART II

The Daily Dramatism
of Economic News

CHAPTER THREE

The News as Figurative Narratives

It is necessary that those things which a man wishes to retain in memory he should consider how to set out in order, so that from the memory of one thing he comes to another.[1]

How did the journalists bring this new idea of "the economy" into the ordinary reader's ken? How did it differ from how they had "theorized" the daily happenings of what had been a grab bag of institutions and organization well into the 1930s? In either 1929 or 1987 the U.S. economy consisted of millions of people, businesses, and institutions, almost all of them standing at a great distance from individual experience. In each year there must have been some explicit or implicit causal force to drive this grab bag or unseen entity into a single "thing." Few readers would have had any familiarity with economics and, as Colander and Coats (1989, 75–105) point out, even fewer would have found anything that corresponds to it in the daily press.

Within a few years, however, the journalists had transformed their prior vocabulary to describe business, commerce, and finance into a rich and highly standardized vocabulary to describe the economy. Much of this vocabulary either before or after this transformation is what we call figurative language, that is, words that, taken alone, might suggest an altogether different topic or set of happenings. They are metaphors, metonyms, synecdoches, or personifications, what Burke (1945, 503–17) called tropes, words that can transform one social reality into another.

Tropes are common even in ordinary speech. The world is full of particular and unique objects and observations. No two of them are exactly alike, so we must use our language in a rather elastic way, anchoring some words with "good examples" (Rosch 1973 and Rosch et al. 1976) and then stretching them almost out of recognition to a world full of questionable examples.

In Burke's dramatisms these tropes combine to form a story, to turn what may be obscure, mysterious, or difficult into a tale composed of familiar parts. One familiar and essential part of this story is its plot, action, or narrative. Once you know the plot or narrative much of the remaining parts, the characters, their purposes, and the locations with their essential implements, fall into place. Like the hook line in a popular tune, familiar narratives are unforgettable and the most essential part of a literary genre. Much of the remaining parts become so essential they can be anticipated.

In this chapter I will describe and compare only the "tropic" narratives that made sense of the 1929 "grab bag" of business, commerce, and such, and the 1987 economy. I will first construct the 1987 narrative because it will be most familiar to the reader. But the 1987 narrative is also more interesting because it shows how one narrative of the economy can slip into another to avoid a certain awkwardness in the choice of tropes. I will then turn to the 1929 narrative for comparison. The following chapter will fill in the narratives with the essential actors (or personae) and their purposes. Chapter 5 will then describe the tropic setting for these narratives. That chapter goes still further to show how cartoons draw on business or the economy to provide the reader with a visual vocabulary that enriches and replicates the mnemonic force of the dramatisms.

The Narrative of the Marvelous Economic Machine

> Lord, Thou has made this world below the shadow of a dream An', taught by time, I tak' it so—exceptin' always Steam. From coupler-flange to spindle-guide I see Thy Hand, O God—Predestination in the stride o' you connecting rod.[2]

By the early 1940s the economy was a measurable, bounded thing. It was also the central topic of a new journalistic dramatism that would last until 1987 and even the present time. The narrative trail of the 1987 dramatism reaches back to the 1940s, but since it closely resembles the 1987 dramatism, it will be most useful and less redundant to make comparisons with the dramatisms of 1929. To compile a representative sample of these figurative terms I searched all the "front page" articles on the economy in the 1987 *Tribune* (N = 443) and those on business, commerce, finance, and so forth in 1929 (N = 1,049) for what seemed to me obvious figurative language. A number of these words or phrases conveyed some action on, for, or by the economy or business, and they could be placed in a sequence that told a story. It's not that they actually occurred in the newspaper in this narrative order, but that they were used repeatedly, often daily, to advance news stories. These daily narrative movements, however, could be spliced together to tell what you might call a "master narrative,"[3] a lengthy story only portions of which were told each day. It was a story that had a beginning, middle, and an end (see the Economic Machine Narrative list below). The daily entries moved the story forward even if news on the following day did not pick it up at exactly the same place. Taken together, however, you could tell a story that would satisfy the Aristotelian requirement of a "probable or necessary sequence."

After constructing this "master narrative" from the front page articles I went through a large number of other articles (some reaching back to the 1930s and others described in the Methodological Appendix) to search for different or marginal terms that might not fit the narrative. The articles proved to be a storehouse of obvious figurative language that fit the narrative; indeed, the narrative itself was generally decisive in assigning the less obvious or near dead tropes. Although not every action by, for, or on the economy was consistent with this narrative, but surprisingly few exceptions occurred in the 1987 and 1929 articles. Other samples will be used later to interpret these inconsistencies but, in general, the search left me with the very strong impression that (1) the tropes that obviously don't fit the dramatism but continue to reoccur belong to an alternative dramatism, and (2) the tropes that do not fit even an alternative narrative are rare and they seldom reoccur with any frequency.[4] As the search for tropes continued, however, the decisive unit did not seem to be the narrative alone but the *entire dramatism* with its personae, their implements, and the stage on which the dramatism occurred. I will introduce these parts of the dramatism in the following chapters and only then will we get a full sense for how each trope fits into the dramatism.

The Economic Machine Narrative: 1987 *Tribune*
economy fueled
heats up
steams up
expands
strong
makes gains
gains on two fronts
gains speed

takes off
shoots up
goes into overdrive
finely tuned
booms
warnings haunts
slows
cools
tinker with
rehcats
takes slow road
roading rough
takes down turn
plays follow the dollar
runs out of steam
hit by triple whammy
sinks
plunges
hard (soft) landing

revives
grows
creates

Since the 1987 dramatism will be most familiar to contemporary readers, let us examine it first (see the Economic Machine Narrative list above). As in a good novel, the 1987 narrative falls within a recognizable literary genre. It is the story of the marvelous machine, a machine that is capable all kinds of stunts that defy the obvious. Suspense and surprise are built into the narrative in keeping with the genre of the marvelous machine. In 1987 the economic machine is something that can be fueled, that will reheat, steam up, make gains, and so on. Keynes actually anticipated it with his "economic machine" in *The Theory of Employment, Interest, and Money.*[5] Of course the exact order I have imposed on the narrative can be altered somewhat but however you change it, it will be the narrative of the machine that puts the reader "in the frame" (Goffman 1974, 21–39).

The narrative in the above list is not at all something out of the dismal science. It is instead a recognizable plot that fulfills Aristotle's requirements. The genre is that of modern folklore where machines are anthropomorphized into near sentient beings. It is a modern version of Vladimir Prop's Russian fairy tale (1968) that has been revised by the inclusion of contemporary equipment. It is a tale that builds from a promising arousal, gets off to a dramatic start, discovers both inner weaknesses and terrible obstacles, and has both good and bad fortune before confronting the ultimate challenge. Then, we have either a happy or a sad (but never fatal) ending. The reader can either rejoice or be overcome with anxiety.

It is a very familiar story, something quickly recognized, indeed hard to forget and, in its modest way, builds the reader's suspense. For the reader familiar with such stories—a "competent newspaper reader" to use Noam Chomsky's conceit—each step in the narrative is a gradation of suspense. Each episode, however, is not just tantalizing; it brings almost instant comprehension and a form of understanding. It "theorizes" the economy in that most universal of paradigms, the narrative story of the hero who is roused by challenge, journeys into unknown and dangerous regions, meets the enemy, escapes overwhelming odds, and either returns home laden with honor or, in the adult version, becomes a chastened adventurer.

As it turns out, we don't have to learn anything new to understand the American economy. The statement is not facetious, for what I want to claim is that the way public knowledge is shared and our news reading culture made common is largely through such narratives. Something that we do not know is made into something we do know; in this case, it's "the big machine that can." And, once that is done, the news story is fixed into our shared knowledge in an extraordinarily durable way. Indeed it was already there. Not from the family car or any actual machine or personal experience but from the nursery and grade school where we read about the "the little train that could" and other stories or films like *Herbie* where machines serve as characters faced with difficulties but win the struggle to overcome them.

The machine is a flexible narrative and can be fitted easily into this genre but the narrative in the above list cannot be radically changed without making it incoherent or destroying the causal texture of the tale. Marginal utility and Phillips curves would add nothing and not move the action one bit. Experts may say that this is not understanding at all and, on their terms, they are right. The inexpert reader, however, finds in it an instance of a very general progression that he or she understands quite well. Some expert readers may even be able to "reverse" the analogue and superimpose a more analytical or technical interpretation on this skeletal narrative. That is something that takes both literary and economic learning. In their own idiosyncratic way, however, the inexpert reader like me is only able to share his or her understanding with other inexpert people. For the pragmatic purposes of shared comprehension and reassurance in an uncertain world, this little narrative is part of popular economics. Once you get very far from it you get beyond shared awareness and the possibility of communication, agreement, and public reassurance. Communicability is what counts in everyday behavior. Even when readers concoct an alternate story, in all likelihood it will be constructed out of a similar vocabulary.[6]

Readers need not be able to recite the narrative. I could not do so myself. All they need to be able to do is to recognize that, like so many storybook machines, the economy is in some familiar progression, speeding along on its own, imperiled, in need of intervention, confounded by increasing obstacles, headed for the dramatic test, and finally at the point of resolution. Just as one need not to have seen all the previous episodes of the Perils of Pauline to understand a single one, the newspaper reader need only to imaginatively place today's episode among likely preceding or following ones. Former episodes—yesterday's headline—need not be actually remembered, but only sensed vaguely as a formulaic sequel with a likely beginning and a problematic or reassuring outcome.

The phrases in the above list did not actually occur in that order. All of them occurred several times and in several sequences. The chronological order is something the "competent" reader (in this case, me) adds. The fit need only be approximate. The competent reader also brings to a single episode a much richer narrative than is evident in a single article or even an entire newspaper. The reader is actually coauthor (Fish 1980). The newspaper has provided him or her with a vocabulary that will work almost anywhere outside of a university classroom.

That said, not all the obvious figurative words fit the narrative of the economy as a machine. Machines do not "revive" or "grow," and "create" seems doubtful at least in the above narrative. Although these words were very scarce in the 1987 *Tribune*, I knew from issues in other years that they were not at all uncommon. Accordingly I made a search of the 1930–86 samples (one article each year) of the *Times* and *Tribune* (see the Methodological Appendix). The results are shown in the list titled The Medical Emergency Narrative of the Economy below.

So! There is a second narrative, a medical emergency narrative of the economy. The economy is hit, hurt, upset; it is under strain, weak, sluggish; it undergoes testing, gets nourishment and medicine; then it revives, rebounds, and actually grows—so much so that by the end it is "skin tight." There is additional detail, of course, but this is the big picture.

Notice that a number of episodes or "acts" in the medical narrative can also work in the machine narrative and visa versa. Machines can be set back, placed under strain, unwind, become sluggish, and so forth. So can hospital patients. Thus, while constructing the medical dramatism from the 1930–86 sample, I also constructed a second one of the economy as a machine (see the list titled The Economy as a Machine, below) over the same period and from the same articles to see how nearly each corresponded with the 1987 narrative.[7] As you can see the economic machine roars along with much the same vocabulary after about 1940 as it did in 1987.

The Medical Emergency Narrative of the Economy: 1930–86 *Tribune* and *Times*
hurt economy '71, *'80
dislocate economy + *'47
upset economy *'71
soft spot in economy *'54
set back to economy + '62
drain on economy + '48
economy under strain + *'66, *'75
economy takes a breather *'57
economy unwinding + '80
weakness in economy *'75, *'80
flagging economy *'77
sagging economy *'74, *'81
sluggish economy + '62
economy suffers decline *'76, *'79
troubled economy *'76
economy has languished *'86
testing economy + '41
prognosis for economy *'65, *'86
economy depressed *'47, *'77, *'85
chart course for economy + '44
stabilize economy + '37, *'41, *'44, *'56, *'59, *'64, *'85
nourish economy '49

medicine for economy *'79
aid economy *'51
economy revives *'47
economy improves *'82
economy makes gains + '58, '63, '67, '68
economy makes strides *'65
economy rebounds *'85
economy strong + '64, *'68, *'69, *'72, *'77
economy recovers *'38, *'39, *'77, *'78, *'82
revitalize economy '77
economy restored '34
economy grows *'56, *'57, *'63, *'80, *'81, *'84, *'85
pulsating economy *'66
economy flourishing *'86
economy skin tight *'85
    * Years in which phrase occurs at least once
    + Could occur in machine narrative as well

The Economy as a Machine: 1930–86 *Tribune* and *Times*
set back to economy + '62
economy cools off *'68
drain on economy + '48
economy moves downward *'61, *'62
economy slows down *'64, *'65, *'68, *'75, *'80, *'84
economy slackens pace *'77
economy sluggish + '62
strain on the economy + '66, *'75
dislocate economy *'47
economy unbalanced *'38
economy unwinding + '80
economy sinks precipitously *'75
economy skids *'75
economy slides into recession *'79
economy stalled *'82
wreck economy *'42
chart course for economy + '44
testing economy + '41
economy stable + '37, '41, '44, '56, '59, '64, '85

demand drives economy *'65

take up slack in economy *'64

economy picking up *'71

economy turns around *'85

economy gains + '58, *'63, *'67, *'68

economy progresses *'34

economy running along *'67

economy cut loose *'46

economy spurts ahead *'64

economy expands *'49, *'50, *'51, *'52, *'64, *'68, *'79

economy continues advance *'68

economy gaining momentum *'67, *'81

economy moves up *'67, *'85

economy on a plateau *'62

economy reaches high level *'55, *'65

economy strong + '64, *'68, *'69, *'72, *'77

economy operating at capacity *'85

rein in surging economy *'66

put brake on economy *'64, *'70

dampen economy *'70

economy leveling off *'56

    * Years in which phrase occurs at least once

    + Can occur in medical narrative as well

The two machine narratives do differ somewhat in content; the 1987 narrative catches the economic machine primarily in a burst of glory before a harrowing emergency landing in October and November. The 1930–86 narrative of the machine follows the economy over the long haul, from setback to recession to turnaround and the long journey upward before the brakes are applied and the machine levels off.[8] This should be expected since fifty-seven years more nearly requires an epic while one year is only a daily serial with a suspenseful or reassuring ending.

The more interesting thing, however, is that both economic machine stories are told largely in the active mode. As a machine the economy does things largely on its own, relying upon its internal guidance and self-regulation. Not entirely, of course; there is a course charted for its recovery in the 1930–86 epic: it is tested, demand drives it, and there are drains on it. It even slides into a recession and seems to have wrecked itself. Yet nothing disastrous has occurred and the economic machine picks itself up, turns around, and, with a little help from demand, begins the long journey upward and onward.

The 1930–86 medical narrative is quite different. Here the economy is much more passive and reaches the depths of depression. It is upset, sluggish, troubled, and just lies there at first, languishing. Not until it is stabilized, nourished, and given medicine does it begin to make strides on its own to rebound. From there on, the economy seems to mend on its own and grows so much that it is full-to-bursting. The immortal, self-regulating machine!

In general, what I think this adds up to is that journalists (and their informants) tend to adopt the medical emergency narrative when the economy is in trouble, usually trouble deep enough that it is accompanied by some kind of intervention. As long as the economy's difficulties are modest or considered circumstantial, however, it is treated as the self-regulating machine that requires nothing more than "tinkering." Rhetorically this preserves a limited version of the invisible hand, requiring only some modest repair with the economic machine while deeper trouble allows for intervention as a medical emergency. Normally, then, the economy is a machine that requires only routine maintenance. It's a Keynesian machine.

This was my own reading of the complete articles but there is some support for it in the lists titled The Medical Emergency Narrative of the Economy and The Economy as a Machine above. Episodes in the medical narrative tend to occur most frequently during the stagflation of the 1970s and budgetary deficits of the early 1980s (25 percent in each), while episodes from the machine narrative occur most frequently (42 percent) in the "go-go" 1960s. Episodes from each narrative are about equally distributed in what I called the "formative period" of the late '1930s and the 1940s and 1950s with their mix of recovery, wartime controls, and recession. If the episodes that could occur almost equally in either machine narrative are omitted, those from the medical model are even more concentrated (63 percent) in the 1970s during stagflation and the early 1980s, while those from the machine model are distributed about the same (43 percent) in all the episodes.

These are crude temporal divisions and, in any case, reporters have to go beyond the immediate present, contrast the present to other periods or, more rarely, write about the economy in a timeless way. As well, there is always some division of opinion about the economy. The business pages are usually upbeat but the reporters shop for differences among their informants to assure readers that "both sides"[9] have had their say and, perhaps, to create some suspense over what will happen tomorrow. A sentence-by-sentence analysis along these lines, however, is tricky because journalists can implicitly shift time periods or subjects and objects even within the same sentence. One of the more instructive examples comes from a July 3, 1985, column, "Economic Scene," by Leonard Silk in the *New York Times*.

Deficit's Effect on Growth

Budget Director David A. Stockman, in his June 5 address to the board of the New York Stock Exchange, said,[10] "It is now nearly impossible to see where the political will and consensus will come from that is necessary to *enact any plan* (1) big enough to balance the books—or even substantially close the gap."

Would the (2) United States face *disaster* if, as Mr. Stockman warned, budget deficits of $200 billion or more lie in prospect for the next several years?

A common belief is that big deficits and government borrowing (3) *depress the economy* by crowding out other borrowers. But Robert Ortner, chief economist of the Commerce Department, contends that this is a misconception.

In 1962, he says, there was apprehension that, because of the rising Federal deficit, private borrowing would be crowded out; yet economic activity and private borrowing grew strongly in the next two years. In 1984, despite the growth of the deficit, the Federal government's share of total borrowing shrank to 28 percent from 38 percent in 1982.

"Why did (4) *the economy grow* despite the rising deficit?" Mr. Ortner asks. It didn't (5) *It grew* in part because of it.

The budget deficit is a form of "dis-saving"—a reduction in the proportion of national income saved and an increase in the proportion spent on consumption, which is (6) *stimulative*. Yet, whether less public saving is translated into (7) *real growth* depends upon two other factors; the (8) *rate at which the economy is already operating* and (9) *the ease or tightness of Federal Reserve policy*.

At the end of 1982 (10) *the operating rate of American industry* was down to about 70 percent and the unemployment rate, was nearly 11 percent. With that much (11) *slack* and the accommodative monetary policy, Mr. Ortner finds that the deficit contributed to (12) *growth*, rather than *retard it*. Today, after more than (13) *two years of growth*, with rising business investment, there is less (14) *idle capacity* but (15) *the economy is still not skin-tight*.

(16) *Industry is operating at less than 81 percent of capacity* and the unemployment rate is 7.2 percent. The budget deficit still looks more (17) *stimulative* than (18) *inflationary.*

But this is not the whole deficit story. For the budget deficit is *aggravating* the nations' other great deficit: the international trade deficit. This year, according to Commerce Secretary Malcolm Baldrige, the trade deficit is likely *to soar* above $140 billion and could reach $150 billion, compared with last year's record $123 billion.

With such trade deficits *piling up*, the United States would soon become the world's biggest debtor. The implications, says James D. Robinson 3rd, chairman of the American Express Company, are "very serious"—*financial market volatility*, a compromising of the independence of American monetary policy and the danger of rapid *dollar drops* that could *rekindle inflation.*

The trade deficit is acting as a *drag on the economy* and *damaging American industries* dependent on foreign markets and competing with imports. The trade deficit is by no means independent of the Federal budget deficits. On the contrary, as Martin S. Feldstein of Harvard, President Reagan's former chief economic adviser, observes, "The primary reason that the United States has become a capital importer and an international debtor is our vast Federal budget deficit."

He says that this is a universal story that explains the capital inflows of the Latin debtor nations as well as our own: When the Government borrows on a vast scale, it *creates a vacuum* in the domestic capital market that *sucks in capital* from abroad.

Those huge borrowings in turn *drive up real interest rates* on long-term government and corporate bonds, and the increased demand for dollar securities causes the value of the dollar to rise. The strong dollar causes the trade (14) *deficit to swell, hurting a wide range of American industries* including agriculture and timber, steel and chemicals and even high-technology companies. "As a result" Mr. Feldstein recently told a Congressional committee, "the level of industrial production is actually lower than it was last summer and the level of manufacturing employment has been falling every month since the beginning of the year."

Thus, the big budget deficits are helping to create *America's two-tier economy*, with *strong growth in service sectors* and *slow growth or recession in industries exposed to the international economy.*

The persistent deficits in the Federal budget *endanger the stability of the economy* by making it risky for the Fed to accommodate the huge budget deficits whenever *the economy moves up strongly toward full employment. A stop-go course threatens the economy,* as long as the big budget deficits persist. And if Mr. Stockman is right, they will. (All emphases are added.)

Silk's article is not at all typical.[11] It makes an appeal to introductory economics but figurative language carries the major burden of explanation. Silk aims for a lesson in popular economics, but it is a lesson that shifts dexterously between medical and machine narratives even as he documents his analogies with technical authority. Silk starts off with the recognition of deep trouble (1 and 2) and the question of intervention. As he expands this possible emergency he uses the medical narrative (3–7) when speaking of the economy, explicitly (3, 4, 5, 8) or implicitly (6 and 7). At (8), however, he appropriately shifts to the machine narrative to describe something (the rate at which the economy is operating) that is *already going* on independent of the (9) Federal Reserve's policy or even the "routine maintenance" of *tightening or easing up* on credit.

But the next paragraph (9 through 17) presents some real ambiguities because "American industry" (in 9) seems to be used interchangeable with "the economy" (in 14) in a chain of three sentences. The paragraph starts (in 9) with apparent deep trouble but the metaphors (9 and 10: "operating rate" and "slack") are more machinelike than medical. Nonetheless, the deficit comes to the rescue and the medical narrative appropriately takes over in an episode of growth (11 and 12) that moves the economy (explicitly referred to only at the end of the sentence in 15) toward normalcy and the language of the economic machine (14: "less idle capacity"). But the following phrase (15) finds the economy still in trouble and in the medical narrative (15: its not skin-tight). Thus, in the last sentence, the effect of the budget deficit is more medical (17: "stimulative") than mechanical (18: "inflationary").

This sort of phrase-by-phrase analysis does not really work for the economy in remainder of the article because the economy itself becomes a passive object destined to arrive at Silk's conclusion: that the budget deficit is worsening the trade deficit and together they are imposing a "stop-go" course by the Fed that is creating "America's two-tier economy" (see the last two paragraphs). It is this final state of the economy that directs agency to still other dramatisms in which the trade deficit, budget deficit, interest rates, and exchange value of the dollar play out their own narrative.[12] Sometimes these agents also become machinelike;

they soar, rekindle inflation, create vacuums and volatility in the capital markets, suck in capital from abroad, drive up interest rates, and act as a drag on the economy.

But these are yet other stories, and to examine all these other possible dramatisms would be an endless task and miss the point. What the article illustrates is the almost limitless ways in which two master narratives with only a little help from technical language can be manipulated and made complex even while, in the main, preserving their rhetorical availability to the general reader.[13] Other dramatisms enter in filling a supportive role and the argument is quite convincing so long as one grants the causal power of machines, repair shops, and medical treatment. This is about as demanding as news coverage of the economy gets.

"The Business of America Is Business" — Calvin Coolidge

Reporters in 1929 did not face equal rhetorical challenges. Their most inclusive term was *business*, and although "commerce," "industry," and "finance" were treated separately they were often lumped into "business" when attempting to generalize about economic conditions throughout the country. One can construct separate narratives for each of them, but all of them resemble the one for business.[14] The readers need not be buried in detail beyond those for the stock market and administrative and congressional economic policy toward the end of this chapter. To show them all would only detract us from my main line of argument.

In 1929 business was as much a part of the natural world as the earth itself. As you can see from the following list titled The Natural World of Business, business becomes both animal and vegetable; it waxes and wanes with the seasons and responds to the ebb and flow of life in general like Smith's and Marshall's theory of the self-equilibration invisible hand. The naturalistic narrative of business was unusually flexible, and all the 1929 sample terms fit into it somewhere.

The Natural World of Business: 1929 *Tribune*
business is stimulated
perks up
picks up
takes on brighter color
grows

increases
strong
takes lively strides
at higher (good) volume
at higher tide
stays above summer level
brims
lulls
curtailed
hurt
slumps
aid
given tonic
boost business
benefits
stable
scarcely hurt
sound

Like the machine and medical narratives of the economy, the natural narrative of business is a serial, where each episode resolves a previous one and raises suspense for the next one. They constitute, then, a very mnemonic order where each ending is also a beginning and the whole cycle can coil back upon itself in endless repetitions and variations. For both writer and reader, the prior and subsequent episodes need not actually be known; something like them can be imagined or implied. At its worst, it is like switching between two or three similar television programs during the same period; it doesn't take much imagination to figure out what happened when either program was off screen; indeed, imaginary fill-ins may be the best part of TV.

The organic narrative of business had the obvious rhetorical and ideological value that business existed independent of contrivance and belonged to a grander-than-human design. The difference between intervention and self-regulation was hardly detectable since both were treated as natural or seasonal routines. Tonics, cheerleading ("boost business"), "stimulation," and "aids" could refer to any number of things, ranging from consumer demand to Federal Reserve meetings. The vocabulary of the organic business narrative seemed to repackage economic policy as something scheduled by nature. The World War I reparation payments, for example, were "late" but finally coming "to maturity." Even Hoover's "prosperity pow wows" were recast as primordial ritual. Thus, Smithian and Marshallian economics was remade into something as permanent as the motion of the planets and the fall of the tides.

Perhaps that is one reason the business narrative did not last very long into the first Roosevelt administration. The Roosevelt administration wanted to take credit for economic policy and promoted its "planned economy" in response to a great hue and cry for visible political action. In the 1930–86 sample the natural business narrative vanishes by 1940. It (along with commerce and industry but not finance) disappear as generalized narratives of the business world. Business, for example, becomes something people do in their own firms.[15]

The Democrats also abandoned the planned economy by the early 1940s, but by then the machine and medical narratives had come to the rhetorical rescue. The word *business* continued to be used but it no longer had its summary powers.

High Adventure on the Stock Market

I have presented both the economy and business narratives in 1929 and 1987 as stories where the event structure coincides with the plot. Day-to-day reporting and reading seems to require a chronological storyline without distant flashbacks or strategic omissions, although there is rudimentary foreshadowing ("warnings haunt the economy") and surprise episodes ("business scarcely hurt!"). Still the reader can understand today's headlines without actually having read yesterday's. Any mysteries left unsolved today might be reintroduced tomorrow to sustain suspense and reader interest. The action is also narrowly focused as in a child's story where the main character, business or the economy, moves through time and space without much regard for what lies around them.[16] The business and economic narratives are not very social stories.

It is the narratives for stocks (or stock prices, see table 3.1) that move us toward a more social world. General accounts almost always refer to stocks as plural, and they frequently have parades, rallies, and retreats. The genre is that of a band of explorers, adventurers, or athletes engaged in some hazardous or original feat that takes them beyond existing boundaries. Records are to be made and new heights to be scaled. There remains, however, a subjective side to the narrative, with periods

TABLE 3.I. **Narrative for Stocks or Stock Prices,** *Tribune*

1929	1987
Stocks rise	Stocks rise
Lifted by message	Perk up
News boon to	Buoyed by White House
Pushed ahead	New year rally burns bright
Forge ahead	climb on hopes
Pick up momentum	Dollar helps
Advance from force of habit	Pushed by dollar
Spur stocks	Take off
Advance in snappy fashion	Climb
Drive forward	Record volume spurs
Climb	Rise a record
Surge ahead	Stay aloft
Are higher	Join blue chips
Hit record pace	Surge
Plunge ahead	Leap trade balance
Hit page 1	Laugh at triple witching hour
Hit new high	Stay on a roll
Shatter records	Scale new heights
Go on a spree (or jamboree or make whoopee)	Dizzying ascent accelerated
Credit snarls up parade	Hit new high
Jar stocks	Hit two-month high
Remain on upgrade	(sky)rocket to record
Falter	Soar
Upset	Leap into new millennium
Reverse	More records
Retreat (in dignified manner)	Midday, late day rally
Holiday lull	Biggest bull run (or one day rise or one day record)
Mark time	Await new test
Uneven or irregular	Off for holiday
Badly mixed	Pace cools
On anxious seat	Slows or slow day
Wobble all over	Sluggish
Limp along	Trendless
Erratic	Finish mixed
Upheaval	Take cue from dollar (or slip as dollar sinks)
Bombed	Recede (or lose ground)
Bubble bursts (or cracks wide open)	Register drop
Undermined	Confidence in stocks fall
Bottom falls out	Fears plague
Drop (or tumble, violent swings)	Fear bubble will burst
Wild selling (or stampede, rage)	Gloom rules
Turn on friends	Try to shake deficit blues
Crumble under attack	Deficit slams
Crash (or slump)	Do about face
Strike bottom	Rally derailed
Churn about	Take sharp fall
Bounce around	Hopes fade
Unloaded (or liquidated)	Selling blitz
Drift (or sag, tired, bogged down, stale, depressed)	Bears maul

(*continues*)

TABLE 3.1. (*continued*)

1929	1987
Strike bottom level	Suffer
Still groggy or listless	Keep falling
Acquire new lease on life	Plummet (or tumble, gyrate)
Pep up stocks	Plunge
Revive	Panic selling
Gather strength	Waves of panic
Rebound, bounce up	Engulf
Stage rally	Crash
Peaceful times come	Avalanche
	Aftershock hits, chaos
	Wild week
	Calm jittery stocks
	Life after stock crash
	Claw to gain
	Claw to gain
	On rebound
	Rally
	Markets calm

of gloom, rage, suffering, depression and the like. Stocks have emotions and the reader is invited to suffer or rage with them. The story is less self-contained than that for business and the economy so that the reader is left with the impression that the unknown hovers at every turn. There is room for imagination and the anticipation of obstacles, trials, or intrusions not previously apparent. To comprehend or enjoy the story, one must be prepared for the unknown. More than a child's story, it is probably suitable for adolescents.

There are many more episodes in the stock market narrative than in the business and economy narratives primarily because of the larger sample of articles on the stock market, almost one for every day of the year.[17] But the business and the economy narratives are also more repetitive. Those who write on the stock market must be more creative in devising new twists of fate. They are writing for "fans." But the adventure genre lends itself to this sort of creativity; as in *Star Trek*, a few generic adventures can be multiplied endlessly simply by renaming people and things.

The narratives for each year are in the same genre and are very similar in content. I have presented each of them as a single grand adventure with many tests of strength and solidarity before the climatic engagement where, despite the threat of social division and almost sure destruction, calm and cohesion are finally secured. That is not the order in which they occurred over the entire year, although something came close to it around the 1929 slump and 1987 crash. As with the previous narratives, there is endless repetition. Both are heroic tales of how social solidarity is tested (especially in 1929) but eventually wins out. Despite a random walk and threat of a tribal war between bulls and bears, the stock market recovers its team spirit in the last act.

The Flight of D. Jones

In 1987, there was a narrative for Dow Jones (the following list titled Narrative for Dow Jones) to parallel that of the stock market.[18] Jones is more obviously the solo hero (and male) struggling against a conspiracy of circumstances but still cracking records and averting plunges. Only occasionally taking a day off, Jones never lacks for courage, and even when rising on shaky legs, he is a sympathetic figure worth following. The odds against him make his survival rather breathtaking. The D. Jones narrative, then, is essentially a condensation of the stock price narrative. In this digested form, it also satisfies the reader's requirement of leading characters; here a solitary hero relies on his own resources and swings with the punch. His is a solo aviator story, and there is no ambiguity about whom to watch, where our sympathies lie, or where to find good and evil. The adolescent's stock market story has been "digested" into the child's Jones story.

Narrative for Dow Jones, *Tribune*
optimism buoys dow
deficit plan gives dow first lift
following lead, dow up
propel dow into upswing
jumps
rally spreads beyond dow
takes off
has smashing day
soars
buying keeps dow on record roll
record for dow
up a record
cracks 2,150 barrier
closes above 2,300

cracks 2,400
2,400 mark falls to dow
off for holiday
tariff, dollar woes drop dow
woes jolt dow
skids
averts plunge
rally fades
a downer for the dow
down
off
falls
tumbles
worries rise as dow falls
falls a record
plummets
stops tumbling
rising on shaky legs
moves back
up in record topping comeback

Aside from the Dow Jones digest in 1987, there is very little difference between the stock price narratives for each year. They seem to differ only in occasional vocabulary choices, and these surface differences are near synonyms (for example, favorites or blue chips) or functional equivalents (doldrums or clouds of gloom) within the storyline. A reader from one year might notice some difference if he or she picked up a paper from the other year, but it would not be much. The big change was in the narrative.

In these narratives and others to be examined later, there is a common rudimentary structure. A beginning includes some kind of awakening, arousal, or transition from quiescence to engagement. The action mounts, often (although incompletely in the sample for the business narrative) accelerating sharply on the occasion of some outside stimulus or assistance to the main protagonist(s). There is one or more episode of challenge and near disaster before the protagonists seizes victory against *outside personae or obstacles*. The central characters are blameless. Warnings or omens may foreshadow difficult trials. A supreme test brings the suspense to a head. The suspense almost ends in a final moment of near catastrophe. But all is not lost! The protagonist(s) gathers himself (these are tales for boys of all ages) together, still intact or unified, and the ending establishes another period of order similar to the one disturbed at the beginning.

Some readers will recognize a rough correspondence between this progression and the functional transitions that Vladimir Propp discovers in the Russian fairy tale (1968). Indeed, the progression from arousal and challenge, to struggle, to victory and celebration, and then to rest may be as universal as the circadian cycle.[19] Something like it would seem common to all "plain" storytelling that aims at transparency rather than difficulty. Genre and master narratives in this light are what Goffman (1974, 40–82) calls the *keys* to the story's "frame." Often it is provided by a single phrase or headline ("economy fueled"). Nonetheless, some of these tropic narratives achieve considerable complexity, which brings us to the congressional and presidential economic policies.

The Congressional and Presidential Narratives of Economic Policy

The figurative narrative for the congressional and presidential news story of economic policy for each year (table 3.2) achieve this complexity.[20] To appreciate them, the narratives must be presented as parallel, interacting plotlines rather than as a single narrative including both Congress (or "House") and the president (or "White House") for each year. Here one can read down each column to follow the administrative or congressional story separately but, within each year, one can also read back and forth across the two columns as if one is following the action of one and the reaction of the other. There is no exact standardized correspondence between these exchanges, of course, and no effort was made initially to pair them as parallel, interacting narratives. The discovery of corresponding narratives was entirely fortuitous.

Nonetheless, once the phrases in each narrative are strung out to describe minimal movements through time, an almost eerie correspondence between them becomes apparent. The moves for the president and Congress differ in number, but specific matches are inessential because the moves are sufficiently generic that they can counter a number of corresponding moves by each "partner."

Also, it should not be thought that the separate narratives simply

TABLE 3.2. **Congressional and Presidential Narratives on Economic Policy,** *Tribune*

1929		1987	
President	Congress	President	Congress
H aroused	Call special session	Plan more active R role	100th C begins 2 year life
H takes stand	Off to a flying start	R poised	C gets package
H presses for bill	Situation laid before special session	R moves on (budget etc)	Door open to deal
H parley for bill	Bill launched with troubleahead	R goes on road	Deal faces test
H outlines task	Committee to hustle	R campaigns for agenda	C under D control
H speeds up bill	Stir galleries with spirited debate	R peddles policy	D's eye tax boost
H peps up debate	Endless debate	R makes plea	D's blame GOP & one another
H issues warning light	PN map plan of campaign	R huddling	Entangled in dispute
H's honeymoon ends	Log rolling gets under way	R aides seek deal	C'al squabble
H deplores division in ranks	C makes concessions	WH less flexible on (deal etc)	D's hit on taxes
H takes middle course in fight	GOP may slash bill	P stands firm	Politics put break on drive
H to break deadlock	Bill on rocks	P vows	Drive collides with politics
H defends bill	PN's bill is flayed	R plays hardball	Talks wane
H drives	Coalition slashes (bill)	R targets C	Talks stalled
H orders	h dooming (bill)	R denounces D bill	C & WH mired in acrimony
H demands	Political pot seething	R would slash bill	Tension kills bill
H assails	S indulges in criticism	R orders cuts	Veto upheld
H stirs up a row	PN decries H's stand	R faces PN's rebuttal	Govt unable to pay bills
H plans to slash bill (kill bill)	PN takes sarcastic shot	R to rally his troops	R cuts challenged
H enters fight	S warns H	R mounting offensive	D's struggle to break impasse
H faces fire	PN berates H	R goes on attack	GOP proposal lifts hopes
H wobbles	h leaders vow revolt	R attack rebutted	Deadlock broken
test of H's leadership	h fight on	R loses	Impasse cleared
H staking all	h fight reaches floor	R in standoff	Progress on accord
H drawn into tangle	h fight delayed	R in a bind	H bill tries to cut gap
H supporters fight hard	fight flares up in h	R gives PN new leverage	Tentative deal cut
H wins first round	H farm fight runs gauntlet in h	A softens stand	Bill to face R's veto
H triwcked	Clash, row in S	R willing to compromise	S panel oks bill
H foiled	Bitter GOP rows	R bends	Pns reach agreemewnt
H on defensive	S showdown	R, C reach (uneasy) truce*	Deal cut

TABLE 3.2. *(continued)*

1929		1987	
President	Congress	President	Congress
H beaten in fight	PNs threatens, charges, attacks, parries, wars on, defends	Bill signed	Package ok'd
Blow to H	PN loses fight	Government kept afloat*	Bill zooms past S
H meets defeat	Mellon fight tossed into S		S passes bailout
	Mellon fight in S		Send bill to R
	Mellon wins first bout		
	S reaches crossroads		
	C waits for fight		
	Threat of war		
	Battle lines formed		
	S lines up farm groups		
	Ds map battle		
	S split		
	S radicals organize, mobilize		
	Radicals defeat D's		
	Interests join battle		
	Radicals whet knives		
	Battle opens		
	Rebels launch move		
	Factions clash		
	Radicals likely to win 1st round		
	Radicals win skirmish		
	Radicals join Democrats		
	Keep up bombardment		
	Draw fire		
	Lengthy battle		
	Hopeless deadlock		
	S quits in midst of fight		
	Old Guard surrenders		
	S toss blame around		
	S laments		

H = President Hoover; R = President Reagan: C = Congress
h = Lower House; S = Senate; D = Democrats
GOP = Republicans; PN = Proper name (e.g., Senator Smoot)
() = implicit; (etc) = alternative phrasing: e.g., budget, deal, bill.

* Phrases in which the identity of Congress and the administrations are fused.

mirror the annual chronology of economic debate between Congress and the administration during 1929 and 1987. The entries for the presidential and congressional narratives do not occur in this order, and most occur repetitively. Typically, different journalists write articles about Congress and the administration. It is just that when these phrases are strung out so as to describe minimal movements through time, they seem to make up a single, interactive narrative.

The parallel between the 1987 presidential and congressional narratives is especially close, as if each recorded a single game of tit-for-tat. But most of the phrases are taken from three rather separate encounters between Congress and the president: the 1987 debate over the national budget, the controversy over the trade balance, and responsibility for the declining value of the dollar. There were even more encounters between the president and Congress in 1929: two periods of farm legislation, one on tariff legislation, another on the stock market crash itself, and a fifth on tax reduction. Many of the same phrases are used repeatedly in these "encounters." Regardless of the issue, there is a general purpose language for describing presidential and congressional interaction. Thus, it is easy for two or more journalists to write up the stories separately without necessarily talking to one another.

Since journalists specialize in reporting on either the administration or Congress,[21] they present the story in terms of their protagonists' objectives. The effect in table 3.2, then, is somewhat like watching a televised tennis match where the camera shifts from one player to the other, always alternating by focusing largely on who is serving or returning the ball. Each player thus maintains a distinct individuality so that the viewer or reader can shift his or her support and fears from one side to another. At any one time, then, there is a single hero or villain to follow.

The broader narrative genre is that of a historical novel where multiple plotlines are loosely interwoven. No single individual completely hogs the show, although the reader's sentiments are usually directed to one while the other goes "off screen." Humorous asides (like the Mellon fight) may be told without advancing the action. The story also makes a claim to the "realism" found in historical novels; unique places and historic events are recognizable. The economic machine and the naturalized business world were narratives as endless and timeless as a Greek cycle. Here, as in the historical novel, it is composed of subnarratives that I have arranged to run from matrimony, to dispute or debate, to gamesmanship, to pugilism, to organized warfare and, finally, to victory.[22] But it could go otherwise, starting, say, with matrimony and ending with war. Historical novels are like that.

In 1987, however, there is one subnarrative for economic policy that prompts virtually no response from Congress (see the following list titled Foreign Relations). *Foreign* economic policy is reported in 1987 almost as if Congress did not exist. It is, instead, a narrative in which heads of state, their administrations or entire nations, and their capitals are the protagonists. The dramatism takes the form of an "us versus them" narrative so that both sides are on stage at the same time. In foreign policy, then, the same journalist writes about both protagonists in a single article. It is a tale of high-stakes gamesmanship in which the reader's loyalties are uniformly attached to "our side." The number of moves by "our side" also outnumbers the ones by "them." Our side leads; their side counters. Our side has several representatives; "Reagan," "the president," "the administration," the "White House," and "the United States," and often just "we."

There was no similar separate narrative on administrative foreign economic policy in 1929. Policy issues existed; there were the issues of wartime reparations, pending tariff legislation, a naval treaty and currency values. But all of them were debated as domestic issues on the front page. Other countries were seldom singled out, and in the exchange over tariffs, the naval treaty and currency values were carried out within Congress, and very little public presidential comment was reported. "Silent Cal" lived up to his name on this issue. Later, during the Hoover administration when foreign relations became an issue there was editorial complaint when he was not more outspoken, But In the early part of his presidency only "the White House" or some member of the cabinet entered into the infrequent exchange over foreign economic policy. In 1987 Reagan was often the only one out front in American foreign economic policy. The "Great Communicator" hung a picture of Coolidge in the Oval Office but the resemblance seemed to stop there.

Foreign Relations, 1987 *Tribune*
big 5 session in works
P departs for allied summit
R ups summit ante
U.S. gives allies a push
U.S. turns up heat on Japan
U.S. to slap tariffs on Japan
sanctions get green light
U.S. sanctions could spur trade war
Japan draws U.S. fire
no U.S. rush to lift sanctions
U.S. leak greased dollar's slide

dollar meeting could be off
dollar deal eludes U.S., Japan
summit fizzling
Japan talks stalled
trade tension kills deal
R, U.S. take a beating by allies
R fights perception of summit failure
R shifts policy (on) dollar's fall
U.S. proposal spun out of frustration
WH statement buoys beleaguered dollar
Nakasone gets ray of hope
Nakasone to ask trade truce
allies agree on rates
accord reached on currency
dollar pact reaffirmed
    P = President
    R = Reagan
    U.S. = United States
    WH = White House

Conclusion

Many other figurative narratives can be made from these articles. For example, there is a "dollar narrative" that resembles the heroics of Dow Jones. There is a 1987 "economic indicator" narrative that takes the form of a trickster tale where the interest rate and inflation carry on an endless, elusive chase, switching in an out of the role of trickster. The events in these narratives are easily placed in a chronological narrative that suggests a recognizable genre: the presidential romance of domestic policy, a gallery of triumphant entrepreneurs, the wonders of modern technology, and those roguish but enviable takeover artists (see chapters 4 and 7).

All of these narratives also guide the reader toward a resolution of the "spurious present" into something that is comprehensible and less alarming. Their rhetorical function, however, lies not only in crowd control but also in moral regulation. Except in emergencies the economy can be left to self-guidance; the hazards of the stock market ultimately bring out the best in competition; Congress and the president are worthy opponents; and the readers are encouraged to root for the home team and, in 1987, its captain, The Gipper. Obviously this is "ideology," but little is to be gained simply by saying so. Ideology does not explain itself. The more interesting question is the form it takes and how it permeates and persuades our daily understanding. How, indeed, something like the ideas of Locke, Hume, Adam Smith, Malthus, Darwin, and Milton Friedman make their way into our daily vocabulary without our turning a page in the original texts. Maybe it could tell us something about how that nebulous thing we reach for with words like *worldview* enters into our daily life.

CHAPTER FOUR

Personae and Their Purposes

We ought, then, to set up images of a kind that can adhere longest in memory. And we shall do so if we establish similitudes as striking as possible; if we set up images that are not many or vague but active; if we assign to them exceptional beauty, or singular ugliness; if we ornament some of them, as with crowns or purple cloaks, so that the similitude may be more distinct to us; or if we somehow disfigure them, as by introducing one stained with blood or soiled with mud.[1]

The narrative is the spine of a good news story, but a story must also have a point, a message, or a moral. Of course, a good story cannot just be a sermon. Its moral or message must be acted out with convincing dramatic force by actors who exemplify its message and who fail, succeed, or defy the moral as they approach a decisive moment. The previous chapter gave us the narrative spine of news stories on the economy. This chapter gives us the characters as personae who put a familiar and memorable face on economic behavior and turn making money into a test of individual worth. As the epigraph suggests, it must be a striking presence, much more memorable than the day-to-day appearance of the eight to five occupants in the row of cubicles in an investment house. The gray presence of those in the real world of the economy must be remade into someone you want to read about.

Dramatisms and Memory

For no obvious reason Burke does not include personification as one of his master tropes (1945, 503). Lakoff mentions it but only as a kind of metaphor where human properties are attributed to nonhuman objects (1980, 33–34). I want to argue that personification is a master[2] trope because it gives people or groups new identities that reveal their moral

quality in a way that "correct" names and titles alone would never succeed. Such a trope is essential to Burke's dramatism because it is the
way that the *purposes* as well as the *agents* can be revealed. If we are to
believe that one social world can be transformed into another, we must
reveal the purposes of the agents in this new world. On a live stage this
is done with personification, by naming, dialogue, dress, and appearance
that go well beyond the actor's identity listed on the playbill. In everyday life we do it by labeling actual people with moralized identities (for
example, delinquent, bum, beauty, hero) or by likening them to other
people with "exceptional beauty or singular ugliness."

Journalists invent all sorts of characters to act out their narrative
accounts. Some are animate and some are inanimate or, at least, not
human. But all of them have motives or purposes. Sometimes reporters do this by giving "stage names" that resemble those in the old morality plays where personae like Perseverance and Sloth were explicitly
embodied versions of morality and immorality. These personae leave
little to the imagination but obviously meet the standard set by Fernandez (1986, 73–99) who says that tropes must move subjects in "quality
space" away from some "Archimedean point" of unexceptional usage.
News reporters are not subtle about this.

For example, take Wayne Goforth, a representative of the 1929 Nebraska Sheep Growers Association. His name and title alone were only
Archimedean in the *Tribune*. To call him a "sheep man," however, was to
place him among "cattlemen, oil men, steel men, grain men" and some of
the other prominent "thing men" alive in the 1929 *Tribune*. To call him
a "lobbyist" or "paid propagandist" (he was called both of them) was to
move him toward the space already occupied by influence peddlers and
corrupt politicians. Thus, when personification moves subjects in Archimedean space it also moves them in moral space. Inevitably personification also brings him, her, or it into bolder relief than would their proper
titles. Characters are made more striking, more ugly or more beautiful,
and, thus, more memorable.

Throughout this chapter and the remaining ones I am arguing that
dramatisms fix news stories more permanently in our memory than
would a strict effort at literal description. One of the most persuasive
studies of individual memory is Francis Yates's *The Art of Memory*, the
source of the epigraph heading this chapter. A study of mnemonicists
through the ages, her account might be thought to apply only to a few
experts, but there is a mass of literature in psychology that supports her

findings on individual memory (see the Methodological Appendix). To
pursue that literature, however, would detour us from the main thread of
this study. Yates's study is well stated and commended by Alan Baddeley, the leading expert on memory (1990, 176–99). In my epigraphs, then,
I will rely upon Yates's articulate summaries.[3]

This mnemonic effect, I want to argue, extends as well to social memory, that is, the secondary records that make history of what was once
news. The second, third, and so forth draft of the news in making "history" so to speak. The mnemonic wording of the first draft is lasting not
only because newspaper reporters have a first look at "history,"[4] but also
because "hot news" tends to be dramatic and more appealing to readers.
News has to sell itself to the reader *today*, not in the long run when the
drama may have expired and the readers are only students and professors. The language of the present is likely to stay with popular literature
and to be a tempting choice to subsequent writers.

The daily news tends to fall into a dramatism that is so appealing and
mnemonic that it crowds out dull and corrective prose. Revisionist historians will always find grounds for doubt and calmer minds. But, almost
by intention, their accounts are comparatively dull and more likely than
not to rob some of the characters of their color and deny the reader of
the heights of past excitement. For revisionist historians to capture a
large audience they must adopt still other dramatisms as mnemonic and
exciting as the ones they fault; a rare feat indeed.

Personae in the 1929 Business Dramatism

There is no difficulty of finding Personae in newspapers. There are so
many of them and they are so familiar that they may escape most reader's notice. Table 4.1 shows Wayne Goforth the Sheep Man's location in
the *Tribune*'s 1929 division of labor in the economy.[5] He was not the only
Sheep Man represented there and most had multiple referents. Some,
like Credit, were not even human; Credit was treated as a single persona
although he might be any kind of loan capital. This may seem odd to
the contemporary reader. But Credit was a sentient being in 1929, acting
on his own, tough on business, a real disciplinarian on the stock market, and unquestionably male. Credit became an ogre during the crash.
American Inventive Genius was more than sentient; he (another male)

TABLE 4.1. **Personae in the 1929 Business World Narrative**

Team Players	False Prophets	
Production	Finance	
American inventive genius	American capital	
Big business	Financial forces	
Business interests	Financial interests	
Key business men	Key financial leaders	
Trade chieftains	Financial doctors	
Business heads	Lenders	
Bosses	Credit	
Producers	Products	Labor
Grain men	Motors	Workers
Cattlemen	Coppers	The Idle
Sheep men	Steel	
Building men	Oils	
Utility men	Etc.	
etc.		
Harmless	Malign	
Graybeards	Jazz economist	
Doubting Thomas	Sleight of hand	
Prophets	Professor	
Seers	Paid propagandist	
Oracles		

was an exemplary spirit and, along with American Capital, was guiding the country to the forefront of the business world.

Like the characters in the old morality plays all these personae bare their purposes, virtues, and vices in their names and their relation to other personae. In 1929, they made as much sense as Prudence and Satyr in 1500, or "Corporate America" in 1987 (See table 4.2 below). The personae are arranged in a descending topology that does something similar to what anthropologists do in a componential analysis to reveal the systemic contrasts embodied in a kinship system or native typology. In their way these personae are like kin terms, identities that describe a system of relationships built on contrasts. Unlike a kinship system, however, they are sociocentric rather than egocentric and might be better thought of as something like the journalists' team players and their opponents in the business world. The team players constitute a moral order—as would a kinship system—in much the same way that pitchers, catchers, runners, and the like constitute a moral order in George Herbert Mead's famous baseball game (*Mind, Self, and Society*, 1934, 227–55). Or, following MacIntyre, these personae embody the virtues[6] as do his exemplary individuals. The only difference being that immorality is on the field. Journalists are realists.[7]

Accordingly, the first distinction I have made is between those I call the "team players" and their detractors who I call "false prophets."[8] The latter are divided only between those treated humorously and those considered malign. The false prophets are either laughably incompetent or genuinely civil. Among the team players the first contrast is between production and finance. There are a number of financial personae but they are not further differentiated in any obvious way although their "product," Credit, is an independent agent acting on its own. Production, however, is divided among producers, products, and labor. The latter might include "the Idle"—workers who had been "laid off" but were not considered unemployed by the *Tribune*.[9] The general principal was to personify products and to heroize the businessmen who produced them. Legal, sales, or medical services, for instance, were rarely personified by their services alone.[10] Nonprofits, including the churches, made no appearance in the business world narrative. Things that had three dimensions were of uncontestable value in 1929. At the time freight haulage was the only frequent general measure of economic output available and reported quarterly on the front page of the *Tribune*'s Business and Commerce section.

The 1987 Personae in the Economic Machine Dramatism

The significance of this selective personification is best seen in comparison with the personae in the 1987 machine/medical emergency narratives (see table 4.2). The personae in each narrative are combined because most show up in both narratives in 1987 and there is no reason to think that others might not do so as well in a large enough sample. All the 1987 personae occur in several articles except for two (Job Machine and Baby Boom Spender) who appear in only one or two articles.

The broadest distinction made in 1987 is between personae in the domestic and global economy. However, all further distinctions are within the domestic economy, and, as in 1929, they are subdivided into subsequent tiers: a division between government and private personae, a

TABLE 4.2. **Team Players in the 1987 Economic Machine/Medical Narrative**

Domestic		Global		
		Allies		Adversaries
U.S. policy makers White House		Trade partners Big 5 Big 7	OPEC	
Government		Private		
Capital	Labor	Consumers		Experts (undifferentiated)
Fed chief Top Fed or Fed Commerce boss High Court	Business barons Top execs Raiders	Labor force Jobless		Big spender Baby boom spender Big consumer
Production		Finance		
Corporate America Giant contractor Domestic automaker Job machine		Major banks Key bank Lender		

subsequent quartering of the private personae into a contrast between capital and labor, who stand in contrast to consumers, while experts stand in contrast to all three. Only Capital is further differentiated into production and finance personae.

In both years the *Tribune* had its heroes of capitalism, but in 1987 they are overshadowed by broader national and international policy makers. Government now stands at the apex of the pantheon, and even at the next level it is on a par with the heroes of business. This would have been anathema to the 1929 *Tribune*. For example, rumored meetings between Montague Norman, head of the Bank of England, and George Harrison, head of the Federal Reserve, were treated as a sell-out of American interests, although neither Norman or Harrison were personified as villains for their efforts.[11] Business and government had an open and entirely acceptable relationship in 1987.

Beyond this apex, however, only the private sector is further differentiated. Finance is now on a par with production, the unemployed are no longer just idle but unemployed, the consumer is an essential if some what undisciplined hero, and the expert is an undifferentiated team player. Even at the most detailed level, finance and production are on a par. Almost all the "thing" personae of 1929 have disappeared. Things are no longer the only ultimate symbol of value in 1987.

Indeed, there are no outright villains in 1987. The [corporate] Raiders are treated as regular, if somewhat rowdy players. In the stock market narrative, where they appear more often (see below), they are stars.[12] The Jobless are losers but not obviously aggrieved or combative. The Experts, mostly bank economists, are of a uniform quality. The Business Barons and Baby Boom Spenders are a bit gross but still essential players.

The personae go a long way toward reflecting underlying changes since 1929: globalization, more open cooperation between business, political leaders and lobbies,[13] a growing reliance on services, and the cultivation of consumption. But the 1987 personae are much more than an embodiment of changes since 1929. They make incomplete and graduated changes into a finalized state of globalization. The personae in 1987 are as much a statement of what "should be" as it is a statement of "what is." One of the tricks of language, especially figurative language, is to make gradations into qualitative differences and, thus, a fated presence. Their striking contrasts crowd out images that might be more representative but "vague and various."

Personae in the 1929 Stock Market

In 1929, the *Tribune* could write about the stock market as if it were recreational, like a game of chance among the boys down at what was called the "trading post." It wasn't quiet legitimate but not really sinful either. Like other things in the 1920s, skirting the edge of the law or morality was in fashion. This lighthearted approach put a bright face on some occasional signs of unease that playing the market might only be "speculation" and divert money from "legitimate lines of business." This suspicion would be more openly expressed in the 1930s when "playing the stock market" was retold as "gambling," a "con game," or "mania." But in 1929, the stock market was populated by some of the most appealing and colorful personae to be found in the newspaper.

As you can see in table 4.3 it is really a three-way contest among personae rather than a binary one. At one extreme there are the stocks themselves who come alive to carry out their own sporting contest with

TABLE 4.3. **Personae in the 1929 Stock Market Narrative**

Team players		Stocks see below	Outsiders
Professionals	Amateurs	Worldly	Otherworldly
Wall St. fraternity	The public	(Helpful/harmful)	(Helpful/harmful)
Rank and file	Manic Public		
Wall St. flock	Throngs	Construct. forces	Spirit of optimism
Wall St. tribe		Ract.<??> forces	Credit bogy
Pools			Money specter
Market sharps			Ogres
Wild	Domesticated	Harmless	Malign
Bears	Bulls	Graybeards	Jazz economist
		Doubting Thomas	Prophets
			Sleight of hand professor
		[Stocks]	
		Coppers	
		Steel	
		Tractions	
		Pets	
		Favorites	
		Long shots	
		Leaders	
		Bellwethers	
		Fast steppers	

the Team Players at the "trading post." The stocks' names here (like "coppers") do not always reveal their liveliness and sporting spirit, but they could be fast on the field and turn on their owners. Practically any "thing product" stock could become sentient and turn into a "leader." The list in table 4.3 is only a sampling of these personae. Much more manageable were the Favorites, Pets, and Bellwethers. The Faststeppers, though, could blow hot and cold, and one was left with the impression that they might be females.

At the other extreme were a number of outsiders who for good or ill intervened into the trading post. Some of them, like the "Spirit of Optimism," were beneficial and appeared to be almost supernatural. There were also "Reactionary" and "Destructive" forces who intervened without apparent reason.

The "Credit Bogy" and the "Money Specter" were both from the financial district and not to be trusted. There were a number of Ogres, primarily from Congress and other parts of government. The most serious villains, however, were some personae who insisted on sticking their nose into the stock market with unsolicited advice. The Graybeards and Doubting Thomases were only a source of humor until after the crash, when they became villains. The "Jazz Economist," however, was a permanent villain who some bankers blamed for the October crash. The Jazz Economists had disturbed the natural order of the business world with newfangled economic theories that roused the manic public and stripped them of caution.

In between the stocks and outsiders were the team players themselves. They were a rollicking crowd pitted against one another to rouse the readers' partisan feelings. There were the Pros versus the Amateur Public who thrashed about in "Throngs" and became downright "Maniacs" late in the year. The Pros themselves provided a gradient from fraternalism to the "Rank and File" among the brokers. It was the "Pools" and the "Market Sharps" who were at the bottom of this gradient. As in sports generally, however, those who skirted the rules of the game were sometimes the most colorful. They were more than comic relief; they could make an ordinary fan feel that he was no worse than the capitalist class. Like everyone else, the Pools and Sharps could become "Bulls" or "Bears." They were still a part of the "Wall Street Tribe" or "Flock." Lévi-Strauss could have made it up from first principles.

Personae in the 1987 Stock Market

The 1987 stock market was much more heavily policed (see table 4.4) than in 1929. The SEC Chief had principal responsibility for the entire show. But the Fed Chief could also throw the fear of God into Trade Figures and the Public by raising interest rates or margin requirements. By 1987 most of the Prophets had become Experts. Except for a few Gurus who were singled out after the crash, Experts were no longer suspect and, apparently, uniform in ability. Hundreds of these experts were mentioned but all were granted credence, and invidious comparisons were not openly made. Often two or more were asked the same question but were spared pointed comparison. The Gurus were seldom sought out by the reporters themselves. Rather, they were reported as newsmakers rather than informants.

Throughout the early months of 1987 the Stock Market personae

TABLE 4.4. **Personae in the 1987 Stock Market Narrative**

	Team players		Stocks		Outsiders
Government	Stock exchange	Expert	Newsmakers	Gurus	Triple whammy
Fed chief	SEC chief				
Professional	Amateur	Stocks			
Trade figures		Public leaders			
Raiders		Blue chips			
Insiders		Followers			
		Technologies			
		Industrials			
		Energy			
Wild	Domesticated				
Bears	Bulls				

were less colorful than of the ones in 1929.[14] There were the professionals against the amateurs and everybody against the Whammy. There were leaders and followers among the stocks but entire economic sectors (for example, Industrials) have replaced the single product stocks in 1929. Only the Bulls and Bears remained unchanged and unrepentant. During most of 1987 it was harder to sort out villainy from heroism than in 1929. The Raiders were pioneer celebrities on Wall Street despite their bad manners. The Insiders were beginning to surface but nobody had been caught yet, and some observers argued that insider information only made the market more efficient. Who needs morality when you have efficiency?

However, as the "Insider Scandal" began to unravel in late 1987 and early 1988 the personae do diversify and star in a very different dramatism from the one shown above. Much the same thing happens somewhat later by the early 1930s during the Pecora Hearings when a whole colony of gamblers, con artists, and corrupt politicians are discovered. But these new personae emerge primarily after the crashes and they really star in an altogether different dramatism.

For the 1987 reader, most of the personae in the stock market were a well-behaved crowd. Some, like the "Public," are not far from Fernandez's "Archimedean point" of standard usage, although the "Public" here only includes those in the market. The Public seems to be one of those personae who can be shifted from one collectivity to another for differing moral, political, or commercial purposes.[15] The "Public," then, is faceless persona until made beautiful by "crowns or purple cloaks" or hideous by soil or blood. The Raiders and the Insiders were as bad as it got before the crash in 1987.

International Economic Policy Personae in 1929

During early 1929 economic policy was assumed to be in the capable hands of Coolidge, and the transition to Hoover went without a change of thought or vocabulary. In the cartoons, "Coolidge Prosperity" simply became "Hoover Prosperity." Economic policy appeared infrequently on the front page until the crash and then infrequently on the front page. The same was true of 1987 front page coverage of economic policy. Domestic economic policy was simply "Reaganomics," and general satisfaction kept most news on economic policy off the front page. As a result, trade policies and the people guiding them were seldom brought on stage as *Personae*. In keeping with the title of this book and for comparability I have confined their personae to those mentioned in articles on the front page in both years. I believe that a deeper search beyond the front page would reveal much the same.[16]

Early in 1929, front page news on economic policies consisted mainly of expressions of impatience to settle up the war reparations and a fixed suspicion that Montegu Norman was influencing American monetary policy. On rare occasions Europe and Mexico served as counterexamples to the domestic calm of "Coolidge prosperity." The one exception was the Smoot-Hawley Tariff Bill late in the year. Tariff levels on agricultural products badly divided Republicans from the industrial and agricultural states. Thus, most of the personae brought onto the front page were those who were positioned around this issue, primarily congressmen, the presidency, and lobbyists. The 1929 cast of personae on these policies were ordered on simple binary principles of opposition (see table 4.5). Negotiations on tariffs brought foreign capitals and Washington on stage as indivisible personae who acted without internal division. Presidential regime policies were usually personified as the "White House," "Washington," "American," or, simply "We" or "our policies." Uncle Sam could also be enlisted to represent the presidential regime, although elsewhere he was the embodiment of the American nation and its patriots in 1929. Something like Durkheim's mechanical solidarity was assumed or called for. International economic relations were personified as a kind of "us-

TABLE 4.5. **Personae in the 1929 Presidential and Congressional Narrative on Economic Policy**

Team players		Detractors
Uncle Sam		Paid propagandist
		Factions
		Radicals
		Rebels ·
		Foes
		Tammany
Political Regime	The People	Foreign
Washington	The public	London
America	The little man	Paris
		etc.
Executive	Congress	Lobbyists
White House	Upper House	Sheep men
Custom men	Lower House	Cattlemen
Treasury men	President's man	etc.
	Old Guard	

them" opposition in which the reader is assumed to be on "our" side in confrontations that lacked moral complexity. Those who did not line up behind this solid front were "Radicals," "Rebels," and "Foes."

These Radicals, Rebels, and Foes represented practically any senator or congressman who opposed the White House. It was not simply a political party line-up. Many were "Radical Republicans," the worst of the lot, traitors to their own cause, it was said. Coolidge and Hoover were themselves sheltered from the controversy by references to the unified "White House," "Washington," or, "America," which seldom enter into the squabble going on in Congress. "The President's Man" in the House of Representatives was an unofficial persona, but good guess work by the *Tribune* regularly revealed his identity.

Many lobbyists, however, did figure in the debate, and they were of two sorts: those who were personified and honored by their product and those the *Tribune* called "Paid Propagandists." So far as I could tell, all of them were employed by product associations and were seeking amendments to the Smoot-Hawley Tariff Bill. There were, however, suggestions that some were paid with additional funds and that others might have used those funds to sway news coverage or congressmen. But I could find no personification of this distinction. The title of "lobbyist" was itself usually avoided in favor of their product, as honorable a personification as one could hope for. The term *lobbyist*, however, was suspect and sometimes replaced with "paid propagandist," especially when suspected of bribing politicians.

The Smoot-Hawley Tariff Bill was a front page test of Republican loyalties. Although Colonel McCormick quickly lost confidence in Hoover (Wendt 1979), the *Tribune* continued to give unqualified support to his administrative policies. A sharp line was drawn between the administration and those who opposed it. I do not mean that there was any obvious fabrication of the facts or systematic omissions when compared with the *New York Times*. Rather it was as if the theory of the natural business world was utterly uncontestable and Republican. Behind this sense of certainty Republican opponents of administrative economic policies appeared more comic than outright evil. It was just that they failed to recognize that the *Natural Business World* is the way it is.

In general, then, there was a certain formality in the treatment of individual people in high office in 1929 despite their party. In print they were usually called by their title although the cartoons could be merciless. Their private lives and sins were not dwelled upon. Democrats were expected to be "foes" and on the wrong side of any issue. But it was the "Radical Republicans" who were the Radicals and Rebels. This sort of formalism by the *Tribune* was extended especially to the presidency to the point that it was held in such reverence as to embody an icon before the change in administrations. Even in the early 1930s some of the same courtesy was shown to Franklin Roosevelt, although his policies were treated as wrongheaded and hopeless. As a result, interesting, colorful, or evil personae are scarce in the 1929 dramatism of presidential economic policy.

Economic policies were an extension of the 1929 natural business world dramatism. Economic life was governed by natural laws unless meddled in by "Jazz Economists." The business cycle was a regular, natural, and sometimes a painful but endurable cycle. What guaranteed economic well-being was a sound dollar, low interest rates, frugality in public spending, and the freedom of businessmen to find the best return on their investments. The market would take care of all the rest.

It was Smithian or Marshallian economics made into a part of the natural world. With Coolidge and Hoover in the White House the course was set in compliance with nature. Economic policy needed no more guidance than the White House could give it by low taxes, low expenditures, and a free hand for business.

The 1987 International Economic Policy Personae

Some of this reverence for the president's office continues into the 1987 treatment of Reagan and his foreign economic policies (see table 4.6). His movie-made nickname, "The Gipper," however, conveyed a familiarity that had not existed for Coolidge or Hoover. His appeal to voters, "come home America," also prompted a nostalgia for an earlier age of "Gippers" whose uncritical loyalties to place and team affirmed an equally unquestioned nationalism that papered over Reagan's heavy involvement in globalization and saber rattling with the Soviet Union.

Reagan's trade policies are referred to interchangeably as "Washington's," the "White House's," "Reagan's," "America's," or "our" trade policies. Opposing congressmen, however, are not "Foes" or "Rebels" but simply ignored. One reason for this was that presidential international economic policy almost completely dominated front page news, and any sign of congressional dissent was buried or brief. International policy had simply become an administrative responsibility. Except for the "President's man"[17] and the "Speaker," all congressmen and congresswomen were simple "Lawmakers." Even as lawmakers, however, they rarely appeared in the foreign trade narrative. The "Upper" and "Lower" Houses in 1929 had disappeared from front page coverage. Experts were everywhere, of course, but they did not advise and defend Congress as a unit

TABLE 4.6. **Team Players in the 1987 Presidential and Congressional Narrative on Economic Policy**

Opponents	Trade Allies	U.S.	West	East	
OPEC	Big 5 Big 7	Washington	London Bonn etc.	Near East Tel Aviv etc.	Far East Tokyo etc.

Executive	Congress
White House	President's man
The Gipper	Speaker
Lame duck	Lawmaker
Top Fed, etc.	
Defense chief	
Budget chief	
Commerce boss	
Expert	

as they sometimes did for the administration. Congress was not a single persona brought on stage with the "White House." Some "Leaks" on policy were said to come from the White House or the administration but all others were left unattributed. Congress, itself, seemed to be left in the dark.

International trade negotiations are configured in two different oppositional structures. One equates capital cities to entire nations in a three-way regional opposition between the West and the Far East and Near East. A second contrasts Trade Allies and the opposing oil cartel by their acronyms. One can see again here the lack of any differentiation of the members of Congress and their invisibility.

Compared to a narrative of domestic economic policy that mounts from courtship to war, the one on economic policy reveals an imperial presidency knocking on the doors of globalization single-handedly. The image of an imperial president may rub up uncomfortable with Reagan's homespun declaration of "Come home America," but it still seemed to play well in the *Tribune*.

Conclusion

Northrop Frye writes, "In every age the ruling social or intellectual class tends to project its ideals in some form of a romance, where the virtuous heroes and beautiful heroines represent the ideals and the villains the threats to their ascendancy" (1957, 186).

For both Coolidge and the "Gipper" the *Tribune* painted a kind of romance of economic policy that evoked a golden age redrawn from the past. The heroes were in the White House and the villains were in foreign lands or opponents in Congress. Coolidge was the defender of "normalcy" and Reagan the guide to "come home America." The general tendency of economic news to pit the White House against foreign and domestic opponents was enlarged by each administration's appeal to nostalgia and American self-reliance.

But Frye continues, "The romance is nearest of all literary forms to the wish-fulfillment dream, and for that reason it has socially a curiously paradoxical role. . . . [Its] perennially childlike quality is marked by its extraordinary persistent nostalgia, its search for some kind of imaginative golden age" (1957, 186). Both the 1929 and 1987 romances would come crashing down into a corrupt and costly financial crisis. Yet, even today both periods are remembered and often written of as a kind of golden age (for example, the "Roaring 20s" and the "Reagan Revolution") by returning to American self-reliance. Despite much revisionist history (for example, Chancellor 1999) the myth seems to have outlasted the revisionists in social memory. However, we will not be able to return to this question until we look at the wordscapes in chapter 5 and the way in which the financial crashes were told at the time of their occurrence in chapters 6 to 8.

CHAPTER FIVE

Wordscapes and Toonland

Places are chosen, and marked with the utmost possible variety, as a spacious house divided into a number of rooms. Everything of note therein is diligently imprinted on the mind, in order that thought may be able to run through all the parts without let or hindrance. . . . The first notion is placed, as it were, in the forecourt; the second, let us say, in the atrium; the remainder are placed in order all around the impluvium, and committed not only to bedrooms and parlours, but even to statues and the like. What I have spoken of as being done in a house can also be done in public buildings, or on a long journey, or in going through a city, or with pictures.[1]

Burke speaks of scene and agency as distinct generative principles,[2] but in stage performances or real life they share a single, framed presence. In such performances the setting and implements that actors employ may be given separate, causal weight, but like the actors and their purposes they cannot be separated in space and time. The combination is obvious but I comment on it because Burke's term *agency* has come to mean something like a lapse in social control that allows for the exercise of human will. Here it just means the objects and settings that actors draw upon.

In the two previous chapters I have tried to show how the reader may take a few key words to recognize a larger narrative filled with interesting personae. The purpose in this chapter is to show how journalists also construct and combine scene and agency in word and drawings to complete the dramatism and remake news into a coherent gestalt. In doing so, I argue, they give imaginative and visual forms to accommodate and restate their narratives and personae. What they accomplish, however, is not just a mute picture but also a way of graduating the reader's curiosity, anticipation, attention, alarm, and sense of wholeness.

* * *

In journalism as well as in real life and the theater, the stage and its settings not only enable but also foretell or make more plausible forthcoming or past action. As Burke puts it in describing a doctor's office:

> [W]e could observe that even the medical equipment of a doctor's office is not to be judged purely for its diagnostic usefulness but also has a function in the *rhetoric* of medicine. Whatever it is as apparatus, it also appeals as imagery; and if a man has been treated to a fulsome series of tappings, scrutinizings, and listenings, with the aid of various scopes, meters, and gauges, he may feel content to have participated as a patient in such histrionic action though absolutely no material thing has been done for him, whereas he might count himself cheated if he were given a real cure, but without the pageantry. (1950, 171)

Like current phenomenologists, Burke is arguing that readers and viewers go beyond the mere mention or appearance (1945,- 283–87) of a place and its objects to impute their likely use in an unfolding account. To see the means is to imagine their use in a larger narrative. Phenomenologists refer to this as "intentionality" to suggest how we disambiguate the mere presence of things, words, or pictures by placing them in a more accomplished frame (Maynard 2003, 8–9). In this way the specious present is transformed into a recognizable episode in a defined social world. For Burke's patient, the doctor's "pageantry" is an essential part of the cure if the patient is to walk away "cured" in both mind and body. Similarly the newspaper reader must be given some sort of setting that allows him or her to visualize and perhaps anticipate much of the story.

Most journalists try for transparency, but like any storyteller they are advantaged if they and their readers can visualize what they are writing as if it were in a definite place and time. The journalist's stage is not simply a barren list of objects and places. As I hope to show, it is decorated with visual tropes as if in a theater when the setting is first revealed to the audience. I will call these written visualizations "wordscapes," for like theatrical staging they attempt to create something like what we call landscapes with their foreground, midground, and background.

Wordscapes

All writings use images of places and objects, but we are so used to them we overlook their systematic character. Thus, they may seem rather fantastic or unreal when you single them out, group them together, and treat them as if they were as convincing as the doctor's scopes, meters, and gauges. For at least the moment of comprehension, however, they must be as able to capture your temporary belief as do the opening curtains of a theatrical production. My own drawings of these wordscapes may not be up to the standards of a theatrical production but the reader can fill in their weaknesses by appealing to similar stagings in drawings by cartoonists that depend upon much the same visualizations and interpretation. This chapter includes both kinds of cartoons.

Figure 5.1 provides an example of this kind of invitation in the 1929 business and finance dramatism.[3] In this example and all the following ones, the instruments of agency and the setting are placed before a background. In this instance the background is a magnificent mountain rising from the crosscurrents of business to a glistening peak of prosperity—an open-air illusion ripe with challenge and possibilities for the financial community and the business world in the foreground.

As with all mountains, it must be climbed. This is a wordscape that lifts your eyes from the ebb and flow of business to the heights of prosperity. The means are there: the money market is open, and the barometers and yardsticks measure the progress to prosperity and past all the obstacles in between. There are landmarks to show the way: the billion dollar mark, the summer levels, the half-year mark. Things will look very rosy, indeed, when the business community gets to the first outlook. When they reach the next outlook they are almost there. There are hazards, of course. Even at the start there are the crosscurrents and tides. If the business world or financial community should fail, both could end in a depression. Readers have to be braced for tragedy rather than only adventure.

The suggested story is one of opportunity, challenge, difficulties, setbacks, and ascent—the same story that was told us in the narrative of the business world. As with an opera, it isn't enough to just trot the singers out and have them blast away. There must be a foreground, a setting, and a background. Only then is the listener transported from a crowded theater to a new, visually rich social reality. The journalist may demand more of the reader than the opera does of theatergoers, but having gone

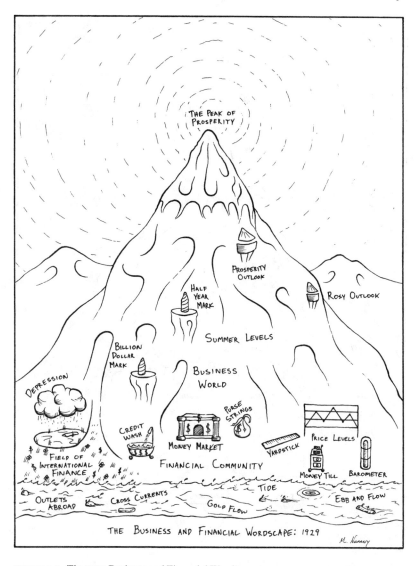

FIGURE 5.1. The 1929 Business and Financial Wordscape.

to an opera will help prepare newspaper readers to enter into the paper's visual imagery as a familiar social reality.

It is this sort of correspondence in the use of imagery that probably allows us to move so easily from one art form to another, one news article to another, and one social reality to another without struggling

FIGURE 5.2. The Economic Machine's Wordscape in 1987.

with each anew. These correspondences are very common among all the
dramatisms of the business world and economy (compare figs. 5.1–5.6).
For example, parts of the 1987 wordscape for the economy are only a
variation on the 1929 wordscape on business. The economic wordscape
(fig. 5.2), however, has been modernized quite a bit for the economic

machine as Keynesian economics replaced Smithian and Marshallian economics. There are paved roads and an electric stoplight, a novelty in 1929. Electric gauges and fancy graphs show the job picture and any number of other economic "pictures" (not shown). The Top Fed has its own spot from which it rations the flow of credit. There are signalmen

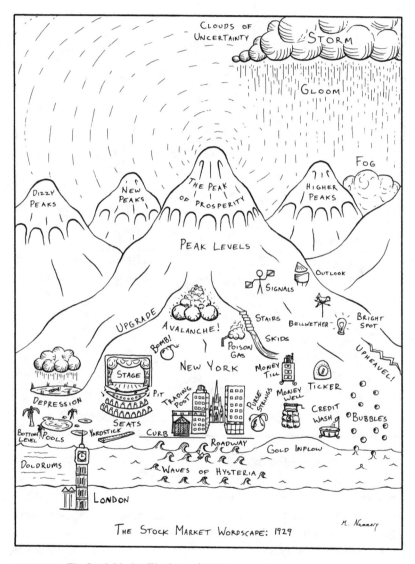

FIGURE 5.3. The Stock Market Wordscape in 1929.

FIGURE 5.4. The Stock Market Wordscape in 1987.

and, once you are past the lower difficulties, there are trade barriers. Beyond that there may be an impasse before reaching the economic summit. It's rough going but there is at least a ray of hope at the top.

The background of the 1929 and 1987 stock market wordscapes is
very much the same as that for the business world and the economy. In

the stock market wordscapes (figs. 5.3 and 5.4) there is also a glistening peak setting a challenge that is even more adventurous for the bulls and bears. There are avalanches and fires. In 1929 bombs and poison gas led to waves of hysteria. There are tremors and aftershocks in 1987. But there are also bright spots and the attractions of record territory. Clouds

FIGURE 5.5. Presidential and Congressional Wordscape in 1929.

FIGURE 5.6. Presidential and Congressional Wordscape in 1987.

of uncertainty and gloom, however, always lurk in the distance in both years. Even more than the business world and economy, the stock market calls for heroism, courage, and teamwork.

The presidential and congressional wordscapes share their background with the other wordscapes, but the setting is quite different (figs. 5.5 and

5.6). The White House and the House (Congress) occupy a prominent position in the foreground with several other distant national capitals across the waves, but only two are shown here. Both presidents have their flags with mottos, "Hoover Prosperity" or "Reaganomics." In 1929 the political pot is really boiling (the tariff hearings) and there is a rocky road between the White House and the House. Some Radical Republicans have roused a hornet's nest and log rolling has ended in a jam. In 1987 Reagan's war chest has proved so expensive there is now a deficit gap that will hinder traffic up the road to the economic summit. Already there are barriers and, in the distance, a likely impasse. In the meantime both the House and the White House have sprung leaks.

All three of the dramatisms are somewhat like a game in which you try to get from here to there in a treacherous obstacle course. But business, the economy, and stock market seem a lot more exciting and fun than the presidential and congressional dramatisms. In this respect the wordscapes restate the absence of teamwork in the tit-for-tat narratives of the presidential and congressional dramatisms in 1929 and 1987. All the wordscapes seem to repeat the comparatively low regard that Americans (and our politicians themselves) have for politics. Politics reveal our differences while business is more like a game against nature and the score is kept only in money.

The similarity of these wordscapes cannot be attributed to the *Tribune* alone because most of the vocabulary is standard in the Associated Press's news releases, the *New York Times*, and my own local papers.[4] Television may be somewhat different, but there is a large overlap with national public TV the only TV economic program I bother to watch. Nor is it simply an artifact of a uniform figurative vocabulary for practically all topics. I have uncovered many quite distinct dramatisms for other topics. The 1929 narrative for organized crime, for example, overlaps some with the business world dramatism, but it also has its own separate figurative vocabulary. Its wordscape, for instance, is mostly underground. Nor can the similarity be attributed to their appearance in the same news articles. The samples for each topic are completely separate from one another. Different journalists tend to specialize in each topic and only occasionally write on one of the other topics (see the Methodological Appendix). It is the topical unity of economic news that unifies much of the figurative language common to each dramatism. This does not mean that economic news is figuratively isolated from other topics, only that the overlap occurs primarily within closely related topics (for

example, white collar crime and Wall Street scandals) and seems to peter out quickly with topics that have different personae or narratives (for
example, Wall Street scandals and juvenile delinquency). The figurative
wordscape for farming, for example, is almost entirely separated from
that of the economy of which it is a part!

The wordscapes are my own visualizations, but the newspaper reader
will have had much the same guidance as I have received. A great pristine
snow-capped mountain is a common icon for calendars (with a preference
for Mt. Fiji, Mt. Blanc, and Mt. Rainier) and, on a mass scale, Mt. Rainier
wallpaper for computer screens. You can hardly avoid Mt. Rainier in
contemporary advertising.

These wordscapes also accommodate the readers' familiarity with
some common conventions in scenographic painting. The background,
midground, and foreground are easily placed. The challenging peak, for
instance, is obviously background for the primary subject, which is in
the midground where most of the important effort is going on. The foreground is less distinct, a sort of platform that places the primary subject
at some elevated distance but central for our attention. These are conventions that readers often use in taking pictures, whether or not they
could articulate them.

The midground is telling us what are the vital parts of the economy.
That is where we should find the business world, the stock market, the
free market, the various gauges and indicators of performance, and the
centerpiece of economic policy. Each of them draw in the reader's attention. The challenge that faces the free market, in turn, lies up the moun-
tainside and gets more and more difficult as one progresses. Meanwhile,
down at the foreground, the earth and water go about their usual un-
rest without much human intervention. The wordscape provides a kind
of gauge to regulate the reader's attention and excitement. Difficulty
and excitement are graduated by height, while importance is signaled
by midlocation.[5] In a rough way, the journalist or the reader can cali-
brate an appropriate response. Avalanches are big news that threatens
the center. A rosy outlook in the foreground allows us to sit back and
relax.

All this may seem to demand a good deal from readers, and, indeed,
I doubt many could articulate similar interpretations. I could not have
done so until I made up the wordscapes. But we often have no declar-
ative knowledge for the things we can do or recognize quite well. How
many of us could explain English grammar whether or not we learned

it in school? What is the pluperfect of "to learn?" Yet, we do quiet well without thinking about it. Recognizing visual imagery, in particular, seems to be the sort of knowledge that most of us practice but cannot explain (Paivio 1990). People must learn some of the same conventions as those practiced in the visual arts; just look at the foreground, midground, and background in the photographs they take.

Toonland

It has been sagaciously discerned by Simonides, or else discovered by some other person, that the most complete pictures are formed in our minds of the things that have been conveyed to them and imprinted on them by the senses, but that the keenest of all our senses is the sense of sight, and that consequently perceptions received by the ears or by reflection can be most easily retained if they are also conveyed to our minds but the mediation of the eyes.[6]

One reason to think that these rather contrived visual conventions are widely understood is that journalists continue to use cartoons despite the availability of photographs.[7] Like figurative language, political cartoons can do more than describe. They can also enliven and go beyond cautious press releases to suggest what may be suspected. Cartoons permit us to say that the emperor has no clothes. Another element to the cartoons is difficult to define. At their best cartoons are not immediately transparent but present the reader with a puzzle. In solving the puzzle, the reader can become a kind of coauthor, and coauthors can be drawn into admiring their own work—a modest triumph but worth self-satisfaction.

There were lots of cartoons in the *Tribune* in both 1929 and 1987. Ordinarily there were three cartoons each day in 1929 and two each day in 1987 except on Saturday when a gallery of "political cartoons from around the world" was printed as well. About 10 percent of these cartoons had something to do with business, the stock market, the economy, or economic policy. In both years most of the cartoons on business and the economy were caricatured by two cartoonists: Orr (59 percent) and McCutcheon (25 percent) in 1929, and Locher (43 percent) and MacNeley (25 percent) in 1987. I took Orr and McCutcheon to be staff cartoonists while the work of Locher and MacNeley was syndicated to several papers.

The cartoon was a well-established convention in both 1929 and 1987, but cartoons differed somewhat between the years. The 1929 cartoons adhered much more closely to the editorial views of the *Tribune* than those in 1987. The 1929 cartoons take a particular position on business, commerce, finance, and taxes and stick with it. It would be more difficult to single out a "party line" from the 1987 cartoons. For instance, the 1987 editorials in the *Tribune* invariably supported President Reagan, but the cartoonists caricatured him mercilessly. In 1929 Hoover was always so heroic and commanding that he appeared something of a bully. Like Hoover, the *Tribune* was unsympathetic with complaining farmers and "idle" workers. Each cartoonist worked with a large stable of stock figures that varied little from frame to frame. I was reminded of the back lot of movie studios where a large stable of props has served hundreds of movies without troubling the viewers by the redundancy.[8] As with movies there was still room for originality and surprise, especially with the more independent ones in 1987.

As I thumbed through these cartoons I came to realize that they were not just still lifes but also that they were meant to tell an active story. They had their narratives, personae, and stages, sometimes repeating the written tropes in chapters 3 and 4. Like television they tracked textual news so the viewers might be "primed" to interpret them. Nonetheless, they varied greatly in subtlety. Interpretation often involved uncovering a correspondence between a drawn figure, an archetypical personae, and then, perhaps, a real person. Or the cartoon might use drawn figures as an implicit play on words. The viewer had to solve or *get*[9] these cartoons before they could tell a story, even if the stories were bold headlines elsewhere. It is here that the viewer shares in the cartoonist's authorship. Since the 1929 cartoons hewed close to the *Tribune*'s party line there was often little to puzzle over, but they made up for it with overstatement to please the more partisan reader.

The Elementary Forms of Toonland

The cartoon not only provides a stage for the journalist's dramatism, it also gives visual form to the narrative, personae, and the stage. We will take them up in order.

Narrative

Cartoons have a kind of syntax that moves the viewer through time and space. For example, in figure 5.7 we see President Reagan loaded down

"An X will do, son. . . . Right here where it says 'cosigner.' "

FIGURE 5.7. Jim Bogan, "An X will do, son."

with weapons from a shopping spree. Just ahead a duplicitous arms seller standing behind his cash register smiles with anticipatory satisfaction at the oncoming sale. Just ahead of Reagan and across from the arms seller is an innocent New Year's babe anticipating the tax payments that will fall upon future generations. Most cartoons are like this. This one even reads from left to right, as would text.[10] Although this is a common bias, the action can start elsewhere. There are all sorts of conventions that define the order of action. "Swish" marks indicate the origin of movement through the air and time. Successive facial expressions like those of Reagan, the arms dealer, and the New Year's babe show a changing awareness over time. Apparent body movement is also a very frequent way of moving the viewer as well through time. Cartoons that seem almost still lifes at first sight (see fig. 5.8) must be filled in with some temporal passage by the viewer. The reader helps to finish the narrative. This is what makes the cartoon fun and seductive. Cartoons are the most interactive part of the newspaper.[11]

Personae

Since cartoons depend upon some degree of ambiguity for effect, all the elements that appear in them cannot have entirely stable referents. Of

FIGURE 5.8. A one-dollar bill showing George Washington with a bag over his head.

course, there are many obvious stock personae who are used repeatedly with slight variation in both 1929 and 1987 cartoons. Some may date from the old Italian commedia dell'arte; for example, the jester (or Harlequin) and the boastful intriguer Scaramouch in figure 5.9 or the pedant, Dottre (not shown). Some have been drawn from other period pieces of literature or the arts: the clown, St. George and the dragon, the knight, the gondolier, the cowboy, the New Year's babe, Santa Claus, and the like. Usually these stock characters are not in the cartoon simply to represent themselves in their original social reality—or unreality—but to enlarge characteristics to be superimposed on some newsworthy person, event, or trend. Occasionally they are "pure" ideal types in the sense that they stand for anyone ("John Q. Public") other than any particular person, class, or group.[12]

By far the most frequent element in these cartoons is some variation of the human form. On average there were about 2 per cartoon in 1929 and about 1.5 in 1987. Sometimes they are not immediately recognizable as a particular person, group, or individual because their identity is newsworthy but not yet conventionalized (an elegantly dressed broker behind bars). But almost always recognition is essential to "get" the cartoon. Other animals—gorillas, dragons, bears, bulls, elephants, mules, monsters—are also popular in both years, appearing in near a third of the cartoons. Their identity is often problematic but also essential to "get" the cartoon. Humans, animals, and monsters are the chief movers and shakers in the cartoons, although occasionally machines (robots), buildings (for example, the White House) and natural objects become sentient and have a mind of their own. Together, however, human and animal forms provide by far the most personae in Toonland. Humans, animals, and monsters rather than organizations or technology usually make toonland economic reality.

The personae in these cartoons on the economy range from grand heroes to utter villains, but the range is much wider in 1929 than in 1987. In 1929, 31 percent of 179 personae were definitely heroes while 13 percent were outright villains.[13] Only 3 percent of 149 personae were heroic in 1987 although 10 percent were sympathetic or blameless figures who had been stymied by circumstances or other personae. There were also very few outright villains in 1987 (4 percent). To some extent, knaves, who were unscrupulous although not evil in 1987, made up the difference from villains in 1929; 20 percent of the human forms in 1987 were knaves while only 9 percent were knaves in 1929. The remaining animals take on various identities with attributes that often lie along dimensions other than just heroism, villainy, knavery, or victimization, or even good and evil. Some possess brute force, others are dupes, and some seem al-

FIGURE 5.9. Dick Locher, "A king, on Wall Street, doing archery with his jester."

most like the photographs (especially in 1929) of real people. Like most photographs the latter are too easy to be fun.

This difference between the years is most extreme in the treatment of the presidents and Uncle Sam (see table 5.1). Hoover was invariably a boisterous hero in charge of the economy. Reagan was sometimes a sympathetic figure despite signs of senility and extravagance. Most often his best-laid economic plans came to naught. In 1929 Uncle Sam usually represented the *American* people and prosperity. He was always a heroic figure even when handicapped by foreigners. Uncle Sam represented the U.S. government in 1987 and was at his best in a cartoon that juxtaposed his World War II performance ("I want you!") with a stoned slob quoting Nancy Reagan ("Just say No!") in 1987. Uncle Sam shared all the frailties of the American government and those of the economy in 1987.

In 1987, untarnished virtue was embodied in victims rather than heroes. Twenty percent of the 1987 cartoons included some victims, and they were about the only completely blameless personae following the crash. The 1929 cartoons included about the same number of victims, but half of them were treated as deserving their fate. Some were those "complaining" about business—the Radical Republicans and the now penniless or imprisoned "get rich" investors.

This tendency to make stronger contrasts in 1929 extends to occupational status, ethnicity, gender, age, and race (see fig. 5.10). In 1987 these distinctions are either avoided, ambiguous, or they reverse conventional social ranks. Underlings may outwit their betters who, in turn, are invariably caricatured without sympathy. Sustained sympathy in a 1987 cartoon is almost a sure sign of inferior status. An ambiguous case was President Reagan. Among the cartoonists, McNeley was unrelenting in caricaturing him as a witless loser. Locher was more sympathetic but there was no sign of hero worship like that for Hoover in 1929. This is a curious reversal of the near deification of Reagan by Republicans following his term in office (see table 5.1) and Hoover's "long farewell" to forgiveness.

Two other differences between the years are the fidelity of drawings and the relative use of ballooned speech. Drawings of human figures in 1929 aim more at representational accuracy, and well-known individuals are usually quite recognizable. Even the settings for the cartoons are more nearly scenographic. In 1987 individuals are more obviously a caricature, and they may also be marred by fussy lines, smudges, or dark

FIGURE 5.10. Stemming the stock stampede.

patches as if to suggest imperfections and ambiguity. Ballooned speech and legends were also much more common in 1929 than in 1987. The 1929 cartoons were not only telling a story, they were also giving authorial guidance to the story (Booth 1961). But the 1987 cartoons were more of a puzzle and more fun for a reader wanting to claim coauthor ship.

The Stage

Inanimate objects—chairs, beds, walls, streets, telephones, and such—in these cartoons are too frequent and too inseparable from one another to be counted with any accuracy. Most often they simply define the location, as would the setting and props on a stage in an opera house. There is a desk and telephone for an office, a microphone and rostrum for a newscast, Greco Roman buildings for the government and banks, and

TABLE 5.1. **Imagery of Hoover, Reagan, and Uncle Sam**

1. Hoover: 7 cartoons in which he was a positive figure as a

1. Doctor (twice)
2. Teamster
3. Heroic figure
4. Teamster
5. Hamlet
6. New resident in the White House

2. Reagan: 36 cartoons in which he was caricatured once or more:

A sympathetic figure as a	A negative figure as a
1. Pilgrim	1. Suited figure (5 times)
2. Stranded motorist	2. Blissful nitwit (twice)
3. House painter	3. Lame duck (twice)
4. Blacksmith	4. Sleeper (twice)
5. Heavy equipment operator	5. Big spender
6. Juggler	6. Stage manager
7. Bar patron	7. Car buyer
8. Stymied figure	8. Cowboy
9. TV actor	9. Pilot
	10. Stuffed turkey
	11. Bookend
	12. Bedtime storyteller
	13. Infant
	14. Dope dealer
	15. Gondolier
	16. Hospital patient
	17. St. George
	18. Customer in brokerage firm
	19. GOP statesman
	20. Resident of White House

3. As a Positive or Negative Uncle Sam

Hoover (all positive):	Reagan (all negative):
1. The American people or nation (10 times)	1. Salesman (twice)
2. U.S. government (3 times)	2. Garbage collector (10 times)
3. American business or free enterprise (twice)	3. WW II recruiter and drunk

A handicapped figure as

1. The U.S. government
2. American business

so forth. They are quite repetitious but a list of them would be even longer than an inventory of all the personae, animals, and ballooned talk.
There is little mystery to these inanimate objects, but they may be dis-
torted in ways that suggest imperfection, irony, and incongruity. In this
instance, these inanimate objects foretell some kind of devious or abnor-
mal course of events.

In 1929 bucolic agricultural scenes were much more common than
in 1987, and a number of the cartoons superimposed parts of the business world onto the agrarian or natural world. This likeness of business
to agriculture was frequent while farming itself was seldom cartooned
positively or negatively (but see fig. 5.11). Elsewhere, the paper was not

FIGURE 5.11. Farm ills.

very sympathetic with complaining farmers despite their important role in the region's economy.[14] Given the conception of the economy as a series of independent institutions in 1929, the use of the natural world as a stage was used separately for finance, commerce, and industry. "Prosperity" was the most global reference for economic activities, and it was almost always cartooned as a glistening peak bidding us onward and upward. In 1987 the economy was a vehicle, sometimes an automobile but also a locomotive or airplane.

The machine is a favorite of cartoonists in both years. Cartoonists in 1929 also favored locomotives, cranes, and suspension bridges for their brute strength, but the automobile was what had caught their imagina-

FIGURE 5.12. Another modern improvement.

FIGURE 5.13. Dr. Ford's prescription may help the patient . . .

tion. In one cartoon the latest models were equated with Hoover's "permanent prosperity" (see fig. 5.12). The self-propelled automobile seemed to have a life force of its own in the race to modernity. This aspect of the automobile was also commonplace in the 1987 cartoons, although no cartoon drew an exact correspondence between the automobile and the economy. The airplane seemed to be displacing it, and at least one cartoon depicted the stock market as a soaring airplane while its engines, the economy, were still lying on the runway (see dust jacket).

Medical intervention on behalf of economic "health" was common in both periods. "Dr. Hoover" brushes aside Congress to save the country's ailing farmer in figure 5.13. "Dr. Henry Ford," in his turn, wrote out what was sure to be a life-saving prescription for the "industrial situation." In 1987, the prognosis was even more serious, but Dr. Reagan was not equally successful. In one carton (not shown) he had given the federal budget an overdose of steroids; "DOA" read the caption. In still another cartoon the federal budget was a trauma victim, and in still another Wall Street was in traction and in sore need of a monetary transfusion.

The props in cartoons give the journalist a great deal of freedom precisely because they can disclaim objectivity, rationality, or fairness. Greater fidelity, such as that in the 1929 cartoons, comes off as more serious, as if the cartoonists expected to convert readers, as if they had found truth rather than just having had fun at the expense of appearances. The 1929 *Tribune* cartoonists often seemed to be "editorializing" rather than just milking the situation for whatever fun they could get out of it. The newspaper was more proprietary and more partisan in 1929 than in 1987, and a glance through a few other newspapers in that period shows similar fidelity to cartoon subjects in 1929. Cartoonists in 1929, I decided, were following editorial policy but ending up "talking" to the converted. You had to laugh at the 1987 cartoons whether you were Republican or Democrat.

Conclusion

Taken together these wordscapes and toonlands fill out the dramatisms of business, the economy, the stock market, and economic policy. The wordscapes appeal to scenographic conventions to regulate the readers' focus of attention and level of excitement. They also give us a stage setting and a set of familiar implements and objects the readers' can share in their "mind's eye" in order to look past the specious present. Together with the narratives and the personae, they help form a gestalt—a story with a beginning, middle, end, and setting.

Appendix 5.1

Philosopher Susanne Langer writes, "all aesthetic experience is virtual, not actual."[15] In the last three chapters I have tried to suggest that something like this emotional and intellectual experience is also created in the "low" art of journalism. Reading and viewing the news can make heavy demands upon the reader's imagination and ability to transpose him- or herself into a world at least as demanding as that of realistic fiction. It also requires much of the reader's memory, for newsworthy narratives, personae, and wordscapes are, at first sight, as unfamiliar as a historical novel. Thus, transposing one's self into this virtual world is only gradually acquired as these strange and unclear references are embedded in what psychologists call a *schemata*. Since it is through memory that individuals gain almost immediate recognition of the news stories' genre, narrative, personae, and wordscapes, journalists must structure them into schemata that may also be learned from many other virtual worlds. To emphasize the importance of this mnemonic structure to facilitate recognition and comprehension, I have headed chapters 3, 4, and 5 with an epigraph from Francis Yates's *The Art of Memory* (1966). A wealth of psychological literature could have been cited, but Yates has captured the most articulate and condensed statements I have discovered.

A full excursion into a vast psychological literature would only detour the reader from my main argument. Some sense of that literature can be found in Paul DiMaggio's splendid article (1997, 263–87) pointing up the importance of psychological schemata to cultural studies. To my mind the best single source on memory is Alan Baddeley's *Human Memory* (1990). Baddeley's combing of the literature as well as his own research shows that perception, retention, and long-term retrieval are much higher for organized material. Indeed, it is often difficult to test memory with narrative material because it has "already been learned" as a common form.

Material can be organized in many different ways: by features, hierarchy, serial order, by "peg words" (say, a place), or by imposing a well-known order (for example, alphabet or cardinal numbers) onto another less well known order (Rosch and Mervis 1977 and Baddeley 1990). Again and again studies have shown that narrative stories, faces, and typical places are among the most easily recognized, retained, and retrieved (Baddeley 1990). Herbert Simon's famous "chunk" (1974) is yet another reference to these schemata. Burke's "dramatisms" would seem to combine all of these mnemonic devices so completely that the newsworthy schemata are hardly escapable.

As mentioned earlier (chapter 4), Hayden White draws a correspondence between Burke's tropes and Piaget's stages of mental development. Later in White's introduction (White 1978, 5) he describes this "deep structure" with such economy that I can only quote him.

> Understanding is a process of rendering the unfamiliar . . . into the familiar. This rendering of the unfamiliar into the familiar is a troping that is generally figurative. I think, that this process of understanding proceeds by the exploitation of the principal modalities of figuration, identified in post Renaissance rhetorical theory as the "master tropes" [Kenneth Burke's phrase].

Appendix 5.2

In looking over these cartoons, I could not help but be reminded of how parts of them resembled some of the stock in the back lot of Warner Brothers.[16] Warner's had a lot filled with virtual reality in all three dimensions. If a director wanted a saloon, the help had only to ask, "You vant a saloon? What kinda saloon you vant? The one from the (old movie)? You vant the hitching post too, right? Yeah? And the stable, huh?" (a lot of the help was Jewish.) If necessary, they could have improvised an impluvium from existing stock. One of the grips would know the entire routine as soon as he knew the first prop. The director, in turn, would put the saloon, hitching post, and stable on film where it could be perceived by the eyes and ears not simply as a piece of back lot social reality but as a piece of an imaginary story that might be better than the real thing. Of course, the pieces that went together to complete the set were reusable, but when assembled the director could "shoot" them in such a way that they were part of his story rather than any story. Cicero, the grip, the director, and the cartoonists knew that you can do something quite imaginative with reusable stock.

The cartoons on the dust jacket ("MORE GLITTERING HEIGHTS AHEAD" and Locher's 1987 jet powered economy) give visual form not only to a revolution in economics but also to how it was reported by the press. They also capture the "spirit of the times"—the undimmed optimism of 1929 and the skepticism of 1987.

PART III

The Telling of the Great Crashes

CHAPTER SIX

The Annual Business Cycle and Its Promoters

The news coverage of the great bull markets of 1929 and 1987 was not simply a dramatism of uphill marches toppled by October bears. In each year the telling of daily news was modulated by expectations that scheduled opportunities, hopes, and reflection. When taken together, it is apparent that these temporal modulations were not simply after-the -fact reporting but were that part of "the economy" that rouses hopes, sets expectations, cheers on expectant readers, and attempts to quiet alarm. Economic news is one of the ways that what is expected to happen does happen.

This chapter looks at four ways the *Tribune* attempted to regulate these expectations, reactions, and disappointments in 1929 and 1987. First, there is the weekly cycle marked by the amplitude of news as it moves from the uncertainties following the weekend to the summing up toward the next weekend. Second, there is the seasonal cycle in the amplitude of news that is paced by shopping holidays and the hopes, government reports, and results that satisfy, calm, or disappoint. Third, when newsworthy perturbations fall well beyond the normal range, the papers may also go beyond the businessman or investment banker experts to invite academic economists to spread their oil on troubled waters. Fourth, and finally, when these perturbations reach the point of national crisis reporters may add the voice of presidents and federal agencies to calm the masses. The years 1929 and 1987 provide occasion for all four ways of telling the great crashes. I will take them up in the above order.

The Daily and Weekly Serial

The weekly business news cycle has a definite rhythm as you can see in figure 6.1. All this graph shows is the average number of pages in the *Tribune*'s business section on each day of each year.[1] Monday had a relatively small business section, about 5.2 pages in 1929 and 10.2 in 1987. It is the Tuesday morning paper that provides the news-hungry with their first reading on what might have gone wrong on the first market day after the weekend. In 1929, the business section reached its peak (7.7 pages) on Tuesday with a close second (7 pages) on Wednesday. Tuesday and Wednesday business sections were also the largest (13.3 and 13.7) in the 1987 *Tribune*. After that the volume of reporting dropped off quite regularly in both years.

There is nothing unusual about this; it is the norm. The usual weekly business news cycle was one during which the initial tests were passed without alarm and the remaining days were treated in less detail. It was departures from this norm that might require explaining. A drop of a standard deviation in the *Tribune*'s industrial index[2] in 1929 or the Dow Jones Industrials in 1987 would increase the size of the business section by, respectively, a quarter and a half a page. Roughly equal increases in

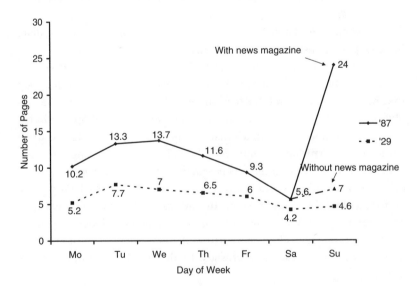

FIGURE 6.1. Average number of pages in business section, 1929 and 1987.

the two indices, however, had no similar effect. Bad news seemed to take more explaining than good news.[3]

"Long weekends" did seem to shift the volume of news coverage to a day or so later in the week. Judging only from my reading of the articles, if nothing untoward had happened earlier both journalists and their informants expected some "profit taking" late in the week to lock up earnings before the uncertainties of the weekend. It was as if the story had fit the weekly plot and everyone could breathe easy over the weekend.

Despite the apparent tendency to increase coverage when stocks trended down, 1929 reporters almost never turned to broadly based quantified measures like the DJIA or NASDAQ. Each weekday, of course, the 1929 *Tribune* did publish daily indexes of stock movements for the previous day in a separate "window." However, they were never referred to until after the crash and, then, only a couple of times. The Dow was also available but it was mentioned only once and, then, after the crash. At the time, many newspapers seemed to have had similar indexes of their own, but none of them had become the national standard the Dow had become by 1987.

In 1987, the Dow had replaced all the *Tribune*'s indexes and was mentioned every day (even most weekends). Accordingly, the *Tribune*'s business section would increase somewhat when the Dow hit "century" or "half-century" marks: during January, or when it "crack[ed] 2,150" in April, and when it "broke through the 2,400 mark" in June as it "hit [a] two month high." By October, however, it was said that "Wall Street awaits new tests" as the Dow declined. By 1987 the Dow could establish "targets," "ceilings," and "floors." As Otis Dudley Duncan (1984) remarks, metrics can become norms even when they are only artifacts.

One significant change was the addition of a Sunday business news magazine in the 1987 *Tribune*. It reflected on the past week and what might happen next week not just on the stock market but also more generally. Much of the news was on specific firms and the views of outstanding businessmen. The glamorization of CEOs as against the major owners was underway in 1987, and the weekend magazine was a vehicle giving CEOs visibility. Their incomes, however, were nothing like those reported twenty years later, nor were they ranked by their salaries, bonuses, options, or payouts like they are now. In 1929, the great dynastic barons and owner-presidents were inseparable from their firms. It was as if they owned the firm, lock, stock, and barrel. Henry Ford, Alfred Sloan, and Thomas Lamont were much more famous than the CEO celebrities of today. They existed on a national stage like that of presidents, and their word on national issues was given as much weight. They were not interviewed by journalists but made press announcements on their own. Their incomes were their own business and what they said was reported in the daily press, often on the front page.

In 1929, the *Tribune* cast about among several indicators of economic performance but granted authority only to the federal government's quarterly industrial index. On a daily and weekly basis stock prices were often taken as the best indicator of economic performance rather than the other way around. News bearing on the stock market made up about a third of the business section in 1929, a little more than in 1987 despite the increase in the number of individual stock quotations in 1987. News on the stock market also made up 40 percent of the stories actually starting on the front page in 1929. By 1987 this had dropped to 29 percent although often mentioned in front page sidelines. But, for daily and weekly purposes the reporters simply had to assume the authority of the market. I must admit it was more fun that way. Had they simply said that business had taken another random walk, no one would have read it.

The Seasonal Promotions

The solstices must be our oldest timepiece (Toulmin and Goodfield 1965, 23–27). The seasons are so embedded in our sense of nature that anything scheduled by their passage seems natural as well. Weather-wise, January may be a lot like December. But not on the financial pages. In 1929 and 1987 everything seemed to have a new urgency about it after New Year's Day, especially the advertisements for the after Christmas sales and, in 1987, gift exchanges as well. There were new and promising reports on the volume of Christmas sales, and soon afterward there were annual estimates of profits, earnings, and, in 1929, freight haulage. The first week of January was also a time for economic forecasts by business leaders, pundits, gurus, and economists.[4]

In a nation where summer weather lasts practically all year in some places and where winter weather can endure into May, standard seasonal "changes" have been scheduled to pace economic forecasts, consumer surveys, government reports, financial announcements, and, above all, consumer behavior. Seasonal celebrations and observances are coordinated to orchestrate this kind of lockstep mass marketing. No holiday passes without some promotional effort and even sacred days of abstinence are usually broken by predictable indulgence. Any number of other consumer activities somehow fall into this schedule—weddings, vacations, family gatherings and, in 1929, the distribution of most dividends in late November, just in time for Christmas shopping.

The Christmas holidays in 1929/30 had already been stretched well into January with after Christmas sales. Then, as now, forthcoming shopping holidays were bunched somewhat in the early half of the year to get things off to a good start. Optimism was not measured by polls in 1929, but the favorable outlooks of several businessmen, including Alfred Sloan and Henry Ford, were given just as much weight as the University of Michigan's measure of consumer confidence in 1987.

In 1929, references to the seasons seemed to carry a certain earthly weight like that of the natural business world. Journalists were especially prone to turns of speech that superimposed seasonal changes upon financial ones. In January, they wrote, "Business picks up with cold weather"; by April, "Spring fever shows up in Wall Street trading"; in July, "Weather fails to wilt starch out of record business"; in September, "Business takes on brighter color as autumn approaches"; and on Christmas Eve, "Trade chieftains give message of Christmas Cheer." The seasonal reporting on business was a continuation of the 1929 natural business world dramatism.

Journalists in 1987 drew much more heavily on "hard data" to navigate the flights of the economic machine. Expressions of confidence and encouragement were more closely timed to monthly and quarterly government reports and a few other respected surveys such as those by the University of Michigan and the Conference Board. This lent to the reports a kind of clockwork scheduling suitable to the economic machine. In the 1987 business section, most holidays (Easter, President's Day, Valentine's Day, Memorial Day, Labor Day, Veterans' Day) were also written of without sentimentality. They were just "sales days" or "long weekends." Seasonal signposts were a time when "the numbers come out." Nature had been accommodated to the self-regulating machine rather than the other way around.

The seasonal variation in the volume of economic news in both years closely resembles that occurring in the weekly cycle. Both years started

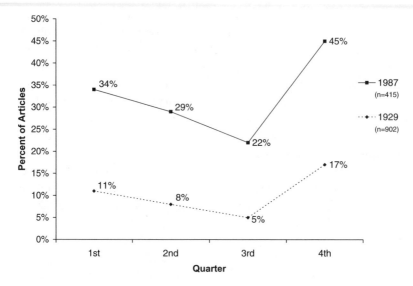

FIGURE 6.2. Percent of articles indicated on front page that actually start on front page.

with high expectations and some apprehension, and news of both reached the front page frequently in the first quarter (see fig. 6.2). As the year wore on, over the next two quarters with some high points and some low points, this kind of variation became the norm. Fewer and fewer articles actually appeared on the front page although there was plenty of favorable news on the business pages. Of course, very good news at first and very bad news later in the final quarter brought a much higher proportion of the articles onto the front page.

This was true of a wide range of topics. News on the stock market did not simply displace other topics but brought them onto the front page in the fourth quarter (see fig. 6.3). The obvious exception was international news in 1929. At that time international news was of interest to reporters and readers because it was written about mainly as a domestic problem. The pressing international issue was how much the tariff should be on molasses, hard winter rye, raw wool, and several other agricultural products. News on international trade fluctuated almost entirely with news on the Hawley-Smoot Tariff Bill in Congress. Coolidge and Hoover both publicly avoided these vexed issues over which a number of farm-state "Radical Republicans" had bolted, party discipline because of the desperate condition of farmers.[5] What made the tariffs and several congressmen newsworthy was an exciting and vitriolic struggle in Congress rather than any wider concern. This kind of entertainment, however, was over when the stock market grabbed the headlines in the last quarter and news on tariffs disappeared.

By 1987, foreign trade negotiations and agreements were treated as a major preoccupation of heads of state, almost to the total exclusion of Congress. Thus, the percent of front page articles on international trade increased during the fourth quarter along with all the other topics. What increased most in the fourth quarter of 1987 was news on fiscal and monetary policy and, of course, the stock market. Front page reports on the nation's economy in 1987 were almost always released by a federal department and were generally accompanied by departmental commentary.[6] A White House spokesman or department head usually commented as well on the same or next day. This pattern introduced some caution in reporting these data but never such as to dampen good or satisfactory news.

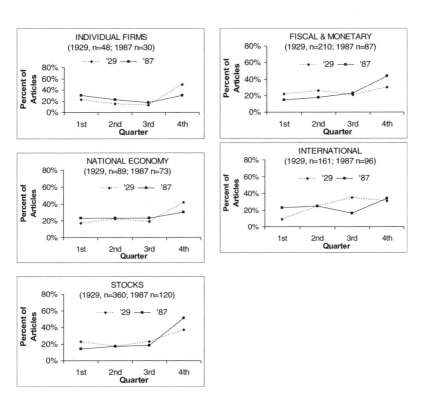

FIGURE 6.3. Percent of front page articles by topic for each quarter.

There was no official pattern of commentary by congressmen in either year, but a few—mostly "Radical Republicans"—did reach the front page in 1929 with complaints of bank failures and the closures on farm loans in the fourth quarter. Their news was not optimistic and rarely reached the front page. In 1987, congressmen were not asked for their views on the economy. Their views seldom reached the front page and were not obviously timed to fluctuations in the economy. They were hardly mentioned at all in the fourth quarter.

To a contemporary reader the reason for the increase in news on fiscal and monetary policies is obvious since they are the main policies used to smooth the business cycle. But there was no agreement on this in 1929 and the conservative position articulated in the *Tribune* was simply to wait until there was a "natural" market recovery, most likely in the spring. The unresolved dispute over monetary policy was what made it newsworthy. At that point the "new era economic theory of prosperity" came in for a good deal of the blame for the crash.

The *Tribune*, however, saw little good coming from the Federal Reserve. What was the obvious source for optimism was the administration's "mellon cuttings" (Andrew Mellon's tax cuts). Conditions were set for another run at prosperity in the spring. What the editorial and staff writers viewed with more immediate optimism in late 1929 was "Christmas cheer," and the seasonal "gloom chasers" (dividends) that would capture the consumer's attention. Since there was little official information to rely on in 1929 journalists could shop around for signs of this springtime recovery. The most available sources for general evaluations of business were the trade reviews or announcements by some business association (for example, the railroads or major chain stores). Even the Federal Reserve's Index of Industrial Activity was sometimes compared to Dun and Bradstreet's seasonal reports in a search for agreement or an alternative, perhaps more encouraging, point of view.

Directly after the crash and in early 1930 the proportion of businessmen among informants in the *Tribune* (as against "experts," politicians, and the White House) increased by about 10 percent. They proved to be very optimistic, and throughout much of the New Year there was considerable dispute among them as to whether or not there had actually been a "slump" in business rather than just the stock market (see chapter 2).

The seasonal telling of economic activity in early 1929 and 1987 was much more on records of consumption than on other economic fluctuations. The scheduling of holidays, the subsequent news on sales, and the monthly and quarterly "round ups" on business paced expressions of confidence in both years and continued right up to the eve of each crash. The 1929 *Tribune* sometimes doubted the reliability of what seasonal reports were available, but they still had great confidence in the forecasts of businessmen as each marketing season approached. Over the longer term it was the forecasts of the great corporate capitalists that counted most.[7] These forecasts were written of as if these men had firsthand knowledge of all industry although no numbers were ever given. The great success of their corporations (called "institutions") in the 1920s was part of the "new era theory of permanent prosperity," but it was the man rather than the theory that appeared on the *Tribune*'s front page.

The Academic Economists

In 1929, it was not uncommon for journalists to write an article that gave absolutely no authority or source (17 percent of the front page sample). In 1987 this occurred in only three brief articles. Quotations and attributions in 1987 outnumbered those of 1929 with about three to one per article and even more per column inch. However, since I have already discussed the seasonal passage of general authorities and sources in chapter 2, I will focus here only upon those periods when the *Tribune* turned to professional, academic economists.

In neither year were academic economists routinely relied upon to interpret the day-to-day events of the economy or stock market. But the reporters needed someone other than just themselves to make their accounts credible or "scientific," especially when so much had failed. As I have emphasized earlier, in 1929, the frontline expert was the businessman who was taken to speak from direct observation. The businessmen tended to be boosterish informants, proud of their recent accomplishments and expecting still more. Before the crash in 1987 journalists relied primarily on "economists" or "experts" who worked for banks or investment firms that closely watched economic reports and the stock market. Curiously, very few were asked what caused the crash immediately afterward in 1987. That task fell primarily to academic economists.

In their separate ways, there were times in both years when the reporters turned to academic economists for a reading on the economy. In 1929 it was primarily in the first nine months to evaluate policy and to forecast the long term. In February, Scrutator[8] disagreed with Jeremiah Jenks (New York University) when the latter said that France's plan to issue gold notes might reduce the supply of money. Shortly afterward Scrutator found an ally in Lionel Edie (University of Chicago) who reassured him that the British would dissuade the French from this folly. A month later L. J. Norton (University of Illinois) said that a 10 cent tariff on molasses would make corn competitive in the manufacture of industrial alcohol, a hopeful sign for midwesterners. In a series of subsequent articles, John D. Black (Harvard) argued that similar tariffs would help U.S. possessions (for example, Cuba) rather than American farmers. In April, Charles Stewart (University of Illinois) explained and promoted his farm debenture plan to Scrutator. Later, in June, R. L. Adams (University of California) was quoted following his testimony on behalf of the California almond growers. Like most other academic experts in early 1929, academic economists were drawn upon to evaluate planned intervention into the economy, and their loyalties to product, state, or nation were relatively obvious.

A month before the 1929 crash, academic economists took a more encouraging role. The first to rise to the occasion in September was that "well known economist from the University of Michigan,"[9] Doctor David Friday, who assured readers that there was little danger in shifting vast amounts of credit from other investments to the stock market. As the stock market became still more volatile the week before the crash, Yale's Irving Fisher offered his "sanguine remarks," which, along with those of the banker Charles Mitchell,[10] provided the "principal news factor behind the day's recovery." Finally, on October 28, a report on Anne Bezanson's (Wharton School) research bore the alarming headline "business heads to read [the] want ads." As it turned out she was only saying that want ads provide a good estimate of the demand for labor. Once the slump on Wall Street occurred, no further academic experts showed up on the front page of the 1929 *Tribune* and reporters felt free to disagree with their past advice.

In 1987, academic economists were called on most often to explain what caused the crash and what to expect afterward. Beforehand, journalists turned to academic economists only three times; all three academics encouraged caution. D. Ratajczak (Georgia State) warned that despite a low jobless rate, "Manufacturing isn't rebounding sharply." A few days later MIT's David Birch was also pessimistic about "corporate America": "It's been years since the Fortune 500 contributed one net job to the economy." Walter Fackler (University of Chicago) was more reassuring when he told reporters that Beryl Sprinkle's resignation was a personal necessity rather than a defection from the Reagan team.[11] Shortly afterward, Ray Marshall (University of Texas, previously President Carter's secretary of labor) pointed out the gross inequities in the "sharing of benefits in corporate buy outs." At best, the few economists questioned by journalists before the crash were either cautious or downers.

After the crash, economists played a more complex role by first reassuring investors, then discrediting some other explanations of the crash, and, finally, taking a shot at some disfavored economic policy that had nothing much to do with the crash. Galbraith's (Harvard) comment was typical. "It was basically simple. A lot of people and a lot of institutions were in the market with the expectation that it was going up and the hope they could get out before it went down." After saying that computer trading was not to blame he argued that the crash was only "made worse by Reagan's economic policies. It's an overwhelming case of institutional fright. Panic is too strong." Merton Miller (University of Chicago) very nearly agreed: "Computer trading is going to get the blame but this is the same [i.e., reckless investments] as [in] 1929." Alan Binder (Princeton) observed that markets often fluctuate widely and that "this one is big enough [to] knock a half to two-thirds of a percent off" the GNP but that was all. Frank Levy (University of Maryland) assured readers that while "many pension funds lost asset value . . . Americans will keep their future pension benefits. Many are not fully funded [by stock investments] anyway." Four days after the crash, Lawrence Summers (Harvard) said that a better than expected report on "U.S. [economic] growth, confirms what everybody is saying. We are not going to have another depression. What we see on Wall Street is a jolt that should awaken us to the reality that our debt binge can't be used forever to support inflation-free growth." However, Paul Romer (University of Rochester) cautioned that "good economic statistics are backward looking and it is possible for good things to happen like low inflation and good growth while bad things are on the horizon."

When the world's stock exchanges remained volatile a week later, Reena Aggarual (Georgetown University) assured the *Tribune* that it should be expected, and James Scott (Columbia) added that computer trading "did not have as much to do with the current volatility as the way institutional investors follow a price momentum strategy . . . bailing out the market when their portfolio falls below specified levels of valuation." When stock price fluctuations were linked with the dollar's decline, Gary Haufbrauer (Georgetown University) responded in a series of articles that ran from late October to late November. "The Louvre pact," he said, had "set an unsustainable high value on the dollar." But twelve days later, after Reagan said that the dollar had fallen enough, he added, "My guess is that with the strong depreciation in the dollar's value we've seen, that maybe its time for a pause." When good news on the trade deficit arrived two days later: "The improvement is there . . . but this doesn't look like a big march downward [in the trade deficit]." A few days later he cautioned against setting the dollar's value too high and later that month recognized that the deficit agreement in Congress was insufficient but, "if the administration had agreed to a . . . significantly larger deficit package, it would have risked a recession." Then, when an arms agreement with the Soviet Union seemed in the offing, a note of almost unequivocal optimism crept into his colleague William Harris's statement that a reduction of defense spending by "$100 billion for 2, 3 or 5 years . . . would be very beneficial." But George Stigler (University of Chicago) had the last word for the year: "If military spending were cut . . . it wouldn't make the economy more productive if the money were spent on catastrophic health insurance or other spending programs."

After the crash in 1929, economists did not fare well. Dr. Friday was revealed as a promoter of stocks, and it was said of Roger Babson that "he kept predicting a crash until we had one!" At the national meeting of bankers late that year one member declared that the whole mess was caused by the theories of "jazz age economists." According to the bankers, every great slump had been preceded by a "new era school of prophets,"[12] and the present one was no exception. "Jazz age economists," the bankers said, had argued that "with the Federal Reserve Board to control commodity prices, the earnings-to-price ratio of stocks was no longer considered important because investors were . . . merely discounting future growth. Necessarily this got the market in an overbulled position."[13] The bankers and the *Tribune* were merciful only in not mentioning any names. Perhaps they were too close at hand.[14]

By pouring oil on troubled waters and hedging their bets the 1987 academic economists fared much better than the 1929 ones. *Tribune* reporters treated them respectfully and, unlike Scrutator in 1929, never disagreed with them. They always listed their Nobel prizes, their specialties, and their prestigious institutions.

The Presidents

In every Age the ruling social or intellectual class tends to project its ideals in some form of a romance, where the virtuous heroes and beautiful heroines represent the ideals and villains the threat to their ascendancy. (Frye 1957, 186)

Each of the presidents was closely identified with economic policy and the bull markets during their terms. "New Age prosperity," "Coolidge prosperity," "Hoover prosperity," and "Permanent prosperity" were mentioned only as alternatives to one or the other. In the remaining time left to his administration, Coolidge reached the front page only once when he gave his farewell budget address, warning "that the nation's prosperity can only be continued . . . by the practices of rigid economy in local, state and federal expenditures." His tax policies were much praised in the *Tribune* business section and there was no mention of the discontent among Illinois farmers for his having recently vetoed a farm relief bill.

In his campaign, Hoover had chided Americans that "prosperity is no idle expression," seeming to imply that his own understanding of it ran rather deep. With his election, he automatically assumed Coolidge's mantel as "Hoover prosperity" replaced "Coolidge prosperity" before even the latter was out of office. Brief rallies on the stock market were attributed to his election: "Hoover bull market," one headline ran, "the bears became bulls and the bulls became rich."

Reagan was equally identified with his administration's economic policies. Arthur Laffer's "supply side economics" quickly became "Reaganomics." Two slogans captured his economic policies: "all boats rise on the same tide" and "tax cuts pay for themselves." How could you lose? Even after the "insider scandal" broke in 1986, Reagan started the New Year with a State of the Union address that envisioned nothing but blue sky ahead. "The calendar can't measure America because we were meant to be an endless experiment in freedom, with no limit to our reaches, no boundaries to what we can do and no end point to our hopes" (quoted in Chancellor 1999, 264). The Dow hit 2,000.

It was Hoover who inherited the difficulties subsequent to the 1929 crash. At first he was relatively silent and distant to the press. News of his administration usually came from one of his department heads, often Robert Lamont, secretary of commerce. After the "slump" he did have Julius Klein, assistant secretary of commerce, quote him as saying, "The fundamental business of the country, that of production and distribution of commodities, is on a sound and prosperous basis" (reported on both October 26 and 30 in the *Tribune*). Apparently there were further pressures on him to make known his position on speculation (Galbraith, 1955, 21 and 40.), but only indirect indications of his attitude reached the *Tribune* (for example, "Hoover's backing claimed for Federal Reserve increase in rediscount rate").

In April, however, an article by Henning, McCormick's closest confident, blamed one of Hoover's speeches for a slump in wheat.[15] By July, there were "conflicting views on Hoover's popularity." As uncertainty increased, he called a special session of Congress to address farm aid, but congressional leaders only complained that he had given insufficient direction. Subsequently, some Republican senators did invite the "leaders of business" (for example, Henry Ford, Charles Schwab, John D. Rockefeller, and Andrew Mellon, secretary of the treasury) to give the senators and "America's farmers" direction. During the hearings Senator Carraway (Arkansas) roused his fellow Democrats by declaring, "[They] don't know the difference between a horse and a cow."[16] Several other congressmen, including some "Radical Republicans," sided with the farmers against these "so-called spokesmen of farmers."

In an attempt to rebuild confidence Hoover called several "prosperity meetings" with different business leaders in banking, manufacturing, and transportation as well as the state governors, urging each to "spend now." The meetings were taken as obvious efforts to raise public confidence, and the *Tribune* quickly labeled them "Prosperity pow wows." Having laid claim to "Hoover prosperity" and the "Hoover bull market," he was tarnished by their failure. The long descent of his identification with the "slump" that would become the "Great Depression" began in the first year of his administration before the word *depression* was hardly mentioned. Despite private misgivings, however, the *Tribune* unfailingly backed his tendency to lecture Americans for complaining. It may have done him a disservice.

Shortly after the 1987 crash Reagan made no immediate effort to say anything until asked by the press. "Well," he said, "I have only one thing to say. I think everyone is a little puzzled because—and I don't know whether, what meaning it might have—because all the business indices are up. There is nothing wrong with the economy. Maybe some people see a chance to grab a profit. I don't know" (October 20, 1987). Reagan's statement was completely disingenuous and accepted as such in subsequent business reporting in the *Tribune*. However, according to Chernow (1991, 700), "Reagan, eager to echo Hoover, said, 'the underlying economy remains sound' for a November 2 issue of *Time* magazine." I could not find this repeated in the *Tribune*. Hoover's declaration also turns up during the Clinton administration when the Dow fell 7 percent and Robert Rubin, secretary of the treasury is said to have employed "the same language Herbert Hoover used" (Chancellor, 1999, 229). Why the presidents were encouraged to repeat Hoover is puzzling. Certainly it did no service for Hoover other than to more closely identify him with the slump and depression. Reagan simply dissociated himself from the stock market. No one seems to have learned anything from the "Great Communicator's" clincher.

Summing Up: The *Wall Street Journal* and the SEC

As the end of 1987 approached, the *Wall Street Journal* published an analysis ("Before the Fall," December 11) of the rise and fall of the great bull market. A lengthy article, the narrative stretched from the last months of 1986 to the immediate period after the crash. The argument essentially detailed a sequence of cumulative events, each of them playing an incremental role in hoisting stock prices beyond credible levels.

Initially, the *Journal* stated, experts believed stocks were only responding to a favorable economic climate in late 1986 and that there would be a "correction" in early 1987. But when the correction did not occur and "the market soared 44 points" on January 5 and "51 points" on January 22, it lent credence to the "esoteric" ideas of forecasters like Bob Prechter, George Soros, James Freeman, and David Herrlinger. As the market passed other "tests" (interest rates increased) in April, customary methods for valuing stocks were abandoned for alternative "predictors," such as "break up value" or, by July, "takeover value." A flood of money, some of it from Japan, much of it domestically produced at the urging of the Reagan administration, required yet additional theories as to why stocks had gone up. The rise of stock prices in other countries confirmed these theories. The Federal Reserve Board declined to raise margin requirements. Then, when the Federal Reserve did raise the discount rate, it came on top of the struggle to stabilize the dollar, the erosion of the takeover boom, and a "chilling fear" of legislative curbs on takeovers. Still, "sentiment indicators hit new peaks of bullishness" until, "the bears finally climbed on top of the ladder and fell off."

Essentially, the *Journal* presents us with a value added explanation of both ends of the stock boom and bust. With the passage of each test, the plausibility of passing the next increases; once a test has failed, the passage of all the previous ones becomes spurious. As with all value added catastrophes, the positive evidence that accumulates in the first part of the cycle depreciates precipitously in the next. What tipped people into this "sleigh ride," the *Journal* headlined, was "the predisposition to believe."

It is instructive to compare the *Journal*'s account with that of the Securities and Exchange Commission's several-hundred-page *The October 1987 Market Break* presented three months later after a voluminous examination of the transactions during the two day "break."[17] Again one is given a narrative (see chapter 2 in *Market Break*), although it is scaled down to the microlevel of moment-to-moment transactions over the period, October 19 and 20.[18] Like the *Journal*'s account, it is one where a number of factors coincided as time moved on: "a variety of factors came into play during the key trading days that affected investment and trading decisions . . . changes in investor perceptions regarding investment fundamentals" were the "trigger," while "institutional stock selling was the largest single direct factor responsible initially [for the] opening declines. . . . Finally, panic selling in a broad range of stocks . . . caused by a broad range of factors . . . coupled with a complete absence of buyers . . . was responsible for the free fall decline . . . [in] the final hour" (*Market Break*, xiii). The remainder of the report goes on into far greater detail than these quotations from the executive report, and eventually there are dozens of "factors which compounded together with the passage of time to take the market into "free fall."

The commission's report, however, does include a comparison between two other "volatile" periods (September 11 and 12, 1986 and January 23, 1987). The first is dismissed as the result of "investor perceptions of fundamental economic conditions—primarily, concerns over possible rising interest rates" (*Market Break*, 1–8). But no such news justified the "mid-afternoon plunge on January 23." The last of these comparisons is used to introduce a "cascade scenario" (a "systematic computer-driven market break"), which is ultimately discarded in preference for "many factors" that happened together. The crash, then, was an accident, an accident driven systematically by several independent human errors.

Conclusion: The Normal Bubble

My point here is not to argue with the *Journal*'s or the commission's reports, but to ask if it is possible that almost every weekly cycle, every shopping holiday spree, and every quarterly assessment produces a kind of periodic bubble followed by a correction, followed by another bubble, and so on? What happens if a bubble slips through and grows on the evidence that it has done so? And it does it again? And again? Random walks are not without pattern. What it seems to depend on is how people talk up or down the market. What are the stories they tell?

The journalists and their informants tell each of these stories as a daily and seasonal dramatism that they can tell equally well for bubbles or corrections although usually with some caution toward the end of each period.[19] It is the seasonal shopping holidays when the news comes closest to obvious promotion and a noticeable bias in favor of bubbles. Who wants to be a downer just before Christmas or Valentine's Day?

The academic experts played a very different roll in each year. The 1929 academic experts took or were given a much more obvious role in hyping the market, and their status suffered from it. Babson, the only notable dissenter, suffered all the more for his dissension. In 1987 most of the academic experts were ignored or laid low through most of the year and simply joined everyone else at calming the masses after the crash.

Of the two presidents, Hoover seems only to have insured a closer identification of himself and the crash by assuring the public of his own knowledgeable certainties and abilities. Apparently other presidents have been encouraged to make the same mistake, but Reagan's admission of ignorance seems to have left his reputation intact despite Chancellor's enticing homolog, "Cowboy Capitalism" (1999, 233). Fortunately, the damage has usually already occurred before the presidents are given a chance to make it worse. Bubbles and corrections seem to be a chronic aspect of investments, and any sudden, new talk of correctives may be just more talk.

Appendix 6.1

To give a rough sense of what reasons were given when the Dow Jones went up or down, the following codes were used to simplify a very heterogeneous day-by-day news coverage. Figure 6.4 gives their distribution on days when the Dow went up or down.

Reasons Given for Changes on the Stock Market: 1929 and 1987

Market Makers consist of any economic data released by the government or private sources other than interest rates or inflation. Included, as well, are those participants (bulls, bears, pools, institutions, foreign buyers, bargain hunters) in the market who are treated as rational human beings but not celebrities or gurus. They move the market up or down for what are assumed to be good reasons.

However, there are some differences in what was considered rational in the two years. In 1929 leading stocks were often taken to be a reasonable sign of a general rise or fall in stock values and were market makers. In 1987 leading stocks were usually referred to as "glamour" or "household" stocks thought to be popular only because of their familiarity. In 1987 they were just normal winners or losers that changed primarily because of their visibility or to provide a stable alternative in the absence of better opportunities.

Trouble Makers includes *exogenous* changes in interest rates, money supply, precious metals, and uncertainties about the actions of the Federal Reserve or other federal departments. In 1987 this included information on international relations, including OPEC, GATT, the trade balance, foreign banks, value of the dollar, gold shipments, and foreign stock markets. In 1929, however, nothing good was expected from international relations and news on foreign trade was a *Trespasser* (see below).

Normal Winners and Losers are endogenous conditions in the operation of the market that influence stock price levels regardless of any specific information on them (profit taking, correction, over-bought, momentum, resiliency, bandwagon, technical position, computer trading, Dow Jones values, witching hour, and such). Some of the reasons ("corrections" or "bandwagons") are taken to be a kind of collective behavior by traders. Normal winners and losers include *Glamour or Household Stocks in 1987*.

Trespassers are conditions, actors, or actions that lie outside the normal course of rational calculation because they are arbitrary, irrational, accidental, or novel. Included are celebrity forecasters (for example, Prechter, Babson, Soros), regime changes, and natural disasters. Sometimes, however, they were

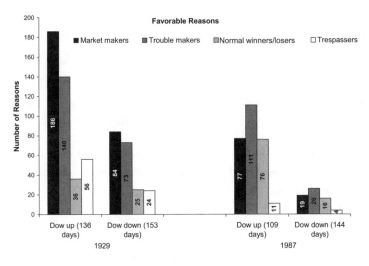

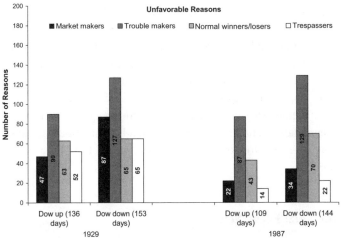

Note: On some days more than one reason of a given type may have been given so that one can get both favorable and unfavorable news of the same type on the same day.

FIGURE 6.4. Number of favorable (top) and unfavorable (bottom) reasons given by whether Dow is up or down, 1929 and 1987.

just called "psychological," "panic," or some other outbreak of irrationality. In 1929, practically all of the news on international finance was regarded as a trespass on rational conduct.

The following figure gives the number of each of these reasons given when the Dow Jones Industrials increased or decreased in each year. In general, when the Dow was up in 1929, journalists and their informants tended to attribute the reason to a disproportionate increase in favorable news on market makers and less news on potential troublemakers. On balance, they also found more good news than bad news on the trespassers, although the usual winners/losers were no better than when the Dow was down. When the Dow was down in 1929 they found only about as much bad news as good news on the market makers and quite a bit more bad news on the troublemakers. Worse, yet, they found over twice the amount of bad news than good news among the normal winners/ losers and trespassers. For 1929 reporters and their informants, a general upward movement in stocks was most often attributed to the market makers and little bad news from the usual winners/losers. A general downward movement in stock values was attributed to a disproportionate rise in bad news on everything but the market makers.

To sum up, the findings suggest a variant of Thaler's confirmation principle, "[T]hat people . . . search for confirming rather than disconfirming evidence" (Thaler 1987, 197). Which is to say that people search for rational reasons to explain good news and irrational reasons to explain bad news.

Appendix 6.2: Farm News

In both 1929 and 1987 reporters had a very routinized way of covering "business" news. They had their standardized indicators, their regular informants, and a substantial list of causes and consequences. None of these causes and consequences included agriculture. In 1987 it was virtually ignored on the front page and, for the most part, elsewhere except for commodity prices or when mention of "non-farm" income or commodity prices reminded the reader of its absence.

In 1929, however, it was the lack of fit into business reporting routines that made farming occasional news. When mentioned, farming was usually said to "follow its own trends," but it was in no way thought to diminish "Coolidge prosperity." Although praised for its "individual-ism" it was treated as an atavism in an age of "institutional capitalism." Yet farmers made up about a quarter of the population, and communi-ties dependent on them must have added a good deal more. In this last outpost of pure capitalism, farmers were losing money and pleading for public aid while "the nation was at the peak of prosperity." Although an occasional embarrassment, there was never a standard list of causes for the "slump" in farming, a trend line for commodity prices, or a lit-tle behavioral dramatism of the farmer himself. The situation became tragicomic by the end of the year when Alexander Legge tried to re-strict output among these capitalists. Eventually he failed to corral them into corporations resembling International Harvester, which he had pre-viously headed.

Nonetheless, reporters appreciated the irony of some of the con-frontations between business leaders and representatives from the farm states. It was a break from the routine of self-congratulation.

CHAPTER SEVEN

The Voice of the People

The *Tribune*'s "Voice of the People" added yet another account of the great crashes. What might the more active readers make of the news? How do they act upon what they have read?

Since the media studies during and following World War II, the active reader or viewer has drawn a lot of attention. Even the early studies of propaganda made allowance for boomerang effects when the doubtful listener or reader took the reporter's slant on the news as evidence against anything else he said. Then, there was also the two-step flow of communication where the credibility of the news went begging unless passed on by a friend or acquaintance. Subsequently, there was a flood of ethnographic evidence, much of it from England, that news is only a kind of provocation that people jointly reinterpret to confirm alternative beliefs. Television had only grouped its skeptics for immediate satisfaction on this count (Morley 1993).

Stanley Fish (1980) went even further in arguing that the reader is really the author of written texts. In previous chapters, I have suggested that dramatisms are so familiar that the reader is at least a coauthor, filling in any missing parts to the daily dramatism. Schudson (1995) has conceded that it is events reported in the news that influence people, not what is said about them. Readers can make up their own dramatisms.

In the background, of course, there was always the looming presence of Elisabeth Noelle-Neumann (1984) nagging us with the observation that people do not so much "believe" or "disbelieve" the news as find in it what is safe to say. And there were also the Marxists who argued that there is only one story in the capitalist press anyhow. Even Fish concedes that a standardized universe of discourse is all the reader has at his disposal (1980, xxi–xxv). So what if you are a trained English major? Your rules for reading are only all that much more explicit. And you will be held to the same standard as all the other English majors.[1]

The subject of media effects does not yield easily to theoretical closure. A renewed empirical approach may be called for. One of the more rewarding of these approaches is that of David Nord, who's *Communities of Journalism: History of American Newspapers and Their Readers* (2001) strives to discover who these active readers were and what they were making of what they read. The historical evidence is scattered and often unrepresentative, but like Robert Darnton (1989), Nord is able to distill out of it a promising direction for cumulative research.

Nord's *more or less* active readers—readers who leave some trace of themselves in history—seem less like independent authors or empty vessels than people who want to engage in newsworthy exchange. That is, like some of Morely's TV watchers, they want to talk things over, disputing one point, agreeing with another, adding information from their own experience, or bringing up an entirely new and sometimes a wandering path of argument.

The best illustration of Nord's work comes from an analysis of unpublished letters written to the editor of the *Chicago Tribune* and *Chicago Herald* from 1912 to 1917. Most wanted to be helpful if not agreeable and, if not that, to be amusing or at least protect other readers and the editor from further faulty news making. In a way they remind me of sociologists having to comment upon each other's papers. You can't just agree and sit down. Blanket disagreement, however, is very bad form and occurs only in the security of written, anonymous responses. Sociologists try to be helpful while arguing the case of other colleagues on the other side of some theoretical or ideological divide; they naturally also argue their own case. Despite disagreements there is usually the sense of a common project that keeps them on talking terms. Most of Nord's newspaper readers do the same, only more briefly.

The letters in Nord's study were written in a critical period (1914–17) in which American newspapers were changing from being the voice of a particular political party to being a commercial enterprise selling itself to a general market. Nord shows that these letters reveal not only the readers' desire to engage the editor in evenhanded discourse but also that some of them—perhaps most—seemed to belong to interpretive communities that had their own take on public events.

Interpretive communities is an important concept in media studies because it escapes the uniformness (all readers are alike) of so much of the "media effects" or "reader versus text" literature. The text may not determine the message but readers are not so empowered that they approach it individually. Reader responses gain conviction and become consequential when they draw upon an extant rhetoric, whether "ours" or that of the media. Speaking of his study of the letters to the editor of the *Tribune* and *Herald*, Nord says: "[T]he letters suggest that readers responded to the newspaper according to interpretive strategies made available to them by interpretive communities and that those communities were sometimes overtly political. . . . [M]ost reader response was determined neither by the text nor by idiosyncrasy. . . . And often these interpretive communities were inspired by formal political organizations and interest groups (248)." Nord is not just arguing that readers come to the newspaper from existing interpretive communities but that newspapers may be a principal instrument that breaths public life into such communities. Nord's interpretive communities are very much imaginary ones; some would hardly exist unless made visible in the media. Nord adds: "Through the act of publication itself newspapers asserted that a particular issue was no longer a private matter" (145).

Nord's early twentieth-century newspapers gave voice to readers who otherwise could hardly be self-conscious of their scattered existence. It is in the nature of imaginary communities that most of their members must learn of one another through some third party and, thus, in modern societies, mostly from the media.

It is possible that twenty-first-century newspapers are evolving away from Nord's commercial press and toward a niche press media that preaches only to the converted. But the 1929–30 *Tribune* undoubtedly falls within the commercial press era that Nord has in mind. Although the 1987–78 *Tribune* was already moving toward a more departmentalized press geared to serving separate segments of its markets,[2] it was still the kind of paper that was widely subscribed to, and Chicagoans could look to it for "all the news."

Methods

In 1929–30 the *Tribune* published about seven letters daily in its "Voice of the People" section; in 1987–88 they numbered about eleven. This expansion seems to have been partly due to a somewhat longer introductory letter that was invited or singled out since it was often from an "expert" although frequently the writer was not obviously different from most other writers who simply signed their names or gave some cognomen. But the letters in 1987–88 were also slightly longer on average.

Unlike Nord, I do not have a collection of unselected letters to the editor of the *Tribune*.[3] What I have is a sample of all letters selected for publication in the *Tribune*'s "Voice of the People." I read and coded the letters in that section every eighth day for the period October 1929 through December 1930 (N = 402) and October 1987 through December 1988 (N = 615).[4] I read them all, kept detailed notes, and coded them according to: (1) What was the primary issue that drew the reader to write and were there other readers writing about the same issue; (2) did the reader respond to (i) a specific article, reporter, or position taken by the *Tribune*, (ii) only some issue currently newsworthy, or (iii) an issue or topic that had only a very general relation to newsworthy topic within the year.[5] I also coded, where possible, how the readers identified themselves, their supporters for whom they might be speaking, and their adversaries. Finally I collected what I considered their figurative vocabulary and searched it for shared dramatisms. Finally, I also searched the letters for how readers conceptualized the great crashes in 1929 and 1987. These data are hard to count or summarize but let me take them up starting with views on the economy and the crash.

Popular Economics

As far as these selected writers were concerned the economy was a big story but not the biggest story either just before the crashes in 1929 or 1987 or during most of the following year (see figs. 7.1 and 7.2). In terms of letters published, 1929 news on the economy ranked third just after prohibition and public transit among eighteen topics. In 1987 and the following year, however, it was only ninth among thirteen topics, and just below the Middle East. Also, despite the larger sample in 1987–88 there were somewhat fewer letters (N = 32) on business than in 1929–30.

One reason there were fewer letters on the economy in 1987–88 was that the news on the market soon improved and the newspaper and subsequently the readers (or those selecting the letters) turned to other topics. The stock market also improved in 1930 but unemployment and

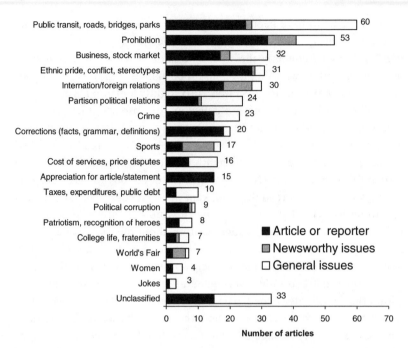

FIGURE 7.1. Number of readers' letters by type of cue: article or reporter, currently newsworthy, or general issues, 1929.

the newsworthy conflict between the "Radical Republicans" and Democrats kept the issue alive in the paper. No similar division or opposition occurred among the Reagan Republicans.

The letters during the crash and the next year followed roughly the same course as the news released in the *Tribune*. First, there were general explanations of the crash. Then, there were disputed assignments of blame for the crash followed by criticisms and alternatives to economic policies to stabilize the market and broader economy. Finally, other economic issues were linked to or attributed to the crashes. The readers' letters were paced by the newspaper although not usually in obvious agreement and often accompanied by original interpretations and especially recommendations for recovery.

In both years the earliest explanations of the crashes were among those that were already being repeated by the press. The first explanation in 1929 was among the briefest: "Barnum was right. So was Babson" (John A. Aarvole). The idea that ordinary people were suckers was also among the most enduring newsworthy formulations in 1929–30. Closely related was the view that "people let their imagination run away with them" in an "orgy of greed" and "short selling." The only structural explanations were the "chaining evil" and growth of "institutions" (that is, chain stores and corporations) that displaced local (and presumably less speculative) businesses. Except for the chain stores and corporations, these early 1929–30 writers sounded just like Hoover. People had let their imaginations run away with them.

However, there was also the readers' arguments that the newspapers, even the *Tribune*, had been "financial touts" for the stock market. This view had not been aired by Hoover or the *Tribune* and would not appear prominently in the *Tribune* until much later during the Pecora hearings. Hoover's "political pow wows" had encouraged investment and consumption, but the writers had even more extreme ideas of how to boost business. One (F. Walt Young), went to extremes: "Eat, drink and be merry for tomorrow we die."

Disputes on recovery began before explanations of the crisis were over. In 1929 there were disputes over acreage reductions, tariff "dis-

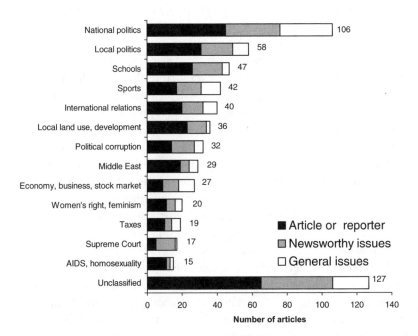

FIGURE 7.2. Number of readers' letters by type of cue: article or reporter, currently newsworthy, or general issues, 1987.

crimination" against agriculture, and Hoover's "prosperity program." Toward the end of 1930 the writers turned to specific make-work efforts (for example, washing parked cars in hope for voluntary payment) or charity. The word *slump* slipped into a few of the letters in 1929–30 although *depression* was not mentioned by any of them. Some writers, however, were suspicious of the beneficiaries of charity and one complained that schoolteachers were eating free with some students. A succeeding letter explained that it was the teachers who had collected the money among themselves so that some students could eat at all. None of these issues or positions had been widely aired in the paper.

The further you got along in the 1930s the more original were the letters. Solutions became a bit desperate: cutting wages to "share jobs," assigning a second man on the buses to collect fares, or the use of unemployed men for jury duty.[6] Recrimination also became a bit desperate: poverty was deserved among those who had not saved; a major employer was said to have coerced employees to give to a relief fund for which the employer took credit. But there were also letters recounting acts of exceptional, heartwarming generosity, like that of the teachers. Although some of these letters were in response to newsworthy issues, they were quite original in their responses and proposals.

Only about a third of the 1987–88 letters were directly in response to an article in the *Tribune*, but another third were in response to an issue frequently appearing in the paper. Even before the crash the mayor of Darien (Ivan Von Zukerstein) forecast a depression and called for rigorous antitrust enforcement against the big government–business "cabal" (that is, leveraged buyouts). Unlike Babson in 1929, Zukerstein was not subsequently blamed or credited with foresight. However, his argument was repeated among readers who saw leveraged buyouts ("legal confidence games," they wrote) as government-sanctioned monopolies leading to the crash. Computer trading and manipulation, however, were the more frequent explanations of the crash in the 1987–88 letters. As in 1929, "doomsday sayers" came in for criticism. Very few of these letters were in response to articles in the paper.

Solutions to the decline in stock values in 1987–88 ranged from boosterism ("Say someone's buying out there," recommended J. W. Hermann) to "forced savings" to reduce the deficit (the president emeritus of Roosevelt University). As the evidence of fraud began to come out, the value of teaching ethics to MBA students was debated. The regulation of plant closings and "high" wages and job fairs were both criticized and defended. These topics or positions were usually original to the authors.

Taken together the topics chosen by the writers are paced by the newspapers, and the readers' explanations of the crashes are similar to those that were prevalent in the newspaper. The difference in the letters was in their solutions to the crisis or proposals for economic policy. In 1930 the paper hewed to the "natural recovery" and Hoover's "pow wows" and proposal. The readers showed little agreement on solutions among themselves but were much more supportive of innovative charitable efforts and political reform.

In 1987–88, there was also little agreement on economic policy following the crash, but there was a sustained critical attitude toward buyouts, computer trading, and "hype." Like the writers in 1929–30 there was some call for federal regulation rather than just monetary policy. One gets the impression from the writers in both years that they were in agreement with what might be called the "facts" presented in the *Tribune* but rather less so with the succeeding explanations of why the crash occurred and what might be done about it. But, once again, there was no convergence among the writers on solutions and policy.

The Active Readers' Dramatism of the Crash

In 1929–30 the readers used much the same figurative vocabulary (see the following list) as the *Tribune* did. The sample is too small to give us a full-blown dramatism,[7] but as a sample it is enough to make the case. The narrative starts with the merger and chain store evils. Despite apparent overproduction, people let their imagination run wild. Touts lure them into gambling and short selling. Investors panic and the crash occurs. Liquidation begins and charitable groups are reduced to panhandling for the jobless. (No letter writer used the *Tribune*'s "Idle.") The government tries price fixing while boosters urge people to buy now for "speedy recoverage." Neither the *Tribune* nor the readers mentioned the prior Florida land bust or the widespread bank failures before 1929 or the long-standing depression of the farm economy.

The 1929–30 Active Reader's Narrative of the Slump
The merger evil
The chaining evil

People let their imagination run wild
Overproduction
Stock gambling
Short selling
Stock crash or slump!
Liquidation
Wallowing in debt
Workers laid off
Charities panhandling
Price fixing
Buy now!
Boost recoverage!

The cast of personae (see table 7.1) is small but fits the narrative. There is the investing public who are suckers. They have been brought to this sorry state by financial touts (some of them reporters) and their "race track brothers" (brokers), hunchback economists,[8] and Wall Street bears. Hoover poses as Superman (used in irony by only two readers), and "the Inquisitorial Committee and Amateurs" (Congress) look for scapegoats. The members of the Farm Board are Price Fixers. There are no heroes.

TABLE 7.1. **The Active Reader's Personae, 1929–30**

Stockholders	Stock Promoters	Policy Makers
Investing public	Financial touts	Superman
Suckers	Race track brothers	Inquisitorial committee
Doubting Thomases	Hunchback economists	
	Wall Street bears	Amateurs
		Malefactors

TABLE 7.2. **Landscapes for 1929–30 and 1987–88**

1929–30	1987–88
Wheels of commerce	Stock market roller coaster
Rodeo stocks	Hard realities
Rainy day	Dark Monday
Idle capital	Gloom
Slump	Depression

TABLE 7.3. **Narrative and Personae for 1987–88**

Narrative
Business cabals
Takeover games
Legal confidence games
Program trading
Computer trading
Trading paper
Gambling
Greed
Stock market overheated
Stock market slide
Chain reaction
Star Wars
Stock market crash!
Media scare!
Media fallout
Worn out rhetoric
Yuppie bashing
Economic nationalism
Revive work ethic!
Forced savings
Flexible freeze (on taxes)
Jobs fair
Recession

Personae			
Victims	Promoters	Press	Government
Jobless	Money manipulators	Doomsayers	Big government
Job seekers		Doomsday prophets	Decision makers
Starving child	Gurus	Bookworm economists	
	Yuppies		
	Crooks		

Like the *Tribune* writers in 1929–30, those in 1987–88 tended to initially fix upon the *Tribune*'s focus on computer trading and buyouts and their resemblance to gambling as the cause of the crash (see table 7.3). As in the newspaper, the Yuppies came in for criticism by the readers for their consumerism. Both the newspaper and the writers also tended to villainize some personae (Gurus, Economists) who had been heroized before the crash. At the level of vocabulary the 1987–88 readers closely follows the text.

The Landscapes in both years is so limited that I have not tried to visualize them (see table 7.2 for a word list). What I think they do show is

some indication of the writers' (or whoever selected the letters) attempt
to write persuasive prose by avoiding hyperbole. They might disagree
with the *Tribune* but they did not want to appear naive or as cranks. This
avoidance of dramatic staging is evident in both years. Also in both years
the readers scarcely ever mentioned terms borrowed from economics or
from the "experts" mentioned by the reporters.

On the whole, the readers in both periods followed the flow of news as
it came to them from the *Tribune*. Their figurative vocabulary was largely
a selective borrowing from the paper and it combines to match something like the narratives in the newspaper. Innovations like leveraged
buyouts and computer trading in 1987, "monopolies," chain stores, and
corporations in 1929 were enduring reasons given for the crash by readers and the newspapers. Where they differ is in the readers' solution to
the crash and subsequent "slump" or "recession." In both years the readers' solutions imply greater control over economic institutions (particularly banks, investments firms, and large corporations) and some kind of
social mobilization to remedy the hardships of lower-income people.

Despite their willingness to offer their own solutions in both years, I
got the impression that economics was one of those subjects the writers
felt least able to tackle. None of the writers claimed any technical knowledge of economics except, possibly, the ex-president of Roosevelt University, and he was the only one using any academic jargon. None mentioned
a newsworthy economist, economic analyst, or school of economics. Nor
did anyone other than the ex-president of Roosevelt University give
any impression of speaking for an interpretive community well learned
in economics. This was sufficiently different from some other subjects
covered in the period, so I take the liberty of briefly contrasting some
other findings although they have little to do with the economy. But they
do reveal topics on which the readers felt freer to show their expertise.

Local Knowledge

In 1929–30 the issues that moved most people to write letters were local.
What troubled them more than anything else was how to move around in
the city and get to work (see fig. 8.1). Suburbanization and the automobile had combined to make travel and parking an adventure, and it was
something that writers did not wait for the *Tribune* to tell them about.

Over half of the sixty letters on the issue came without obvious prompt-
ing. The letters were full of notifications of bad crossings, poor train service, and the need for the electrification of trains. The letter writers did
not hesitate to tell other readers of the opportunity for converting vacant
land to parking lots or how to make changes in the scheduled raising and
lowering of bridges or how to accommodate traffic during the forthcoming World's Fair. Well over half of the letters on this issue seized upon
solutions without mentioning any article or reporter. At some point the
Tribune also began a campaign to electrify trains. Yet, no one mentioned
that campaign either.

Transportation is a very local issue, and it is to be expected that readers would tackle the issue with confidence and originality. But international relations are not local and 1929–30 readers showed much the same
confidence in responding to the *Tribune*. What was primarily at issue
was a treaty on the reduction of sea power, but readers did not always let
that keep them from writing on the broader issues of that treaty. This was
also a subject that some writers approached with references to a literature other than the *Tribune* (which was supporting the U.S. proposal on
the international naval reduction treaty). Over half of the readers wrote
without any specific mention in the *Tribune* although it was newsworthy
throughout much of the year. Many writers took sides on the proposed
treaty depending upon specific *local* ethnic identities (mostly Irish, English, Italian, and French). The Irish took exception to England's continued control of the seas. Some Anglo-American admirers of the Empire
defended it although an isolationist branch of Anglo-Americans was
distrustful of the continued British "ruling [of] the seas." The Italians
were offended by the exclusion of Italy from the treaty, and the *Tribune*'s
criticism of Mussolini. The writers were also quite original in their proposals to amend the treaty.

Much the same thing occurred in the letters on international relations (including the Middle East) published in 1987. Letters on the Middle East and the Soviet Union roused Israeli and Arabic partisans on
the first issue and roused the "hawks" and "doves" from the Vietnam
War on the policies toward the Soviet Union. Ethnic relations in general tended to draw letters without any mention of a *Tribune* article or
the paper's position. Once again, however, there was little agreement or
shared choice of vocabulary beyond that within each ethnic or national
group.

Considering all of the letters, most of them were not elicited by an identifiable article, although most were responding to newsworthy topics (87 percent to 95 percent, 1929 and 1987). Still, some seemed to stake out an entirely original subject. There was little agreement among them except within relatively well-defined groups.

Identity and Interpretive Communities

The writers in each period differed sharply in their self-identification and their reference to any interpretive community. The tendency of the 1929–30 readers was to adopt a kind of "common man" persona. About 9 percent gave only their initials. Another 10 percent signed themselves off as a kind of everyman: A Taxpayer, An Ordinary Citizen, A Reader, A Housewife, An Observer, A Straphanger. Only five did this in 1987–88, three of them sports fans, one a postman, and one more signed only as "two women." Many of the writers in 1929–30 gave only their last name. Even Anton Cermak did not give his title in 1930, but neither did Saul Bellow in 1988. Perhaps they did not need to.

None of the writers in 1987–88 gave only their initials but about 13 percent gave an organizational title or membership (Professor, President, Director, as such) that conveyed authority. About 10 percent were credentialed or claimed expertise in what they were writing about. About 7 percent also gave titles in 1929–30, but the titles had nothing much to do with the issue they were writing on. Some doctors added "MD" to their name no matter what the topic was. The titles given in 1987–88 titles outranked those in 1929–30. There were senators and the heads of foreign consulates writing in 1987–88. The few writers with titles in 1929–30 were from volunteer associations.

Conclusion

Surely people who bother to write letters to their local newspaper are active readers. They are neither so apathetic they do nothing nor so alienated they think it hopeless to try. Judging from these writers about 50 to 70 percent, perhaps a good deal more in 1929–30 than 1987–88, write with some awareness of a wider, imaginary community who share their views. By and large they want to negotiate differences, although more so in 1929–30 than in 1987–88. A majority of these writers in both years are neither Panglossian nor polarized. Rather, they seem to know that there is no self-evident truth in the daily news and that interpretations are achieved only by edging toward a "workable truth." They do not simply "decode" the "news code" into their own code (Morley 1993). Rather, they seem to be searching for an interpretation "for all practical purposes." Like Harold Garfinkel's conversationalists (1967), they are experimenting with words where "truth" means only agreement.

As you might expect, the readers were most confident and most likely to speak out on local issues or international issues when they touched on ethnicity. Economic policy, however, was one of those issues the readers seemed least sure of, and they were least likely to mention a supportive interpretive community. They approached the great crashes and their aftermath from a moral rather than an analytical point of view. In that respect not even the popular slogans of Reagan's economic policy (for example, "tax cuts pay for themselves") reached them. Nor did the language of the bank and investment experts mentioned in the press show up in their letters.

But not all the writers appear to be aware of some larger, imaginary interpretive community. Perhaps they were in search of a community, but in the context, they read like "voices in the wilderness." There seemed to be more of them in 1987–88 than 1929–30. Nor was every reader in the mood for easy compromise. In 1929–30 views seemed to harden when the issue was ethnicity, and in 1987–88 views had hardened on a number issues; on race, the Supreme Court, on Israel and the Palestinians, on women's rights, homosexuality, and AIDS.[9] I took this to mean that writers in both years were less willing to compromise on moral or primordial claims than on economic and regulatory issues. However, it was not just that the writers' views had hardened in 1987–88. Both presidential candidates and the ward politicians, as well as their supporters seem to have increasingly seized upon such zero-sum contests and their visceral appeal. At the fundamental level of this vocabulary the writers were repeating the language of their political leaders.

TABLE 7.4.

1929–30 National and Local Politics	1987–88 National Politics
Lunatic wife	The dispossessed
Malefactors	All -star candidate
Propagandist [historian]	Super wordster [J. Jackson]
Parasites [schoolteachers]	Know-it-all [J. Jackson]
Masters of the mouth [senator's critics]	Right winger
Blackleg	Radical Right
Vote mongers [campaigners]	College crowd
	Draft dodgers
	Super patriots
	Big Labor
	Pinko lawyers
	Professional poor
	Entertainment chief [Bush]
	Liberal cohorts
	Losers
	[Two-bit] drug pushers
	Drug czar
	Average joe
	Ideological fanatics
	Dr. Strangelove [Kissinger]
	Reaganites

Appendix 7.1: A Selective Listing of Repeated Vocabulary Items (not including those in the preceding text)

The readers in both periods avoided extended figurative Landscapes as a way of dramatizing their claims. The personae they used, however, were sufficient to bear some comparisons. They help reveal the less compromising tone of the 1987–88 readers.[10]

Local Politics 1987 only
Racist [Mayor Washington]
Titular Mayor [Sawyer]
Mob [demonstrators]
Bloodthirsty Gangs [demonstrators]
Crazies [demonstrators]
Amateurs [Washington Administration]
Hardcore Bigots [whites/blacks]
Uncle Tom
Crook [Mayor Thompson]
Four Flusher [Mayor Thompson]

Taxes, Public Expenditures, or Debt (1987–88 only)
1987–88
Big Spender [Governor]
At Risk Students
Big Vote Getter [Governor]
Budget Bloater [R. Reagan]

TABLE 7.5. **Political Corruption**

1929–30	1987–88
Entirely Local	Mostly National
Ringleader [Mayor Thompson]	Uncle Ronnie [R. Reagan]
Rascals	Do-Nothing Congress
	Dupes [congressional representatives]

TABLE 7.6. **International Relations**

1929–30	1987–88
Clerical agents [pro-British ministers]	Scum [boat people]
International gumshoe	Thugs [communists]
Foreign powers	Useful idiot [R. Reagan]
Draft card burners	
	Fonda bashers
	Extremist
	Terrorist

TABLE 7.7. **Women**

1929–30	1987–88
Wifey	Warrior women
Taxi dancer	Preborn child
Gold star mothers	Rising stars [in corp. America]

TABLE 7.8. **Sports**

1929–30	1987–88
Rotter [owner of Cubs]	Legend [Ditka]
Whiners [players]	Whiners [Cubs]
Fans	Pawns [ticket holders]
	Megabucks actors [players]
	Fans
	Spare Bears [replacement players]

TABLE 7.9. **Topics that are not Comparable**

1929–30	1987–88
Transportation, Parking	Land Use Change

Straphanger	Dictator [aldermen]
Taxpayer	Derelicts [slum residents]
City gang [city council]	Junkies
Professional optimist	Muggers
	Slum Lords
	The Powerless
	The Far Right
	Bigots
	Snobs

1929–30	1987–88
Crime	Middle East

Blue coats [police]	Socialist puppet state [Palestine]
Newsy [newsboy victim]	Anti-Semites [pro-Palestinians]
Gangsters	Terrorist critics [critics of Israel]
Hoodlums	Pretender [Arafat]
Brigand	
Slicksters	

1929–30	1987–88
Ethnic Pride/Conflict	Schools

Woppies	Homeless
Undesirables	Street gangs
Criminal class	Tomorrow's truants
Hillbilly civilization	[Next year's] dropouts
Night riders	Burned-out teachers
Town loafer	Chronic truants
Alien race	Racists
Unregenerated foreigners	At-risk students
Class of degenerates	Buffoonish honcho [sec. of education]

Supreme Court (1987–88)

Extremist

True Ideologues

Demagogues

Gays/AIDS (1987–88)

Gay Bashers

Homophobes

CHAPTER EIGHT

Congress and the Courts
Have Their Say

Each in their own time the journalists, the cartoonists, the experts, the presidents, and the readers had their say on the great crashes. But there were two other tales to be told about the crashes. First, there was the legal aftermath of each crash as Congress and the courts attempted to normalize the remaining disorder. Then, there was the literary canon of books that continued to work over the traces of all the previous tales.

This chapter is about each of these last two tellings and how they have frozen a mnemonic language from the past into the authority of the present. I do not want to say that the mnemonic daily or seasonal dramatisms, the cartoons, the voices of presidents or readers, or even that of the high courts froze the past beyond historical recovery. What I do want to say is that these accounts have provided an almost irresistible resource to any popular version of our collective memory. If it is not the final word, then, it is almost so.

Crime as Innovation

In his study of corporate takeovers, Paul Hirsch (1986) shows how established investors and stockbrokers first used figurative language to construe corporate takeovers as acts of low barbarism. Then, as these profitable takeovers spread to more reputable investors and brokerages, relatively modest but systematic changes in language remade corporate takeovers into high-risk acts of high finance. This was accomplished by only extending the moral range of personae and by evening out the odds of victory while leaving the genres unchanged. A brutish attack, thus, was remade into a rousing but fair fight.[1]

Hirsch argues that language and behavior mutually facilitate each other and that figurative language is especially suited to morally condemn or pave the way to a clean conscience and heroic appearance. In the business world, figurative language can reposition disreputable or even illegal practices into understandable "innovations." Individuals who practice these innovations are then relieved of any stigma that might separate them from other practitioners. Institutional relations, initially threatened, are repaired by a shared rhetorical conventionalization of the new practices (Hirsch 1986, 823–29). Deviance becomes innovation and innovation becomes business as usual. It would seem that business ethics track business practices rather than the other way about.

More than anyone Hirsch has taken the use of figurative language into the dynamics of changing business practices (see also Fiss and Hirsch 2005; Hirsch and Soucey 2006; and Hirsch and Thompson 1994). In his work language does more than disguise, justify, or normalize new and often questionable business practices. Language is the opening wedge, the verbal equivalent of George Herbert Mead's "exploratory gestures" that allow their spread at the outset (1956, 182–91).

In this chapter, I do not want to look at the incipient steps taken toward Wall Street crime in 1929 and 1987, but I do want to look at the linguistic aftermath of each crash and its duration into the present. The 1929 stock market crash was followed by a lengthy U.S. Senate investigation and was conceived of as a market failure. The language developed in that investigation created a dramatism in which the regular practices on Wall Street were only a politically protected form of gambling. This language took the form of a coherent dramatism and worked much of its way into the press coverage of the *Tribune* and *New York Times*. It was not to displace contemporary news dramatisms of the stock market, but it was to become an essential literary genre in the "canon" of book-length treatments of the 1929 crash.

The 1987 crash was also followed by a series of investigations of individuals. Here the classic contingencies of scandal (Adut 2005), including the newsworthy language of the investigations, served to confine the scandal to something "extralegal" but nothing like a system failure. Taken together, the two cases suggest that the public language that developed around the scandals following the 1929 and 1987 crashes became a kind of frozen source for history. The subsequent histories of each crash do not lack for revisionists, but the vocabulary of the period is too attractive, too colorful, and too mnemonic not to creep into all but those works so technical they have few readers. This is one of the ways that history or culture is passed on to become part of the future.

Innovations in 1929 and 1987

In business, ethics and morality are always somewhat under siege by competitors who can profit by relaxing them a bit. For example, innovations like extending installment payments to common workers or selling stocks rather than bonds to widows were unethical but not illegal in the early 1920s. By 1929 they were business as usual. The years leading up to 1929 and 1987 were periods of rapid innovation. The big news before 1929 was the Harvard School of Scientific Management, the "institutional" (corporate) form of production, and the Federal Reserve's capacity to control the money supply and interest rates. A "New Era of permanent prosperity" (or more often "Coolidge" or "Hoover" prosperity) had arrived and had unleashed any number of other innovations sheltered by the same word magic.[2]

Before 1987 there was supply-side economics, or Reaganomics (or, by some, "Voodoo economics"); tax cuts became a way of increasing tax revenues; and, of course, the takeover boom was to discover "synergy" and weed out the less competitive firms. All of these boats would rise in the same tide. These "post-Keynesian" innovations invited all sorts of others, especially those in marketing securities.[3]

After 1929 and 1987, the stock market crashes revealed widespread "irregularities" that seemed like crimes to onlookers. Businessmen (and they were men) were not just running close to the law with one another but also with widows, the retirement accounts of workers, and the "trusting public." The relative magnitude of the two crime waves is impossible to compare, for the way they were investigated and the way they have been retained in our collective memory is entirely different.[4] I want to document that difference here.

I first examine the contending dramatisms developed in the Pecora hearings in both the *Tribune* and *New York Times* during the early 1930s. I then turn to the play of comedy in the *Tribune*'s coverage of the insider scandal in the late 1980s. I conclude with a brief look at the more durable literature that has survived each crime wave.

1929: The Pecora Hearings and System Failure

The Pecora hearings were something of a President Hoover fluke and miscalculation.[5] Hoover had earned the dislike of the "Wall Street Bears" by blaming them for flooding the market with stocks they did not own so they could buy them back at a lower price. Hoover may also have been led to believe that the bears would retaliate by driving stocks down again to embarrass him in the forthcoming presidential race (Burk 1988, 36–37). Investigating the bears could kill two birds with one stone: confine the investigation to a small number of unpopular bears and warn off others like them from supporting Roosevelt.

The investigation was apparently staged for what we might call the "normal scandal": an investigation that was bound to turn up some shocking individual instances of fraud and to single out one or a few "bad apples" for punishment. The investigation would go no further than to expose a few bears.

Initially, that was exactly how the hearings progressed. When it first hit the front pages of the *Tribune* the investigation was called "the great bear hunt." William Gray, counsel for the Senate Banking and Currency Committee, had been a criminal prosecutor and came with a reputation for getting indictments. From the outset he tried to reveal individual fraud, but he could not find a single guilty bear. The trouble was that practically everything done on Wall Street—insider trading, wash sales, pools, dummies—was legal. Gray seemed hapless and the press soon lost interest in it altogether. The hearing could have ended there with nothing more than a few frightened bears.

But some members of the senatorial committee would not let it rest. Although majority Republican, the senatorial committee was somewhat divided by the presence of "Radical Republicans" who were populists (Cowing 1965) from the farm states where low farm prices and high interest rates made them a natural enemy of eastern Wall Street. The chairman of the committee, Senator Norbeck from South Dakota,[6] would not allow the investigation to flounder and appointed a new counsel—Ferdinand Pecora, a former chief assistant district attorney in New York.

At the outset Pecora announced that this is "a fact-finding, not a head hunting expedition." He knew that most of what could be revealed was legal or so often left unprosecuted that the law could not be enforced (Pecora 1939). His aim was public outrage and reform. The son of Sicilian peasants, Pecora had a commanding presence despite the contrast he made to the rather tallish, stylish bankers and brokers (both papers would call them "thoroughbreds") he would face. Reporters found the comparison with J. Morgan irresistible:

[When] Mr. Morgan appeared . . . [h]e came down the aisle, massive and dignified but less grimly masterful than his father, in a manner which could not fail to be impressive. His head is large and rather handsome despite the bulky neck and the Morgan nose. His nearly bald head is fringed with thin, white hair, his mustache gray, his eyebrows black and bristling. With him [was] Mr. Davis, the former Democratic candidate for President [Morgan's attorney]. The banker's antagonist . . . was a short, swarthy, determined-looking man, Ferdinand Pecora. He has tightly waved gray hair, a thin mouth, with slightly protruding lower lip, and a square chin. The name of Morgan held no terror for him. (*New York Times*, May 24, 1933)

Pecora's questioning of witnesses was quite gentle; when a witness's memory failed or ignorance of "Wall Street language" was professed, he would simply approach the topic from another direction, eventually hemming the witness into so many denials and lapses of memory that credibility became hopeless. He was also more articulate than any of the witnesses. Take his questioning of Morgan:

Mr. Morgan don't you know as a matter of fact one of the reasons for the filing of this income-tax return on behalf of the firm for the two-day period of Jan. 1 to Jan. 2, 1931,[7] showing losses of over $21,000,000 against the taxable income for the ensuing two years, that is for the years 1932 and 1933?

"No, I do not know that of my own knowledge," Mr. Morgan replied.

Mr. Pecora dropped the subject at this point and asked Mr. Morgan . . .

And, again with Edsel Ford:

"According to the annual report of the Guardian Detroit [banking] Union Group for 1930 you were also a member of the advisory committee of the group. Do you recall that?" Mr. Pecora asked.

"I think so," Mr. Ford replied.

"Did the advisory committee frequently advise with the officers of the group?" Mr. Pecora asked.

"I could not say; I cannot remember." . . .

"Well," asked Mr. Pecora, "do you recall generally any such conference that you had as a member of the advisory committee, with officers of the bank?"

"No Sir," was the reply. . . .

"Do you consider that during the years that you were director of the group you were active in the discharge of your duties as a director?" Mr. Pecora asked.

"I was in close touch with the members of the operating organization," was the reply.

"Were you in your own opinion, active in the discharge of your duties as a director?"

"I thought I was. I was counseling with officers on the policies of the bank."

"How much counseling did you do?"

"I do not remember."(*New York Times*, January 12, 1934)

Some witnesses responding by sparring over words. Both Richard and George Whitney tried to change Pecora's vocabulary. George strongly objected to the word, "pool."

Whenever Mr. Pecora described the operation as a "pool" Mr. Whitney insisted upon calling it a "suspense account."

"You apparently do not want me to use the word pool?" Mr. Pecora said.

"We are gun-shy of certain words," witness said.

"The newspapers referred to it as a bankers' pool, did they not?"

"And," rejoined witness, "we did our very best to make them change but they would not change." (*New York Times*, June 3, 1933)

However, a few witnesses, like M. C. Brush, were more forthcoming.

". . . no one is on Wall Street for his health," . . . "Dummy accounts are a common practice and . . . the basis on which the general public operates in the market is pitiful."

He admitted the market could be manipulated and termed some activities in the market "a racket that makes Al Capone look like a piker." (*New York Times*, April 23, 1932)

Mr. Brush added that the public's mania was encouraged by brokerage firms: "They [the public] get a circular saying stock XYZ is good . . . and there are undoubtedly some crooked circulars put out—dope sheets"

(*New York Times*, April 23, 1032). Without going further, Mr. Brush stopped, "as if he visioned the Gotham reception committee awaiting when he returned" and said, "Gosh, gentlemen, I wish you'd buy me a ticket for the south instead of New York" (*Tribune*, April 23, 1932).

Readers quickly became interested in the parade of monied celebrities. Important dignitaries, like John Raskob, chairman of the Democratic Committee and a prospective witness, dropped by just to see how Percy Rockefeller, a faithful Republican but good friend, bore up under questioning. Despite his discomfort, Percy did well, calling himself a "retired bear." Yes, he had participated in a "little syndicate" now and then but only to lose money.

The news coverage of the Pecora hearings was like nothing I have ever seen afterward in newsprint.[8] For three years while Congress was in session the *Times* and often the *Tribune* devoted several pages to verbatim accounts of the hearings. Many articles were accompanied by "informed" observers and reporters and, sometimes, editorials. In shock value it might compare to the Pentagon Papers, but the Pecora hearings lasted for three years in the *Times* and two in the *Tribune*. The hearings became a kind of national soap opera, filled with political and business celebrities as well as characters from Wall Street's demimonde.

The figures below give a numerical impression of the news coverage. These articles are only those that quote the hearings at length or discuss them as their main topic. The *Tribune* was initially reluctant to take up the story and let go of it entirely in 1934. But, during the heat of the hearings, in 1933, the *Tribune*'s coverage usually added up to nearly a full page each day the hearings were in session. Coverage was often much greater in the *Times* (see below).

1932
Times: 61 articles on 61 days; almost continuously from April 1 to late June.[9]
Tribune: 27 articles on 24 days, mainly from late April to late June.
1933
Times: 209 articles on 149 days; almost continuously from January through March; May through July; October through December.
Tribune: 156 articles on 102 days; almost continuously May through June and October through November.
1934
Times: 58 articles on 51 days; almost continuously January through March; scattered from April to October.

Gamblers and the Manic Public

Even before Pecora became counsel, the metaphor of gambling had begun to appear in the discourse between the members of the committee,
the witnesses, and the newspapers. The senators and Pecora wanted to
know the difference between playing the stock market and gambling.
Pecora directly asked some witnesses what the difference was. The most
forthcoming, Otto Kahn (of Kuhn Loeb), considered that it was essentially a matter of motivation. Those purchasing stocks expected to make
a profit; those gambling wished to win. This early version of labeling theory was not lost on Pecora.

The gambling dramatism (see the list titled The Committee's Narrative) was pursued primarily by the senators and Pecora, but a number
of witnesses adopted a language that seemed like gambling or a confidence game; there was market rigging, wash sales, bear and bull drives,
sales against the box, dummy accounts, dope sheets, pool operations,
and so forth (see the list below titled Narrative Terms Used or Protested
by Witnesses). Several of these terms aroused resistance by other witnesses who protested their accuracy or tried to find alternatives: syndicates[10] or joint accounts for pools, investor for speculator,[11] publicity man
for propagandist. Nonetheless, incautious witnesses often found themselves using most of the terms or admitting that they were used "on the
street." Indeed, the street language that surfaced in the hearings fit very
well into a gambling or confidence game dramatism (see the list below titled Narrative Terms Used or Protested by Witnesses).

The Committee's Narrative
ballyhoo stocks
play the market
boom stocks
bull operations
use window dressing
wash sales
pool (bear/bull) operations
peg prices
market rigging
give insiders favors
big bear drive

short selling
insiders sell short
sales against the box
unload worthless bonds
trim the lambs
Americans played for a sucker

Narrative Terms Used or Protested by Witnesses
In Wide
New Era thinking
Coolidge prosperity
Public mania
Short selling
Distress selling
Syndicate operations

Used but Also Protested
Ballyhoo stocks
Bear or Bull drive
Bull or Bear operations
Pool operations
Sales against the box [pool] to the rescue!
Bankers' Pool
Suspense Account

Mostly Protested
Wash sales
Peg prices
Gamble in stocks
Unload worthless stocks
Americans played for a sucker

Pecora and the committee composed the most elaborate, coherent, and most often repeated vocabulary during the hearings and in the press. Essentially, the committee's vocabulary of motives was that brokers and bankers had lured "the trusting public" into buying worthless bonds and playing the market by ballyhooing over priced stocks, bulling prices with wash sales, pool operations, and market rigging, while buying off politicians and regulators as "preferred customers." The result was a speculative "mania" promoted by brokers and investment houses followed by big bear drives to sell stocks they did not own to "trim the lambs" during each fall in prices. The crash was just one of these deceptive runs that got out of hand.

The witnesses were at the disadvantage while being interviewed one by one so they could not easily construct a joint response. The most common story by the witnesses was that "good times" and a rise in stock values had roused a gullible public who bought wildly and on margin to "get rich quick." The more reckless of them were forced to dump stocks back on the market when it fell. The crash was a matter of self-entrapment or "distress selling" that spread to knowledgeable investors and responsible brokers. There were variations on this theme. Otto Kahn, for example, agreed that the bankers and brokers were also victims of "new era thinking." "Coolidge prosperity" had promised "permanent prosperity" and investment houses unthinkingly gave in to the public's irresistible urge to get rich quick.[12] Another variation was an effort to construct a more heroic narrative in which the market was actually rescued from the "manic public" by the "bankers' pool." Richard and George Whitney subscribed to this version and also insisted on calling the "bankers' pool" the "rescue pool." The "rescue pool," however, remained only their language.

The witnesses were more active at protesting the committee's terms than at presenting their own. Some especially objected to the idea that there were wash sales and that Americans had been played for suckers with the sale of worthless stocks. This riled some witnesses and prompted Richard Whitney to attribute the entire stock boom and bust to a greedy mass mania "indulged in by a hundred and twenty million people" (*Tribune*, April 12, 1932), seemingly every man, woman, and child in the country.

Even more hotly debated between the committee and the witnesses were the personae that emerged in the hearings. The committee's personae consisted only of bad guys and victims (see tables 8.1 and 8.2). In the course of their inquiry, some of the personae from Wall Street were villainized as gamblers or cheats: for example, Bears, Shorts, Preferred Customers, "old Friends" and "Propagandists." The press picked up most of the personae, especially the "Preferred Customers" or "Old Fiends," and treated them with irony. Although some witnesses described the public as gullible and greedy, they never went past the "manic public" in elaborating their personification. The committee, however,

TABLE 8.1. **Personae in the Committee's Narrative**

Financial Community	Victims
Corrupters	Gamblers
Favored customers	Pool promoters
Special friends	Propagandist
Preferred customers	Publicity man
Payoff man	
Fair-weather bankers	
Manipulators	
Dummies	
Bears	
Bulls	
Shorts	
Speculator	
Wolf of Wall Street	
Innocent	**Gullible**
Shorn lambs	Lottery players
Trusting public	Suckers
Average man	
Common man	
Little fellow	

TABLE 8.2. **Personae in the Witnesses' Narrative**

Brotherhood	Work groups	Proletariat	Manic public
Banking fraternity	Syndicate	Two-dollar brokers	
Brokerage fraternity	Joint account	Chiselers	
Wise heads	Suspense pool		
Committee of elders			
Leading bankers			
Colossus of finance			
Special friends			
Rescue party			
Old friends			

Resisted		Used but Also Resisted	
Shorn lambs	Shorn lambs	Bears	Wolf of Wall Street
Little fellow	Suckers	Bulls	Preferred customers
Manipulators	Propagandist	Pools	Dummies
Pool promoters		Speculator	
Fair-weather bankers		Special friends	
			Old friends
			Publicity man

progressively personified the general public as representative citizens; they were the "Common Man," the "little fellow," or "Shorn Lambs." As hard times had spread throughout the country the "Common Man" emerged as a representative American and an icon of hard work, responsibility, and hardship. The witnesses, well dressed and well groomed "thoroughbreds," were at a loss to protest that personification.

The dominant self-description of the witnesses was that of a loyal brotherhood headed by that "Colossus of Finance," the House of Morgan. Presiding over the brotherhood were "Wise Heads" and "Elders." Affiliated were "Special Friends" and "Preferred Customers." "Special Friends," like themselves, just happened to be in high places. They also formed collectivities, mainly "Syndicates" and "Joint Accounts." The "Suspense Pool" did not travel very far beyond the Whitneys. They did grant that there was a Wall Street proletariat called "Two Dollar Brokers" and "Chiselers." It was said that they traded on such small movements in the market that they could not influence it. Together, they claimed, the Brotherhood did its best to control the Manic Public and a few Chiselers of their own.

Of course, not all of them subscribed to these personae, but neither did any of them resist their inclusion except for the Whitneys. Several of them, however, denied the existence of the Shorn Lambs and the Little Fellow by implying that entering the market was a sign of mental weakness or uncontrollable greed among ordinary people. What some witnesses had called "Preferred Customers" were later disclaimed in favor of "Special Friends" who, in turn, became "Old Friends" who just happened to be in the Senate, House of Representatives, or elsewhere in the federal government. The witnesses' personae were not just a reversal of the committee's, and they steered clear of offering any personifications of the committee itself.

All of the committee's terms made it into the newspapers not only in verbatim quotations but also as personae to populate their own coverage. Sometimes they were still bracketed in quotation marks, sometimes they were treated with irony, and sometimes they were simply adopted for use. The most widely and continuous use was for the changing cycle of "Preferred to Old Friends." Although coverage of the "Preferred Customers" had occurred early in the hearings, references to them were sustained in the press and by Pecora, who incorporated their presence into the committee's wordscape.

For over two years the *Times* and the *Tribune* gave extraordinary coverage to the Pecora hearings. Yet, the tone of the coverage was usually subdued, occasionally critical, ironic, or humorous, but more often revelations were left to stand for themselves without outrage or high drama. Pecora ran a disciplined hearing. There were no figurative cyclones, no earthquakes, no volcanoes, no Mt. Blancs—almost nothing to stir the reader beyond the sometimes ironic descriptive and verbatim coverage. The wordscape they summarized was at first sight hardly figurative at all (see fig. 8.1). One could have found almost every object in it also in the daily accounts of business or the stock market. There was the White House, the Republican Cloak Room, the Rockefeller Bank and House of Morgan, both bear and bull markets, all kinds of pools surrounding a growing depression, an open market, curb exchange, Wall Street, Congress, and much of the rest of the "hardware" that showed up in wordscapes already in use in reports on business in the *Tribune*.

No one, except Pecora, ever recited all of the wordscape at one hearing, but parts of it were used by the witnesses who spoke in both descriptive and figurative language. There was no effort to avoid much of it. What gave the wordscape shock value was a single, sinister "web of influence" that had infected every nook and cranny of the political landscape: the White House, the Congress, the federal departments. All were under the influence of the celebrities of Wall Street; the House of Morgan, the Rockefeller Bank, the Open Market, and practically all the Wall Street firms represented by the witnesses were entrapped in this web of influence.

The web of influence had caught the newspapers' attention early in the hearings after Pecora took over. Each celebrity witness seemed to know another celebrity witness or, more often, a helpful member of Congress. The newspapers handled it rather gingerly at first, referring frequently to the "Preferred Customers," but mentioning the web of influence only in direct quotations. Pecora's creation, it was a striking visualization, especially when Pecora went so far as to diagram it—with real names—in open hearing before an appreciative audience and press. After that the papers reported on the web of influence in detail and listed hundreds of names along with their position in government and business. The newspapers never independently elaborated the web of influence but once it was introduced in the hearings there was no effort to depreciate the hearings or treat them as comedy.[13]

FIGURE 8.1. The web of influence.

By that time Pecora was a formidable presence, and only once was he seriously challenged.[14] Senator Glass, a member of the committee and whose name was on practically every existing piece of banking legislation, was perturbed when Pecora probed into Morgan's interests in a holding company that controlled 30% of the electricity consumed east of the Mississippi (*Tribune*, May 27, 1933).

> "I do not care anything about the house of Morgan but I do not intend to see any injustice done to it or to any other house . . . " flared Senator Glass. His thin veined hand of a 75 year old man banged upon the table. His white hair bristled in a crest: his face glowed an angry red as the wattles of a bantam game cock.
>
> Pecora's rejoinder, "I did not seek this assignment as counsel to the committee. I appreciated and I still appreciate the honor. . . . I have been happy to render whatever service, modestly, I could . . . the compensation of $255 a month is no incentive to me to render these services or to continue to render them," brought the crowd to its feet with applause "loud and long continued." (*New York Times*, May 27, 1033)

That day the *Tribune* gave Pecora credit for establishing that the holding company

> . . . was controlled by the Morgan firm, and that the Morgan influence virtually governed the policies of the operating companies. He established the fact that the Morgan house had been given in return for its advance of funds a million option warrants at $1 each, good for the purchase of United corporation common at $27.50 a share, and that United corporation stock was selling at twice that price and more shortly after this transaction. (*Tribune*, May 27, 1933)

Three days later the *Tribune* headlines ran, "ROOSEVELT PUTS O.K. ON PRIVATE BANK INQUIRY." It was Glass, not Pecora, who would retreat.[15] The day following that headline, Arthur Krock wrote on the editorial page: "the inquiry will resume tomorrow, no longer a mere Senate hearing before a divided committee but shining with the notation: 'O.K.F.D.R.'" Krock went on to say that a mysterious "distinguished visitor" ("a member of the nation's top intellectual stratum") from New England, "had told the President that the Senate inquiry into private banking had already been of deep service to the administration . . . that the President had been able to obtain unprecedented executive powers from Congress" (*New York Times*, May 31, 1933).

This was not the first or last time Roosevelt stepped in to support Pecora. Earlier that year, just when the *Times* thought the Democrats would drop the inquiry, Roosevelt spoke out to endorse Pecora's managing of the inquiry (*New York Times*, February 7, 1933). Later, when the stock exchange refused to distribute to its members a questionnaire prepared by Pecora's staff, the *Times* had only to remind the exchange that "many members of the Stock Exchange must know . . . that the vigorous support of the public, Congress and the Roosevelt administration is behind this investigation" (*New York Times*, October 22, 1933). Richard Whitney agreed to "send the revised questionnaire to its members with a recommendation that they answer it."

Roosevelt did not hesitate to use the authority the hearings had granted him. That same day he would sign the Securities Act. On June 16 he signed the Glass-Steagall Act, which Senator Glass had revised to suit him. A year later, as the investigations were winding down, he signed the Securities Exchange Act despite opposition from much of Wall Street and the Senate.[16] As James Burk argues, it is hard to believe that the crash alone empowered the president to take such action. "The crash did not cause people generally to lose confidence in the market. . . . The number of individual shareholders . . . actually rose from between nine and eleven million in 1930 to between ten and twelve million in 1932, more than double what it was in 1927 (1988, 32–44). This recovery compares well with that in 1988. And no one was even indicted in the Pecora hearings.

The 1987 Wall Street Scandal

When we look back to the 1929 crime wave, what we see is a national crisis and a loss of faith in fiduciary responsibility.[17] When we look back to the 1987 crime wave, what we see are the colorful, greedy, and brilliant rogues who helped make business a comic adventure. Like Michael Milken, the greatest celebrity of the age, they were as much heroes as villains. Staging takeovers and insider trading were scandals with all the fascination, intrigue, color, and moral ambivalence characteristic of what Wendy Griswold (1986) calls the "City Comedy." City comedies are that sort of scandal where responsibility for rotten law enforcement is pushed off on a few flagrant violators (see also Jacobs 2005). Claims to complete innocence are everywhere compromised, but only one or a few principals suffer. Only if the litigants or legal proceedings get out of control can something alarming, or even "system failure," occur (Adut 2005).

The crimes revealed after 1987 were drawn out serially in separate investigations and court hearings that were concluded as if independent events. After 1987 a number of individuals actually went to jail. No further legislation was passed until the Sarbanes-Oxley Act of 2002, following another Wall Street crime wave in the 1990s. The Sarbanes-Oxley Act essentially assumes that the stock market cannot be regulated directly by government oversight but only made more "transparent" by actuaries, new reports, and procedures, and vigilant or at least opportunistic lawyers (Lowenstein 2004, 205–15). Already there is a movement afoot to repeal the act. Seemingly it makes U.S. exchanges less competitive.

There are so many "structural" differences between the 1929 and 1987 crashes that the differences in the figurative language used to report them may seem unavoidable or only "descriptive," but "description" was one of those differences. Social structures do not move through time and space guided by their own weight in an electromagnetic field. Language must evaluate their "weights," and figurative language seems especially apt for the task of giving them this weight. To say that figurative language is "only descriptive" seems wrongheaded on the face of it. Such language becomes figurative only by exploring something other than literal similitudes. (If such "literal" weights exist.) The problem is to find out how different parties shape a language to report differences; they do not exist in raw nature.

One of the differences between the 1929 and 1987 insider scandal was that the latter scandal broke before the crash. The chain of indictments that started with Dennis Levine, reached Ivan Boesky, and eventually led to Michael Milken straddled rather than followed the 1987 crash. The legal arrangements for separate trials were already in motion when the crash occurred. Since some of them took the rich man's plea of guilt with a fine and a reduced sentence, their newsworthiness was limited. Exactly what Hoover might have hoped for and almost got in 1930–31.

Although other forms of fraud were revealed before and after 1987, from start to finish it was called the "insider scandal." Indeed, the *Tribune* and *Times* had a name ready made for it because they had been reporting on insider trading ever since the 1981 election of Ronald Reagan (see fig. 8.2).[18] Most of the coverage was only on the business pages until 1986, by which time insider trading was a well-established business-page genre. Although those indicted were active in "takeovers" and "bundling mortgages," there was never a "takeover scandal." Nor was the "Home Savings and Loan scandal"[19] merged with any of the other scandals during the Reagan administration.[20] There seemed to have been an effort to avoid bundling the banking and stock market crashes into one "super scandal." However, the 1920s and 1980s were both periods of pervasive deregulation, lax enforcement, and deep corruption in Congress (Allen 1931; and Calavita et al. 1997). The spread of a 1987 "super scandal" would have had almost no limits. Congress and the Administration had every reason to confine the scandal to the "insiders." The Reagan administration, however, did not repeat Hoover's miscalculation for an investigation.

The stage was set for a comedy of good boys gone wrong under the influence of some great corrupter. There were plenty of candidates[21] to fill the roles, but two starred: Ivan Boesky and Michael Milken. Together they filled the principal roles of the "great rogue" and the "young gallant" in Wendy Griswold's (1986) city comedy. There were other young gallants. Dennis Levine was the main subject of three books, one of which he wrote. (The bibliographic appendix [8.2] that follows gives a sense of the literature surviving both the 1987 and 1929 crashes.) But none of the other young gallants measured up to the "Wunderking" Michael Milken, nor was there another Great Goliath to measure up to Ivan Boesky, "the King of the Arbitragers." When it was reported that Boesky had pleaded guilty to insider trading on November 14, 1986, that day was christened "Boesky Day" and has remained so in the following literature. The literature that follows in Milken's wake is much more sympathetic, often taking the form of a genius gone wrong. "So what," one response was, "he created value, didn't he?" George H. W. Bush saw fit to pardon him.

Although the crash made the insiders more newsworthy, they were never blamed for it, nor were there any official efforts to explain the crash other than the SEC's report that it was an unhappy coincidence.[22] To a contemporary reader that may seem very different from the 1929 crash, which is generally thought to have been followed almost immediately by the depression and revelations of gross misdoing.[23] The situa-

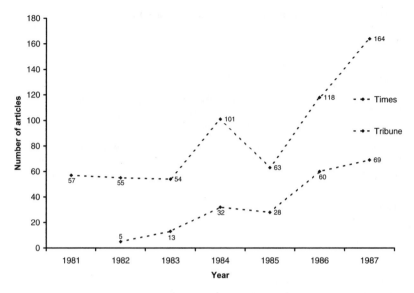

FIGURE 8.2. Number of articles on insider trading, *Chicago Tribune* and *New York Times*, 1981–87.

tion in 1929 was different but not that different. Thousands of bankruptcies had occurred in the farm states and had split the Republican Party by 1929. The Florida land boom had gone bust by 1927, but it was hardly mentioned in 1929 and not at all in the Pecora hearings. But, as you can tell from chapter 2, the *Tribune* and urban Americans and their representatives remained optimistic right into the Pecora hearings. None of the witnesses in the Pecora hearings blamed the 1929 crash for a depression. And, they never called it the "*Great* Depression."

1987: The Insider Scandal

The insider scandal was reported in similar ways in the *Times* and the *Tribune*; I will present only the *Tribune*'s dramatism (see table 8.3).[24] Only one article on the insiders made the front page. Four more made the front section but all the remainder were on the business pages. Murder, robbery, and burglary did much better in gaining front page coverage.[25] As in 1929 there was no overlap between the reporters writing about the insiders and those writing about either organized or common

TABLE 8.3. **The Narrative of the Wall Street Insider Scandal, 1987**

Insiders	Investigators	Wall Street
Tip off a relative	Target insiders	Wall St. fiasco
Pass tips to friends	Roaming investigation	Wall St. on defensive
Accommodate customers	Widening probe	Wall St. rocked
Dual trading	Move into takeover arena	another blow!
Piggybacking	Tackle esoteric violations	Wall St. circles the wagons
Front running	Put customers on trial	Wall St. shell shocked!
Team up	Talk tough	Shocking aberrations!
Orchestrate efforts	Stand pat	Wall St. debates ethics
Profit sharing	Insider snared!	Wall St. soul searching
Prop up prices		Wall St. gets tough
Park securities		
Filter money		
Money laundering		
Judgment proof!		
Cuts deal		
Pays penalty		

TABLE 8.4. **Personae in the Wall Street Scandal, 1987**

Leaders	Followers	Investigators
Goliath	Small fry	David, legal super star
King of the arbitragers	Copycats	Insider watchdogs
Key figures	Bad boys	Secret informant
Central figures		
Dealmakers		

Bad	Bold
Bad apples	Corporate samurai
Malefactors	Fast buck raiders
	Good hitters
	Wall Street wunderkind

crime. Most of the credited reporters at least occasionally wrote on business and the stock market.

The 1987 Wall Street Insider Scandal is carried out by three protagonists (table 8.3). The Insiders and Investigators are the chief personae, but Wall Street itself comes alive as a sort of Greek chorus to deliver judgment. The articles move back and forth between these parts as if separate characters until they come together at the final showdown. The insider is snared, he pays the penalty and Wall Street gets tough.

All personae (table 8.4) use the same wordscape (fig. 8.3) and the in-

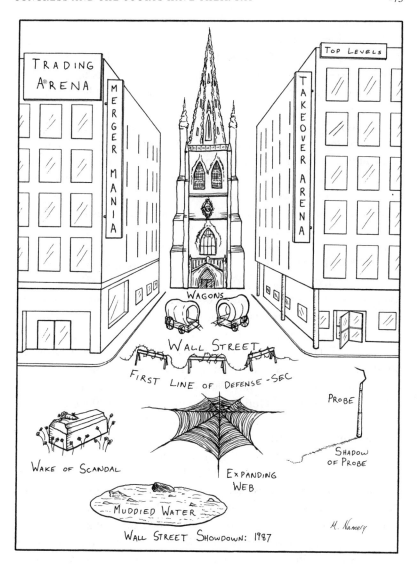

FIGURE 8.3. Wall Street showdown, 1987.

siders and investigators make up a single population of personae who collectively define the moral contrasts: bully:underdog, leaders:followers, and bold:bad. Wall Street is always a single, unified persona, and, while beleaguered at first, it stays on the sidelines almost to the very end.

Although reporters use these phrases repeatedly, many of the insiders and some of the investigators are placed (at least initially) in quotes as if to use insider rather than newspaper language. Some terms are defined in early articles: Piggybacking = to follow a client's investment with one's own; front running = to do the same thing before investing for the client; park securities = secretly agree to buy and hold securities for another broker.

However, there is almost no overlap between the terms used here and those reported by Hirsch (1986) for the "merger mania," although most of the insiders were also engaged in or used information about takeovers. It is unlikely the reporters coined the terms since their first appearance was in quotation marks. More likely they are drawing upon the language of informants who are avoiding the more colorful terms uncovered by Hirsch. What we are getting in tables 8.3 and 8.4 is an expurgated dramatism where nothing really muscular or heavy-handed occurs.

Still, it is easy to see here a later-day version of Griswold's Elizabethan city comedy (1986, 14–54). A variant of the trickster tale, the city comedy is a story of bold youth who are misled by a great rogue into some shady enterprise by visions of easy fortune. There are the young gallants (Corporate Samurai, Fast Buck Raiders, Good Hitters, and the Wunderking). There is the great rogue (Goliath, King of the Arbitragers, Boesky). Some of the young gallants are little more than minor cheats and swindlers (Small Fry, Copy Cats, Bad Boys), the equivalent of Griswold's "coney catchers." Goliath (Boesky), of course, is the great rogue, but virtue appears as the biblical David (Gary Lynch, head of the SEC's enforcement division) who fells Goliath with legal arsenal.

As in most comedies, morality is not black and white here. Things go, almost inadvertently, from bold to bad only to end in a humbling and moralizing rescue. It is that timeless tale of bold youths caught up in their own unguarded aspirations only to be drawn further afoul by a devious rogue. The great threat on the horizon is the investigative probe "zealously wandering in esoteric and uncustomary" directions (see fig. 8.3). But in the end a kind of rough justice worthy of popular feeling is meted out. The gallants cut a deal and the great rogue pays the penalty. The Wall Street chorus rises to intone its restored moral standing.

The Elizabethan city comedy has to be Americanized for a contemporary audience, and that is done primarily by the wordscape. It is something like a western showdown in the middle of Wall Street. A wandering probe is advancing against the first line of defense (the SEC). Two houses of disorder—the takeover arena and merger mania—flank the street. The probe, accompanied by an expanding web, crosses the muddied waters, casting its ominous shadow over the wake of the scandal. Already there has been a fatality. Ahead are the encircled wagons and, presumably hovering behind them, both the young gallants and the great rogue.

Griswold provides a synopsis that is easily adapted to the insider comedy:

> [City comedies] offered a quasi-resolution to make everyone happy. [In them] the smart and aggressive, be they younger sons, servants or con men, achieved wealth, forgiveness, and sometimes even respectability. At the same time those who profited from the loss of lands and the downfall of others, the [Goliath] types, were punished. Most important the gallants reclaimed their . . . social status by relying on their wits to accumulate the necessary capital. (1986, 52)

Northrop Frye provides a broader statement of the genre:

> If superior neither to other men nor to his environment, the hero is one of us: We respond to a sense of his common humanity, and demand from the poet the same canons of probability that we find in our own experience. This gives us the hero of the *low mimetic* mode, of most comedy and realistic fiction. . . . On this level the difficulty in retaining the word "hero," . . . occasionally strikes an author. (1957, 186)

The First Draft of History

There is no single way to tell a story. Journalists recognize this when they call upon informants of different persuasions to tell their story. It isn't just a matter of bias; language is only a form of approximation and, in the rough-and-ready world that journalists face, it is easy to justify several approximations. Thus, whatever vocabulary journalists and their informants use, the words will carry with them a provenance, a lasting first draft for others to use in their own stories.

If journalists are to tell a story—and there is practically no other way to reach their readers with any lasting impression—they must mold this language into something like a genre with a familiar line of narrative action, recognizable characters, and an appropriate setting. Also, if the story is at all to capture the reader within the next twenty-four hours, the action, the characters, and the setting must be somewhat larger than life, providing drama and suspense. However, since most news making is a form of realism, there must be data, evidence, and learned testimony to suggest the very smell and feel of place and people. The journalist must balance all these ingredients so that they are hardly visible to the reader.

Not all journalists manage to do this. Indeed, the Associated Press makes a practice of avoiding it. Some, however, are remarkable at doing it almost every day with considerable originality in the use of many genres accompanied by a sense of personal judgment. For most reporting, however, the genre, the narratives, the personae, and the word-scapes have already been outlined, and the problem is to superimpose upon them some more or less ill-fitting data, evidence, and testimony. After all, the object is not to list some facts but to fit social happenings into a mnemonic dramatism that might leave some traces by the next day.

In the early 1930s Pecora told a very mnemonic dramatism of system failure and, for much of the time, the newspapers allowed him to go directly to the readers with verbatim accounts. It was a powerful telling not of the crash but of the men and institutions made visible by the crash. Could Pecora have told a very similar story following the 1987 crash? I think so. All the ingredients were there except the senatorial committee. Reagan, also, was fortunate. He did not pretend to understand the stock market and he did not make Hoover's miscalculation. Contingencies, always there are contingencies. But it was not Pecora alone who left this mnemonic package. It was also the remarkable journalistic translation that made it so memorable and unavoidable to historians. The first draft of this piece of history is still making history.

A Canon of Corruption

The *Tribune* journalists had a good story to tell about each crash, and they told it well. Both come to us in a familiar and interesting form. The two accounts of the crashes differ greatly, and they have left very distinctive stamps upon on the literature that has followed over the years (see appendix 8.2). It is very hard to evaluate the large volume of literature that has followed each crash. I confined myself to book-length, nonfiction[26] treatments that could be found in one or another of the Indiana University libraries using a small number of terms that seemed—after some experimentation—to turn up most post-1928 and 1986 book-length accounts[27] of each crash that might have a continuing readership.[28] I pruned this list to exclude reports by the government or research foundations, books by economists meant only for economists, and I omitted books that had less than a full chapter or its equivalent on one of the crashes, crime waves, or investigations.[29] I then took the books published on the 1987 crash between 1987 and 2000 and combed their bibliographies and footnotes for references to any similar books published after 1928 and 1986. I wanted only books that were still available and within the range of "active readership." I skimmed all the books and eliminated those that did not directly address either the crashes or subsequent investigations.

One cannot draw any safe conclusions from the number of books on each crash or crime wave. Fewer books were being published between 1928 and 1986 than after 1986, but the telling of the crashes and Great Depression have made the 1929 crash much more memorable. In 1997, when I taught an undergraduate class of about thirty-five very bright University of Chicago senior sociology majors, few of them had heard of the 1987 "insider scandal," although some did remember that "something had happened" on the stock market when they were about twelve years old. Practically all of them knew that there had been a stock market crash in the late 1920s.

In any event, the number of books on each crash is nearly a tie, twenty-eight for 1929 and thirty for 1987. Both lists of books follow a pattern of frequent publications in the first decade or so with a quick drop-off thereafter (see the list of titles in appendix 8.2). For the 1929 crash the drop-off continued until the 1950s, after which there is a small stream of two to five books for the next three decades. Then, attention to the 1987 crash in the 1990s seems to have awakened attention to the 1929 crash for the next decade or so. Five of the twenty-one books published after 1989 bring the two into comparison. Several of these books also touch briefly on previous crashes and Wall Street crime waves, but the 1929 crash seems to have become the standard against which all lesser ones are compared.

There are some interesting differences in authorship. Most of those writing in the first decade after the 1929 crash were well-established writers (Allen, White, Noyes, Fisher) or well-known prior to the crash (Schumpeter). Those writing in the immediate period after the 1987 crash were less established writers with the exception of Robert Sobel, who has written a book on practically every turn of the market, including three on the 1929 crash. Bruck and Lewis have become well known but were made so by her *Predator's Ball* and his *Liar's Poker*.

Since I have weeded out economists writing only for other economists, Galbraith, Schumpeter, Kindelberger, E. N. White, and Miller are the only ones left. Galbraith's story of the *Great Crash* is everywhere called a "classic," even among his many critics. Schumpeter, of course, is very well known, but Rendigs Fels in his following summary (425–39) of the three-volume *Business Cycles* says that the work was poorly received and seldom read. References to Schumpeter elsewhere (for example, Chancellor 1999, 122–23) usually mention only his view that crashes are usually preceded by technological innovations. In fairness to Schumpeter, however, it must be said that no one else has singled out *financial* innovations as an initial condition contributing to the moral ambiguities that seem to precede each crash. But, like all the books on the 1929 crash, he regards it as a national crisis. The distinguishing feature of all these books is the seriousness of their treatment. The 1929 crash was the great crash and a national disaster. To some (for example, Galbraith), it need not have been a disaster except for poor fiscal policies. The remaining literature on the 1929 crash is basically historical although sometimes drawing on comparisons with other crashes. They are not very polemical but all tend to situate the 1929 crash as the standard against which all other crashes are to be judged. The little humor to be found in their treatments of the 1929 crash is ironic and singles out a few notorious figures who were well known but not central to the crash.

The books on the 1987 crash are often quite polemical but also very amusing. Irony occurs but so does every other form of humor. The writers debate, defend, or satirize takeovers, junk bonds, government regulation, derivatives, and the moral standing of Michael Milken and the market. It is hard to find a single representative example, but they range from Fischel's and Kornbluth's (1995 and 1992) unqualified defense of Milken to Martin Mayer's meticulous reader's guide (1992) through the history and changing habits of brokers preceding the 1987 crash. Writing on the 1987 crash, the Nobelist Merton Miller makes an extended argument in favor of futures and derivatives while also rehabilitating Michael Milken and the junk bond industry. His argument goes on at great length and, though at the margin of popular appeal, it does include some op ed pieces aimed in that direction. He seems to be the only one who is dead serious. White and Kindelberger are quite readable and both of a mind to let crashes "burn them selves out." Crime just fuels the purifying flames. Still, even in their account, the 1929 fire was an exceptional national cleansing.

It is the literary form of these books rather than their specific vocabularies or characters that distinguishes them from one another. The 1929 crash is told as a great tragedy in a period given to excess and corruption at the highest levels. The literature on the 1987 crash is overwhelmingly a comedy confined to Wall Street. Many more of the books on the 1987 crash focus on one or a few characters who are more than colorful—they live at the boundaries between brilliance, danger, and outlawry. The books on the 1929 crash deal less with individuals and more with social conditions and the political culture that promoted the crash. These differences exist even for those books that treat both crashes. Only Chancellor is self-conscious of the differences in the treatment of the two crashes and the consequences of that difference:

> It was widely expected that after the excesses of the 1980s, the speculative spirit would wane as it had done after the 1920s. In retrospect, the crash of 1987 sent out a radically different message to the events of 1929. The market's recovery appeared to show that buying and holding stocks was the best investment strategy, and that stock market crashes did not herald economic depressions. Instead they provided an opportunity for bargain basement purchases by canny investors "buying into the dip." (1999, 281–82)

Appendix 8.1: Hirsch's Dramatisms

As in my own analysis, Hirsch recognizes the genre rather than the "master metaphor" as the organizing principle for grouping figurative vocabularies. It is instructive to see how nearly Hirsch's vocabulary of corporate takeovers also fits the form of what I have called a dramatism. Hirsch's collection of terms draws from many sources both verbal and textual (Hirsch 1986, 803–4) over two decades while most of mine derive from established journalism in two newspapers about sixty years apart. Still, the dramatism is very similar to that constructed by the newspapers.

TABLE 8.5. From the "Merger Rage" or "Mania" to the "Age of Aquarius"*

The Merger Rage or Mania	The Age of Aquarius
Big gun hunting	matchmaking
Unfriendly offer	friendly offer
Play chess	wooing
Play marbles	courtship
Black book plan	sex w/o marriage
Fight letter	bring to the altar
[Go] nautical	marriage
Hot pursuit	afterglow or on the rocks
Ambush	
Throw up barricades or flak	
[Try] greenmail	
Jewish dentist defense	
Double pac-man strategy	
Shark repellant	
Cyanide pill	
Scorched earth	
Shoot out	
Saturday night special	
Bear hug	
Iron clasp	
Rape	
Takeover	
Mushroom treatment	
Chain letter effect	

* For definitions see Hirsch 1986, 930–34.

TABLE 8.6. Personae in the Era of Merger Mania and the Age of Aquarius

	Aquarian Characters	
Merger Mania Heavies	Supporting	Sacrificial Victims
Big hat boys	White knight	Sleeping beauties
Hired guns	Gray knight	Pigeons
Studs	Seed partner	Raquel
Black knights	Rescue party	Wounded list
Pirates	Summer soldier	LIDOs*
Raiders	Cupid	
Sharks		
Don Giovanni*		
Jaws*		
Mad Austrian*		
Mankiller*		
Faye*		

* Ad hominem references that became generalized to other heavies or victims. See Hirsch 1986, 830–35.

Appendix 8.2: Books on the 1929 and 1987 Crash/Crime Waves in Use after 1986

Books on the 1929 Crash/Crime Wave by dates of publication
(alphabetical within year of publication)

1930S

1. Fisher, 1930, *The Stock Market Crash—and After.*
2. Allen, 1931 (republished 1959 and 2000), *Only Yesterday: An Informal History of the 1920s.*
3. Allen, 1935 (republished 1966), *The Lords of Creation.*
4. White, W. A., 1938 (republished 1973), *A Puritan in Babylon.*
5. Noyes, 1938, *The Market Place.*
6. Pecora, 1939 (republished 1968), *Wall Street under Oath.*
7. Schumpeter, 1939, *Business Cycles.*

1940S

* * *

1950S

8. Galbraith, 1955 (republished 1972 . . . 1997), *The Great Crash, 1929.*
9. Churchill, 1957, *The Incredible Ivar Kreuger.*

1960S

10. Cowing, 1965, *Populists, Plungers, and Progressives.*
11. Sobel, 1965, *The Big Board.*
12. Sarnoff, 1967, *Jesse Livermore: Speculator King.*
13. Sobel, 1968, *The Great Bull Market: Wall Street in the 1920s.*
14. Brooks, 1969, *Once in Golconda.*

1970S

15. Carosso, 1970, *Investment Banking in America.*
16. Schlesinger, ed., 1975, *Congress Investigates.*
17. Sobel, 1977, *Inside Wall Street.*
+18. Kindleberger, 1978 (revised in 2000), *Mania, Panics, and Crashes.*

1980s

+19. Sobel, 1988 (revised edition), *Panic on Wall Street: A Classic History of America's Financial Disasters with a New Explorations of the Crash of 1987.*

20. Burk, 1988, *Values in the Marketplace.*

1990s

+21. White, E. N., 1990, *Crashes and Panics.*

22. Bierman, 1991, *The Great Myths of 1929 and the Lessons to Be Learned.*

23. Sobel, 1991, *The Life and Times of Dillon Read.*

+24. Grant, 1992, *Money of the Mind: Borrowing and Lending in America from the Civil War to Michael Milken.*

+25. Sobel, 1993, *Dangerous Dreamers: The Financial Innovations from Charles Merrill to Michael Milken.*

+26. Seligman, 2000 (3rd edition), *The Transformation of Wall Street.*

+27. Chancellor, 1999, *Devil Take the Hindmost: A History of Financial Speculation.*

2000 AND LATER

29. Kindleberger, 2000 (revised edition), *Mania, Panics, and Crashes.*

28. Klein, 2001, *Rainbow's End: The Crash of 1929.*

Books on the 1987 Crash/Crime Wave by dates of publication (alphabetical within year of publication) (by date of publication)

1980s

1. Frantz, 1987, *Levin and Co.: Wall Street's Insider Trading Scandal.*

2 Madrick, 1987, *Taking America: How We Got from The First Hostile Take-over to Megamergers, Corporate Raiding and Scandal.*

3. Stevens, 1987, *The Insiders: The Truth beyond the Scandal Rocking Wall Street.*

4 Bruck, 1988, *The Predators' Ball.*

5. Metz, 1988, *Black Monday.*

+6. Sobel, 1988, *Panic on Wall Street: A Classic History of America's Financial Disasters with a New Explorations of the Crash of 1987.*

7. Arbel, 1989, *Crash: Ten Days in October—Will It Strike Again?*

8 Lewis, 1989, *Liar's Poker.*

9. Wood, 1989, *Boom and Bust.*

1990s

10. Walter, 1990, *The Secret Money Market: Inside The Dark World of Tax Evasion, Financial Fraud, Insider Trading, Money Laundering, and Capital Flight.*

+11. White, E. N., 1990, *Crashes and Panics.*

12. Levine, 1991, *Inside Out: An Insider's Account of Wall Street.*

13. Miller, 1991, *Financial Innovations and Market Volatility.*

14. Rothschild, J., 1991, *Going for Broke: How Robert Champeau Bankrupted the Retail Industry, Jolted the Junk Bond Market, and Brought the Booming Eighties to a Crashing End.*

15. Stewart, 1991, *Den of Thieves.*

+16. Grant, 1992, *Money of the Mind: Borrowing and Lending in America from the Civil War to Michael Milken.*

17. Kornbluth, 1992, *Highly Confident: The Crime and Punishment of Michael Milken.*

18. Mayer, 1992, *Stealing the Market.*

19. Stein, 1992. *A License to Steal: The Untold Story of Michael Milken and the Conspiracy to Bilk the Nation.*

20. Sobel, 1993, *Dangerous Dreamers: The Financial Innovations from Charles Merrill to Michael Milken.*

21. Mayer, 1993, *Nightmare on Wall Street: Solomon Brothers and the Corruption of the Market Place.*

22. Platt, 1994, *The First Junk Bond: A Story of Corporate Boom and Bust.*

23. Fischel, 1995, *Payback: The Conspiracy to Destroy Michael Milken and His Financial Revolution.*

+24. Seligman, 1995 (3rd edition in 2000), *The Transformation of Wall Street.*

25. Beckner, 1996, *Back from the Brink: The Greenspan Years.*

26. Melamed, 1996, *Escape to the Futures.*

27. Bose, 1998, *The Crash: The Fundamental Flaws Which Caused the 1987–8 World Stock Market Slump and What They Mean for Future Financial Stability.*

+28. Chancellor, 1999, *Devil Take the Hindmost.*

29. Woodward, Bob, 2000, *Maestro: Greenspan's Fed and the American Boom.*

*30. Kindleberger, 2000 (revised edition), *Mania, Panics, and Crashes.*

*Books referenced on both crashes/crime waves.

+Books that examine both crashes/crime waves.

PART IV

The Transformation of Ideology

Normalizing the Economy: Popular Ideology and Social Regulation

It is the function of public opinion to check the use of force in a crisis, so that men, driven to make terms, may live and let live. Walter Lippmann, *The Phantom Public*, 1925.

Ideology seldom comes to us directly as a self-described theory of society and a plan for guiding or changing it. Rather it comes to us as stories, stories that are packaged in such a way that they are almost immediately recognizable, interesting, and possibly convincing. They are recognizable and convincing because they resemble all sorts of other social scripts, some of them normative (that is, prescriptive) but others that just turn happenings into familiar narratives or genres with an implicit moral.[1] They do not necessarily offer empirical proofs or some testable theoretical mechanism (still another machine, by the way) but exemplary cases that are to be taken as both description and proof. As stories, however, they often obscure immediate recognition of their ideological content. To reveal this content takes a research project like the present one or, at least, a trained eye that searches for ideological content.

Taken strictly, the social sciences (excepting Marx, of course) do not offer an explicit ideology that explains social life and also provides a generalized recipe for guiding it. They are analytical sciences that tackle less general problems, and their narrowly defined generalizations hold only if everything else is held constant. Of course, everything else is never constant. One way to go beyond this sort of social science is to find an analogue in which everything else doesn't seem to matter or is at least manageable. The natural world is an especially apt analogue precisely because it includes every thing else. To some, it is all the more persuasive as God's creation or Newton's clockwork (still another metaphorical machine). Naturalizing ideology is probably the most widespread of all our self-explanations.[2]

The machine is another popular possibility because it seems so self-contained and well regulated that it requires only occasional maintenance. There are other attractive unitary possibilities: the human body, sports, the family, the seasons, the life cycle, and so on. If you look for them you will find all of them in figurative models reported in the daily press.

These analogies become less visible yet persuasive if they form an entire dramatism, a complete story that makes familiar the incoherent "rushing flow of occurrences and observations" of reported daily life (Nord 2001, 74). Dramatisms have this power because they can turn a difficult theoretical argument into a social reality almost as persuasive as experience itself. It has a familiar narrative with recognizable personae and an appropriate setting. Dramatisms prompt familiar visualizations that are sometimes realized elsewhere in the newspaper as cartoons. With some supporting facts and expert testimony these stories seem entirely objective except among those who come ready with an alternative dramatism. When Nobel Prize winners and presidents use much the same language, one can hardly doubt their descriptive value.

This transformation of ideology is unidirectional for most readers. Analogies do not reveal their origin unless we mount a systematic search. The "invisible hand" gives no clue to the underlying argument made by Adam Smith. Each figurative extension taken alone is understandable, convincing, and perhaps enlightening in its own way.[3] But you cannot work your way back without a special effort. It is a-many-to-many problem. There are lots of newsworthy topics that can be turned into figurative "machines;; for example, the human body[4] or the political or military machines. The last two might also be turned into organized crime but that hardly serves Lippmann's hope that the press will dampen the use of force. Machines are among those root analogues that, like the natural world, seem to be so self-contained they can be comprehended without worrying about "all other things."

Our elaborated language may be built upon a number of grounded experiences (for example, Thomas Reid's "natural language"), but you cannot work your way back from our unlimited (potentially infinite) concepts to a few root experiences or a single "natural language."[5] What you can do and what I have done is to collect a *dramatism* made up of figurative extensions that reveal a rough correspondence to Marshallian and Keynesian economics. However distant these dramatisms are from the technical details of each theory, they made order out of the buzzing confusion of daily, seasonal, and annual changes in the economy during the crises of 1929 and 1987.

What makes these years particularly interesting is that journalists were called upon to test their skills at getting readers to exercise patience at a time when conflict and force could have made conditions much worse than they were.[6] What these dramatisms did (other than skip all the technicalities, caveats, and most evidence) was to normalize something very uncertain by turning it into something at least familiar and most likely manageable. The 1929 naturalized economy initially moved along with all the determinism of the tides. When it faltered in the Great Depression the Keynesian machine provided a dramatism that normalized government intervention as hopeful as the repair work on the family car. It wasn't that Keynesian economics were a proven policy, or that it was initially very successful. But, as a hopeful dramatism it provided breathing room for experimentation and subsequent government intervention. Nothing like the riots in Germany occurred. Debates over Roosevelt's fiscal policy still continue, but the resurgence of neoconservatism has not yet altered the figurative machine. The new brand of conservatives want to manipulate tax policy, monetary policy, and fiscal policy just as much as the liberals want to manipulate them.[7]

The more serious threat to the popular figurative machine may be globalization. Ever since the Great Depression the operation of the "our" economy and the welfare of the national community have become coterminous. Globalization, however, tears at the boundaries between the American community and its economy. What the European Union has struggled with since World War II may have its dim reflection in this hemisphere. What sort of figurative economic reporting patched over the European nations' gains and losses so far? Can it carry the countries to complete unification? What kind of language is beginning to appear on this side of the hemisphere? These are questions I leave for others.

The Reader

Where does this leave the reader? Is he a social dope or is he like most of us who read the news with a grain of salt? I think that economic news leaves most readers where most of them were beforehand: aware, if not able to articulate it, that the news on the economy is part of the economy. The facts never stand alone in these news stories, and there is almost always a forecast that precludes precipitous action. All the studies of the media show at least one consistent finding: readers read the news as intentional behavior. The news is aimed to achieve some kind of result and readers are very good at reading into the news some such intent.[8] It isn't that they simply translate the journalist's code into their code but that they read into the journalist's code an unwritten objective.

News is read as a claim rather than only a description. The reader may agree entirely with the reported "facts" but that will not keep him or her from assigning an intention to reporting on the economy. Are they being mobilized, reassured, cautioned, or what? Readers are at least as rational about the news they read as they are about their own economic behavior. News on the economy, most of them know, is mostly what the promoters of the economy provide the reporters. Why would it be otherwise? The economy depends on a favorable "climate" of opinion. It is not the "unmoved mover."

Don't get me wrong. This is not a criticism of journalism or of ideologies. What ideologies can do is bring the politically possible alternatives to light while journalists restate them in an available language. Their mission is to regulate the general sense of alarm or quiet. The most alarming of all conditions is the absence of reliable news or the management of it to the point that it loses confidence. Readers are quick to notice that. And I hope they will be equally quick in deciphering my own intentions. For my language is laden with figurative terms. Somebody other than I should make a dramatism of them.

Dramatisms among Cultural Studies

Where do dramatisms fit into cultural analysis? The easiest fit for this study is with Swidler's cultural "tool kit" (1986). Dramatisms are among the essential strategies in the toolbox of the practicing journalist. They are one of the ways he or she can communicate about things that we really don't fully understand, yet, are terribly problematic. They may be so problematic that they threaten peace and due process. The dramatisms studied here are one of the ways collective behavior with all its uncertainties is regulated on a daily basis. The economy and the polity are the modern centers of uncertainty. As Lippmann recognized, the news does not stand, indifferently, outside these centers of uncertainty but is a vital "thermostat" that can restore a rough balance among contending forces. What the dramatisms do is bridge the gaps between ignorance, the very technical and also disputed models of the social sciences, and yesterday's movement on the many social indicators that now flood the electronic age.

But these dramatisms do not stop with the journalists. The journalist's language can also become that of the reader. The evidence here suggests that those readers who are drawn into correspondence with the editors also use much the same toolbox, and some went so far as to offer similar rhetorical help in dampening the reaction to the 1929 and 1987 crashes ("Buy now," said one brave soul).

The findings of this study also fit Swidler's paradigm of how cultural practices become routinized after the crises that gave birth to them. As she points out, once an ideology becomes unproblematic, it becomes a vocabulary more for show than practice. Indeed, the natural world model of the economy outlasted a number of business crises in the 1890s, and it did so as well in the early years of the Great Depression. The Great Depression, however, was such a lasting crisis that a new administration, the sponsors of the Keynesian "machine" and the recently measured "economy"—the national accounts—converged to completely change both popular and professional ways of speaking and writing about what had been conceived of as a number of more or less independent institutions.

The persistence of the machine ideology of the economy may be for show, but "show" is not unimportant in mass societies. A vocabulary that works for professional economists, businessmen, reporters, and the general public is a vital part of the public discourse that makes mass societies manageable. Indeed, ideologies in general may be more important as a rhetoric with which we overcome uncertainty than as a precise prescription for conduct. Christians, for example, need not be very Christian where Christianity has become only lip service. Conventionalization provides a language that smoothes over differences and uncertainties. Once you have conventional religious beliefs there is no need to go to extremes proving you are one of the faithful.

Debates over Roosevelt's fiscal policies now rage with the resurgence of neoconservatives, but this has not altered the figurative language of the economic machine in the daily news. Both sides try to reach the public with much the same vocabulary. The new brand of conservatives want to manipulate tax policy, monetary policy, and fiscal policy in new ways, not to abandon "tinkering" with the economy.[9]

One difference between my study and Swidler's early work is her tendency to treat the cultural "toolbox" as consisting only of "odds and ends" without much overall structure (see DiMaggio 1997, 263–83 for a criticism). That may be true of individuals when they are exploring and experimenting with different lines of approach or avoidance. Unprepared spoken language is usually delivered in bits and pieces. But, when even the private individual shifts to written language, he or she will write in extended phrases if not complete sentences or paragraphs. The news is not at all an individual production. It has behind it a tradition, formal education, and all the constraints of a business that must make money. It requires that understanding and common usage be shared among journalists, informants, editors, and experts and readers. Any change is worth noting and, possibly, revising. We might say that the larger and the more diverse the individuals, groups, and organizations that use a vocabulary of motives, the more structured and durable they are.[10] Swidler's later work (2001) moves in this direction.

In his review of Swidler's work and that of recent social psychologists, DiMaggio also argues for a much more structural approach to culture. Like the social psychologists he relies on, he uses the concept *schemata* to describe such structures. What the social psychological research tends to show is that individuals retain "information"[11] if it is somehow structured and used frequently. The assumption is that what is remembered is what is important and perhaps actionable. I have adopted much the same position although I balk at the term *information*. Information has become a sponge concept that only rescues rational action theory (and the Internet). Rationality is something imposed by the demands of a role rather than a human inclination or a ready-made mental template that imposes itself on understanding, memory, and action.[12] Instead, schemata that use figurative language move us between different social worlds in which a few facts are pieced together with a narrative, personae, and wordscape. It is very hard to tell a news story without using some of this figurative language. Condensation alone forces its use.

Most of the social psychological work that DiMaggio relies on uses language reproduction (that is, memory), which is subject to this kind of figurative transformation. I agree with him that memory and recognition are fundamental to the formation, recall, and use of cultural forms. However, visual schemata may be even more plastic in shifting the viewer from one social reality to another. Visual art need not even pretend to be realistic to evoke compelling emotions or conviction (Wagner-Pacifici

2005). Visual and language reproduction, in turn, are linked to recall (Paivio 1990), as I have tried to argue here. If you can visualize it, you can often speak of it. If you can speak of it you can usually visualize it. Neither need be a close representation of "reality." My cartoons may be more memorable than any other part of this book.

Which brings me to the question of how "big ideas" like those of Keynes or Marshall enter mass discourse and create their own "reality." Like Swidler I think that big ideas enter into usage only in periods of unsettled times. I agree also that once they are conventionalized, they are more for show than practice. But, to recall Goffman, most of what we do is for show. I would add that these big ideas are transformed even as they enter into mass consumption. They are disguised as dramatisms that do not compel strict adherence. Benjamin Franklin's *Poor Richard's Almanac* (that is, Weber's example of the popularization of the Protestant Ethic) is hardly recognizable as a conscientious effort to translate Calvin's doctrine. It is basically a dramatism, remaking Richard's disciplined capitalism into a model of worldly virtue but not an essential to salvation. Undoubtedly it was influential. New Englanders were (unlike Franklin himself) a rather prudish, churchgoing and penny-pinching people.[13] Many other "big ideas" of this sort may be still with us in disguise. Perhaps the ideas of Locke, Dewey, or Adam Smith are not confined to the academy but are still with us in narrative disguise.

This book is obviously much indebted to Goffman's *Frame Analysis*. But Goffman left the impression that frames were rather temporary moments as the individual moved from one situation and one vocabulary of motives to another. Other studies might suggest a similar transient fate for frames in face-to-face interaction. My interest, however, has been in frames that may last for decades, perhaps centuries. In his study of social memory, Schudson has followed somewhat the same interest in his inquiry into the durability of "cultural objects." In summarizing, he says, "a cultural object is more powerful [persistent and memorable, my gloss] the more it is within reach, the more it is rhetorically effective, the more it resonates with existing opinions and structures . . . the more thoroughly it is retained in institutions, and the more highly resolved it is toward action" (1989, 179). I agree with every word and believe that I have made some headway toward a methodology that will meet each of these requirements.

Dramatisms reach the public and are rhetorically effective because they tell a story that belongs to a recognizable genre. The news stories are not creative writing but are as transparent as the perils of Pauline were to my father's generation. *Resonation* is a concept that is often used in studies of political suasion and influence. I take resonation (the apparent provenance is the "sympathetic" vibration of the strings and shell of a violin) to mean that the terms used in dramatisms are tropes that recall a provenance with some standing among "authorities": the church, polity, military, academy, trades, or one of those sources faced with censorship—the underground, the demimonde, or that of outcasts who are taken to be *really in the know*. Dramatisms borrow their authority from those *who ought to know*. Such terms are "grounded" (objectified) either by operation or example. Newspaper text, as I have emphasized, also seems to be extremely durable and is obviously "institutional language." The Keynesian model was not only resolved toward action (policies) but also made its dramatistic appearance in one of our most popular images of action: the machine.

Dramatisms in the news media are not something that changes moment to moment. Widely shared, they tend to dampen social reaction or to quiet what might otherwise be uncertain, disturbing, or alarming news. They are like the governor on a truck motor that regulates its rpm. They do not themselves promote change but capture change by regulating those transitions that might otherwise lead to panic, bitterness, and the abandonment of the daily drill that rational action theory seeks to capture. Dramatisms, however, are not simply arbitrary in channeling social change. The Keynesian machine was a selective dramatism, not the previous ones at hand.

Dramatisms also leave a history of themselves that is difficult to erase. The dramatisms of the events of 1929 and 1987 are recorded in a literary genre that continues in the readable canon of market crashes. They are part of our social memory and are watermarks that gauge subsequent crises. The historians won't let us forget 1929 and 1987. The fit to Schudson's criteria is too close.

What I find much more problematic is the theoretical approach of Jeffrey Alexander and Philip Smith (Alexander and Smith 2001; Smith 2005). Although they make a convincing argument for the autonomy of culture, they make much less headway toward a methodology, or a unit (or units) of analysis, and an operational (or grounded) definition of those units. Also, there is no apparent mechanism of causation although the term is confronted. These are minimal requirements if a "strong cultural analysis" is to match positivist approaches on their own ground.

Yet Alexander and Smith's (2001) strong program is a strong defense of the autonomy[14] of culture. Thus, I find myself agreeing with much that they say. But it is not a design for research or an example of how it would be deployed. Smith does make some headway toward a methodology with his use of Frye's genres (Smith 2005), which I have also used in this book. Frye's descriptions of the major genres are sufficiently specific or diagnostic that they can be used reliably by other researchers (see also Jacobs 1990 and Rosmarin 1985). The contrasting categories used in Smith's *Why War*, however, are too unspecific to identify what even a sympathetic positivist would consider a unit of analysis. These contrasting categories are similar to those used in the semantic differential and the endless binary contrasts in Talcott Parsons's work. My own effort is to use contrasting vocabulary items to construct a typology similar to those documented in the componential analysis of kinship terms in anthropology. But, in fairness to Smith, *Why War* is, to quote one reviewer, a "good read."

What might we mean when we say culture "causes" someone to do something? Is the answer really different from when we say "interests" cause someone to do something? I suspect the answer to each question might be rather similar. Interests are a vocabulary of motives we impute to someone depending upon their role, identity, situation, or reputation, not their physiology or physical state. When we attribute interests to someone, that person does not have to agree with us. The only "hard evidence" bearing on the actor's interests is the actor's conduct, social position, situation, and, in rare instances, his or her reputation. His or her interests are read into a culturally defined role, not something you measure on a metric scale.

Interests are exactly the same kind of evidence that might be used to further a "cultural" explanation of the same behavior. Indeed, it could be claimed that "interests" are a particular kind of "cultural" explanation of conduct. This is the whole thrust of C. Wright Mills's listing of any number of vocabularies of motives (1940, 904–13) that include both "interests" and "values." Whatever you want to call these interests they do not reduce behavior to the material conditions required of strict positivism. That kind of positivism disappeared with behaviorism.

But I do not want to simply merge cultural causation with that attributed to interests. When vocabularies of motives are combined with rational action theory they are easy to formalize and can be extended to a wide range of conduct where the outcomes can be measured in money terms. This is very interesting research and seemingly appropriate so long as it is confined to market decisions. When researchers begin to as-.sign their own values for other exchanges (for example, with "social" or "cultural" capital) they can't lose, but we gain little from it. So long as there is no well-defined market and currency of exchange, social and cultural capital are simply another attempt at popular dramatisms.

Where cultural analysis is lacking is in the difficulty of grounding its units of analysis and in establishing a dynamic in which variations occur. I like to flatter myself that I have made a step in this direction. Dramatisms can be grounded because their elements are well defined. Figurative terms are recognizable departures from conventional use and draw upon their provenance to achieve their contrast. This is not their etymology but the "owner" whose current grounding offers a "play on words." It may be the church, the state, the sciences, the crafts, the demimonde, or the underclass. It is that "owner" who offers a kind of authority and contrast on meaning not otherwise available. If dramatisms endure and dominate a particular usage, they fill a social slot, a kind of demarcated region of explanation: the economy, the White House, crime, celebrities, and so on. They define a stage (in both meanings) in the dramas of life that are very important but lie outside direct experience.

Dramatisms exist as a whole, and, therefore, membership must fit into their narratives, their personae, and their wordscapes. Exceptions will occur. Language in use is an incomplete experiment whether spoken or printed, and new trials are subject to selection in survival. But the general approach has much to gain from that of linguistics and semiotics with their emphasis on contrast, the selective fit of parts to wholes, the fate of sports, and the borrowing of likenesses for variation.

However, it seems to me that the future of studies in language usage lies not in the search for progressively "basic micro units" of meaning, or in word counts or even in the reduction of units of speech to the level of some studies of conversation to micro units (Schegloff 1987). Language, especially printed language, seems to function at the schemata level where memory locks its parts onto an existing ensemble: a story, a theory, a paradigm, or, at least, a parallel. If that be the reduction of the social to the physical, so be it.

My notion of culture is probably not a good fit with Alexander and Smith's "strong program." It is as weak a program as that of positivists. Indeed, it may be a positivist program.

Methodological Appendix

The *Chicago Daily Tribune*—as it was called in 1929—had the largest circulation of any American newspaper at that time and unhesitatingly called itself "the world's greatest newspaper." By 1987 the *Tribune* was still a big newspaper, ranking a little behind the *Washington Post* with its 810,000 daily circulation as compared to the *Tribune*'s 775,000. Both were well behind the *New York Times* and *Los Angeles Times* with something over one million circulation in 1987 each, while the *New York Daily News* and *USA Today* had about 1.3 million circulation. None came close to the *Wall Street Journal* with its 2.2 million circulation.

In 1987, the *Tribune* had not held its own as the nation's largest, but it remained among the top five that carry a general inventory of news. It also continued to be aimed at the country's midsection where one is led to believe that the least exceptional of Americans can be found. Some readers may counter with the claim that the *New York Times* is far more authoritative and read on practically every campus in the country. John Kenneth Galbraith remarks that in 1929, "By far the greatest force for sobriety was the *New York Times* (1955, 78–79). By contrast he quotes the *Wall Street Journal* only to illustrate the extremes of financial enthusiasm in 1929. The *Wall Street Journal* would seem to be inappropriate for my purposes. *USA Today* did not exist in 1929, and the *New York Daily News* was owned by the McCormick family in 1929 and by the Tribune Corporation in 1987.

The *Tribune*, unlike most of the other top five papers, has been given very little attention in work on the 1929 slump or 1987 crash. Sobel 1965 does not even list any of its reporters as on the take during the great 1929 bull market. Galbraith, Allen 1931, Cowing 1965, Brooks 1969, and Burk 1988 either do not mention the *Tribune* or do so very sparingly. There might be some historical value in extending our attention to economic news in the nation's largest newspaper in 1929.[1]

The *Tribune* had undergone some changes between 1929 and 1987 but, in the main, these changes have kept it in step with the big city press in 1987. In 1929, the *Tribune* was a proprietary newspaper, very much under the command of Colonel Robert Rutherford McCormick, who died in 1955. Like most other newspapers, however, it became part of a media conglomerate by 1987 that included the *New York Daily News*,[2] and the Chicago Cubs baseball team.

The "feel" of the 1987 paper does differ from that of the 1929 edition. The "news" is more sharply segregated by topic in 1987: the boundary between the Sports and Business sections is sharper; human interest, entertainment reviews, and advertisements are more confined to a special section (Tempo); and the positioning of most local news in a separate section gives a greater sense of the gradations of importance between local and national news.

These differences extend to content. The 1987 *Tribune* did not invariably endorse Republican candidates as it had in 1929. The ever-present front page "political" cartoon in 1929 had been consigned to the editorial pages. World affairs were more circumspectly described as what happened, and speculation on what will happen was usually attributed to informants rather than reporters. As in almost all current newspapers, honorifics were used to refer to people of different nationality, ethnicity, age, sexual identity, and race and religion in 1987. Individuals were "alleged criminals" until tried and then, often only "convicted criminals." The practice of "naming" was not exactly the opposite in 1929; for example, ethnic slurs were never used even in quotation marks in either year. However, there was no obvious avoidance of ethnicity, and race was always mentioned for Negroes and Asians in 1929. Some people were also "criminals" whether or not they had been convicted. The battle of the sexes was permissible language in 1929.

In a few ways I do think that the 1987 *Tribune* continues to differ from other newspapers in its league. It has a reasonably well-documented history (Waldrop 1966; Wendt 1979), not all of it favorable.[3] As you might expect, the press usually gets a good press. But, like the city of which it is a part, the *Tribune* still lacks a reputation for detachment despite the paper's self-evaluation (May 4, 1990) as "mainstream." The *Tribune*'s

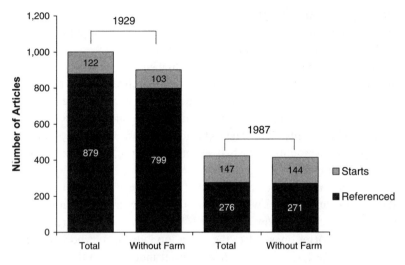

FIGURE A.I. Number of articles starting or referenced on front page, with or without farm, 1927 and 1989.

readership probably is drawn heavily from "the center to the right," or was until the *Chicago Daily News* expired in 1978 and the *Chicago Sun Times* was purchased by Rupert Murdoch in 1983.[4]

My data on the *Tribune* come mainly from three sources—a content analysis, informal interviews with some reporters, and a variety of other documents. For chapters 3 to 5 the most important is the content analysis of all those articles in each issue that either start on the front page or are referred there and purport to say something about the "economy" or "business." Several other samples of articles are used in the remaining chapters, but since the procedures there are similar to the ones used in the early chapters, they will be described only briefly.

Most of the "front page" articles (88 percent in 1929 and 65 percent in 1987; see fig. A.I) do not actually start on the front page but are indexed in a center column in 1929 or displayed in brackets or a side column in 1987. This creates some incomparability between the two years, with 1,001 articles in 1929 and only 423 in 1987.[5] The main reason for this disproportion is that the 1929 center column included an average of about forty entries to an average of about twelve entries for the side column in 1987. However, the number (122) of articles actually starting on the front page in 1929 is considerably *less* than the number (144) starting on the front page in 1987. One could take this to mean that news on the economy was given less priority in 1929, and, that by pursuing all the articles listed in the 1929 center column, I am reaching into a more trivial level of news coverage in 1929 than in 1987.

There is probably some truth to the first part of this statement, but the ratio of the total number of articles from each year need not reflect more trivial or detailed coverage from 1929. For example, the 1929 edition included ninety-nine articles on the farm economy while the 1987 edition included only eight. The topic had virtually disappeared. For the most part I have omitted the articles on farming to make the two samples more comparable.[6]

It is also important to mention that the average article in 1929 was about 17.5 column inches while the 1987 average was 25.8 column inches, a difference of 45 percent.[7] Journalists in 1929 wrote more articles, but they wrote shorter ones. Also, the seven top journalists who wrote consistently on the economy in each year differ much less in the number of articles they wrote. Finally, when we compare the total number of authorities or sources referred to in the nonfarm samples, they are also very close. For these reasons, I am inclined to think that 1929 *Tribune* journalists and wire services produced about twice as many articles with about the same amount of information.[8]

The more important reason not to restrict the analysis to only those articles actually starting on the front page is that you cannot "tell a story" with obvious continuity. Occasional events just seem "to happen." If, however, one reads both the articles that start on the front page and those referenced on the front page, one can "tell a story" with continuity, characters, and the stage on which they appear.

After covering the nonfarm 902 articles in the 1929 "serial," for example. I found that I could read John Kenneth Galbraith's *The Great Crash* with hardly any surprises. He adds an interpretive scaffolding, of course, and rings his account with prior events (for example, Churchill's attempt to peg the pound to unrealistic heights) and subsequent events (the balanced budget as high doctrine). But the characters involved, what they said and did, and the aggregate events that overtook them, is about the same. This, of course, may not be too surprising since Galbraith took much of his narrative from another newspaper, the *New York Times*. No account quite like Galbraith's exists for 1987, so I cannot subject the 415 articles in the 1987 series to the same test.[9] All I can say is that if you read only the 145 articles that begin on the front page of the 1987 *Tribune*, you will get a story with several blank spots. Alternatively, if you read all 415 articles, you will be able to tell a story with much the same continuity as that which can be told from the 902 articles in 1929.[10]

I should add here that singling out a topic like the nation's economy and reading all the "front page" articles on it in sequence is a rather different experience from that of going through the same articles day by day. Reading them in a very compressed time period reveals a more interactive or theological texture. It is as though the people making news releases were talking to one another through the newspaper; as if the sequence of news releases were efforts to counter, neutralize, or "put a spin" on previous releases.

These "conversations" are among the narratives I attempt to reveal here. I start simply by laying out a numerical account that reveals the gross, temporal passage of news in each year. Each article was coded according to a topical list of twenty items that were subsequently combined into seven categories (see Topical Codes for Each Article). These codes were devised after reading all the articles for the first month in each year. I coded all the articles for both years, and had a research assistant code the 1987 articles as well.[11] Agreement between us for the 1987 articles was always 90 percent or better on the twenty subcategories and virtually complete for the combined categories.

Topical Codes for Each Article
1. Stocks (including futures).
2. Fiscal and Monetary (federal expenditures, rediscount rate, Federal Reserve actions, federal budget, jawboning, "moral policy").
3. State of National Economy (global statements; trade reports; indicators such as rail volume, trade balance, consumer confidence; general estimates of wages, prices, prosperity).
4. International Economic News (news on other countries, tariffs, gold, exchange rate, World Bank, OPEC [1987 only], debentures [1929 only]).
5. Specific Nonfarm Industry (dividends, earnings, investments, general condition of specific firm or number of firms with no indication of a broader effect on business or the economy).
6. Farm (prices, weather conditions, supply, prices, support prices).
7. Other (none of the above).

To provide a rough sense of the different informants and sources who "spin" their narratives through reporters and news releases, I used the codes in Types of Authorities or Sources below for whomever the jour-

nalists identified as their news source. Individual and organization are
coded only once in each article, although either may have been mentioned more frequently.

Types of Authorities or Sources

1. President, White House spokesman, or just White House.
2. Federal agency or spokesman.
3. Congressman, congressional aide, congressional committee.
4. Lobby: trade, farm, labor.
5. Local politician or spokesman and local public agency spokesman.
6. Church leader, consumer group, nonprofit social service institution (excludes research institutions).
7. Trade reviews, other news source (e.g., *Wall Street Journal*).
8. Stock Index: Dow, AMEX, NASDAQ, Standard and Poors, Tribune index.
9. Expert: economist, statistician, analyst, "expert."
10. Businessman, firm, dealers, traders.
11. Foreign person, firm, organization, politician, and so on.
12. Noise: rumors, too incomplete to code or no authority source for entire article.

Individuals or their titles were given priority over the firms or organizations they represented. Economic indicators were coded only once
although several measures of, for example, the producer price index
might be quoted. One problem, however, was what to do with the Dow
Jones Index of Industrial stocks and the *Tribune*'s 1929 index for twenty-
five rails and twenty-five industrials. Like the *New York Times* and several other newspapers at that time, the *Tribune* provided its own measure of stock fluctuations in the Commerce and Finance section. Yet, on
only four occasions, all of them during the October slump, did the sample articles in the 1929 edition of the *Tribune* actually mention this index. In 1987, however, the DJIA (or the NASDAQ, S&P, or AMEX)
was almost invariably cited as a measure of stock activity. I decided to
code only those occasions when these indexes were actually mentioned
within an article rather than simply published each weekday. One reason
for this was that each time the *Tribune*'s index was mentioned in 1929,
the journalist went on to explain it, seeming to assume its unfamiliar-
ity to the reader despite its daily appearance. Journalists in 1987 bothered to explain the DJIA to readers only twice; first when the DJIA "hit
2000" and later when it lost over 500 points. Again, there was virtually

complete agreement between the two coders once the authorities and sources were combined.

Some of these categories of authorities and sources may obscure revealing detail. "Lobbies," include labor unions and farm lobbies as well as those representing manufactures, distributors, and retailers. Farm lobbies are included because they appear in the debate over tariffs. They were not a part of the farm news. The inclusion of labor unions may be misleading because they were mentioned only three times in 1929 and not at all in 1987. Essentially, one can assume that lobbies refer to another kind of businessman, but lobbyist use a language different from farmers and other businessmen. They argue for the social good of their business rather than individual success and hardships. Most of what are called *experts* in 1987 can also be businessmen since many of them are analysts or bank economists. All of them, however, use a technical language much like that of university economists when they are quoted by the reporters. None of these experts were ever referred to as "a businessman" in either year, and only the newsman's title was used for coding even when the same person was described differently in separate articles. For example, Charles Lamont, undersecretary of commerce in 1929, was usually described as such but was also called an "economist." He became "Dr. Lamont" in one article. It was said that he was the most liked of any of Coolidge's cabinet.

Churchmen, nonprofit organizations, and consumer groups were mentioned only five times in 1929 and ten in 1987. They are excluded from almost all the analyses. I counted them only to impress the reader with the inability of these groups, and the labor unions, to make their way onto front page economics.

"Noise" is a residual category that includes unattributed rumors, individuals, or organizations so vaguely referenced that they could not be coded in another category, (17 percent of all articles in 1929, but less than 1 percent in 1987). I called them "noise" rather than "don't know" because they only seemed to mask rather than reveal the source.

An unavoidable omission from these codes is the gender of authorities and sources. After coding articles from several months of the 1929 edition, I ran into a woman's name and realized that I had not encountered one previously. Altogether there were four women mentioned as an authority or source in 1929: Mrs. Mary Norton, a congresswoman from New Jersey, whose "blows against tariffs" were "parried" by Senator Smoot who described her as typical of those (women?) who look only at the cost to households rather than to the income of working women (September 2); Miss Anne Bezanson, director of the University of Pennsylvania's "research department" (Wharton School) who advised "business heads to read the [help] want[ed] ads" the day before (October 28) the great crash;[12] Mrs. Francis Warva, whose complaints were held up as an example of those whose naïveté attracted unprincipled brokers (October 30); Mrs. Ruth Pratt, a congresswoman from New York, who was duped by soda pop manufacturers into giving a speech favoring low sugar tariffs (December 21). All but Bezanson were treated with pity or humor. The 1929 articles on the economy were all written by men. However, three of the top seven journalists in 1987 were women and, of the total, ten out of thirty-nine were women. There were no women journalists in the 1929 sample.[13]

There was no tendency in 1987, as there was in 1929, to assign the market's fall to the emotionalism of women. On February 12, 1929, Edward Bendere, a Philadelphia banker, made the front page by declaring that "women as a class" had no place in the stock market.[14] Subsequent to the slump, women and shoe shine boys were grouped together as irresistible bait for brokers. Several cartoons elaborated these feminine weaknesses in 1929. Women were also said to have a more general disturbing influence upon the stock market in 1929, and signs of their danger was given wide attention throughout the paper. Their divorces, marriages, scandals, and aeronautical adventures were heavily covered news. Photographs were more plentiful then than now and the cheesecake ad was a well-developed form. With their boyish bobs and impish faces, they strode forward in gowns that were flat and bodies that were not.

There was also a brief "conspiracy theory" of the 1929 crash when the news of James Riordan's suicide ("Gotham banker kills self") was suppressed for one day. Male suicides, however, were taken as normal, and as early as October 30, people were said to be passing around the joke about hotel clerks asking clients, "Do you want the room for sleeping or jumping?"[15] The suicide myth survived into 1987 only in the cartoons.

In both years, however, reporting of the crashes quickly settled down to a formulaic pattern with a rather fixed inventory of "causes." This was especially so for the articles filed each day after the market's close. These articles seldom reached the front page, but since they constituted the most frequent and most standardized way of writing and thinking about the market, I read and coded all of them for a separate analysis in

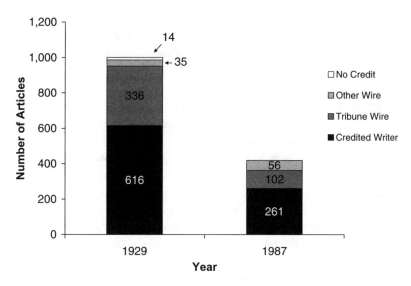

FIGURE A.2. Number of articles, by type of article credits, 1929 and 1987.

which they were compared to a sample taken from the *New York Times*. The difference was so small I do not report it.

There are several other samples used in this study, including one from *Tribune* and *New York Times* articles from 1930 to 1986 to trace out the popularization of the concept *the economy* and its figurative dramatisms. Several other samples are described when they are presented.

Those who wrote the front page economic news for the *Tribune* in 1929 and 1987 show more similarities than differences. In both years almost exactly the same proportion (see fig. A.2) of the sixteen sample articles was authored by a credited journalist. These percentages do not change if the farm news is excluded from each year. The main difference was the much greater reliance on the 1929 *Tribune*'s wire service. The *Tribune* "out sources" much more of its news from other wire services in 1987. However, the 1987 *Tribune* also makes greater use of its own reporters and has them coauthor articles more often—something that never happened in 1929. The 1929 writers wrote shorter articles, but their articles were not half the length of those written in 1987.

One's first impression is that the 1929 journalists must have been filing regular copy on a specific topic while those in 1987 were moving about somewhat from different assignments on a greater number of topics. There is some evidence for this but it does not quite capture what seems to have gone on in either year. The general pattern seems to have been that a small number of journalists wrote or signed off on the bulk of credited articles on business or the economy while the wire services filled in when needed to cover the "budget of news."

Neither of the two financial editors, O. A. "Cotton" Mather in 1929 and William Niekirk in 1987, were not specialists in the usual sense of the word but "generalists" who wrote about the most important macro-economic topics in each year: fiscal and monetary policy, the national economy, and stocks for both with the addition of international economic news for Niekirk in 1987. Although both wrote almost daily on the economy they were not columnists with a set location in the newspaper.

"Cotton" Mather, in 1929, was more obviously "slotted" so that readers could usually find him at about the same location, although he sometimes contributed articles elsewhere. Still, his columns were not headlined by his name. Niekirk's articles were much more scattered throughout the 1987 newspaper.[16]

More obviously slated as columnists were Scrutator in 1929 and William Gruber in 1987. Headlined by their names, their columns appeared almost every weekday, but hardly ever on the front page. They were also generalists but tended to write about very timely events. Scrutator[17] was by far the more omnivorous of the two and became my favorite. In his daily article, about ten inches long, at the top center of the Finance and Commerce section, he held miniature seminars on economic policy and its current application. Scrutator defined and illustrated the "farm debentures" that were so much a topic of controversy in Congress. He explained the Federal Reserve Board's "rediscount rate" and its intentions. He noted the tendency of business toward institutional (corporate) lines and assured his reader that it was no cause for alarm. He spoke from his own authority relying hardly at all on other "experts." No one quite like him existed in the 1987 *Tribune*. I could never find out who he was. Surely that was not his given name.

Gruber was a much more familiar columnist, writing on business personalities and newsworthy changes or events in corporate management and ownership. Seven other journalists made up almost all the remaining division of labor in both years. In 1929 Fred Harvey wrote almost entirely about the stock market, and he hogged the show, writing well over half of the sample articles on that topic. Although not explicitly a columnist, he was carried almost every weekday and his article was placed on the opposite side of the Finance and Commerce section from O. A. Mather's contribution. Between them, they usually framed the page, with Scrutator in the middle. Harvey wrote almost exclusively on stocks, but when the task became too much for him in late 1929, Tom Petty filled in with ten articles. Otherwise the *Tribune* wire service took up most (26 percent) of the slack. Together, Harvey and the *Tribune* wire service filed 83 percent of all front page articles on the stock market in 1929.

In 1987 one reporter, Pat Wider, also wrote most (85 percent) of her "front page" articles on the stock market, but this was a small percent (18 percent) of the total. The *Tribune* and other wire services far exceeded (54 percent) her contribution, although she was writing elsewhere in the paper on a daily basis. Her articles followed a standard form that was virtually anonymous on most occasions. One could anticipate the order of presentation: the movement of the DJIA, the volume of transactions, which economic indicator came out, bond prices, the announcement of analysts, the value of the dollar, the price of gold, and which "household name" stocks went up or down. Only when there was some exceptional movement on Wall Street did Wider improvise, as on October 24, when her article headlined, "Stocks End Wild Week—Whew!" The article continued in this vein: "A battered and bone weary Wall street ended its historic week." By the next paragraph, however, the article had settled into its standard form ("The Dow industrials ended at 1950.76, up .33 . . .").

Arthur Crawford was the most productive journalist after Mather, Scrutator, and Harvey in the 1929 sample. He wrote primarily (75 percent) about international economic news, especially tariffs, which may be why none of the histories of the *Tribune* say anything about him. International news was important to the *Tribune*'s management in 1929, but not international *economic* news. International news on the economy was frequently (29 percent) obtained from the wire services. Unlike the stock market, responsibility for international economic news was not centered on a prominent journalist in 1929. Arthur Sears Henning (ASH), bureau chief in Washington, DC and among Colonel McCormick's closest advisors, scarcely wrote about it at all, and the same is true of Mather, the financial editor. The 1929 *Tribune* wire service was the next most important source of front page news on international economic events. William Lawson, the least productive of the top seven 1929 journalists, wrote all of his five front page articles on international news.

In 1987, international economic news was the chief preoccupation of the financial editor's front page articles. Elaine Povich and Michael Arndt also wrote most of their articles on the same topic. But I do not mean to suggest by this that 1987 *Tribune* journalists had come to focus on international economic news as they had on the national economy. They still depended heavily upon the wire services (22 percent of all articles on the subject), and the more detailed textual analysis suggests that reporting routines paralleling those for reporting national economy have not been developed for international news. Accounts of the Organization for Economic Cooperation and Development (OECD) were rarely mentioned.

In 1929, Henning wrote about national fiscal and monetary policy. Judging from Wendt (1979, 444) he may also have had a hand in many of the *Tribune* wire service articles that provided the largest single source (42 percent) on this topic. Mather, and Arthur Crawford, also contributed to this topic. Altogether, they wrote 86 percent of the articles on fiscal and monetary policy. Thus, despite the localism we usually associate with the period (Cowing 1965, 258–71; Friedman and Schwartz 1963, 357–62) and with the *Tribune* itself, management of the "*nation's* prosperity" seems to have had a high priority in the paper. The distribution of attention to fiscal and monetary policy in 1987 follows a similar pattern but has lost ground to international economic news. William Niekirk, financial editor in 1987, wrote heavily (31 percent of his articles) on fiscal and monetary policy. Dorothy Collins wrote most of her articles (86 percent) on the same topic. George de Lama wrote most of his articles on fiscal and monetary policy, but he was the least productive of the 1987 "front page" journalists who wrote on the economy. The contribution of other wire services to fiscal and monetary policy had grown by 1987.

Beyond the financial editors and the *Tribune* wire services, seven journalists in each year authored, respectively, 95 percent and 82 percent of the sample articles in 1929 and 1987. The obvious differences are the growing importance given international economic news and the increase in the outsourcing of news.

In some ways 1929 journalists seemed more aware or explicit about the use of their newspapers as a forum for consecutive exchanges between those making news releases. Tom Petty, for example, observed with satisfaction how, "Wall street laughs at U.S. credit warnings" (February 13, 1929) the day after the Federal Reserve Board was said to want more constraints on call loans. Reporters in 1929 were also more inclined to allude to some level of conspiracy or tit-for-tat practices among invest-ment groups or political leaders. As the crash approached, Fred Harvey declared, "Powerful foreign interests had combined to break the mar-ket" (October 5). When he chose to quote a financial expert he added that he used the term "to mean a man of wide experience not a slight of hand professor on the stock exchange."

This sort of journalistic license was not totally absent in 1987, but the pattern most often was one of treating economic news as the outcome of impersonal "forces" to be understood from the standpoint of cre-dentialed observers. Even specific actions by the president or the Chi-cago Futures Exchange were often referred to as "agendas" or "policy changes" rather than as the willful choices of individuals. It was, as I ar-gue in the last chapter, part of the more general pattern of representing economic life as a lawful mechanism that marches to its own drummer.

I must add that I learned to like these journalists. I enjoyed reading them and came to recognize their style in their articles. I hope my study has not dampened their enthusiasm for their work or that of readers who still look for news with a human face.

Notes

Chapter One

1. Robert Nelson's argument that economics has replaced religion may be the most extreme statement of this viewpoint (2001). See George Soros 2002 for a statement and critique of the outlook. Somers and Block provide a study of how the language of market fundamentalism has invaded the general debate over welfare policy (2005).

2. James 2001 argues that it was from the start a worldwide monetary crisis of early globalization. However, he does not share Soros's view that something like it is a necessary outcome of globalization (1998, 200–217).

3. For an even more remarkable florescence of multiple realities see Christopher Hill's study of the English revolution in his *The World Turned Upside Down* (1972).

4. The argument is similar to that of Thomas Reid's for a "natural language" (1997, 50–53), but where Reid takes the "natural language" to have been the root words used to reach agreement on all subsequent "artificial words," Lakoff assumes that these "artificial words" are also grounded in this source domain. Reid's natural language, however, is grounded in the collective primordial experience of early man and is now lost among their various extensions.

5. The general approach is best described in an earlier book with Mark Johnson (Lakoff and Johnson 1980, 3–68). The adoption of the concept frame appears in a more recent book (2002).

6. Snow and colleagues (1986) report that social movements involve a great deal of music, cheering, and body language that gives additional form to what is said.

7. See Stephen Toulmin and June Goodfield's *The Architecture of Matter* (1962) for an even more torturous tracing of the word "atom." My account is based on only Webster's dictionary.

8. See Hoyt Alverson's much more thorough critique of the concept "source domain" (1991, 94–117).

9. And, of course, there are "dead" metonyms, personifications, and attempts at irony. Some figurative terms are so near death that the contrast has to be pointed out. Which, one may ask, is the more defensible reference?

10. According to Erin McKean, editor in chief of the *Oxford English Corpus*, newly coined "technical jargon, medical terms, or complex ideas" are among words most likely to enter the corpus. "Slang" has a high mortality rate before getting to the corpus (*University of Chicago Magazine*, October 2006, 56).

11. The term comes from a clerical or judicial practice in which the defendant's own narrative story is taken as mitigating evidence during a confession or legal proceeding. It is, thus, calculated to persuade.

12. What some psychologists call a "chunk" of meaning.

13. See Mills's "Language, Logic and Culture," and his "Situated Actions and Vocabularies of Motive," in *Power Politics and People* (no date). Goffman draws upon Burke several times in his *The Presentation of Self in Everyday Life* (1959). Becker draws upon him in *Outsiders* (1963). When I was a graduate student both Dan Glaser and Joe Gusfield encouraged me to read Burke's work. Apparently, it was required reading at the time they attended graduate school at the University of Chicago.

14. Burke, like Lakoff, tends to assign special significance to one of these tropes (i.e., a "master trope") rather than the entire ensemble. As one reviewer of this manuscript points out, Hayden White, like me, also focuses on the entire ensemble of tropes (White 1978, 1–23).

15. For no explicit reason he leaves out "personification." Like Lakoff and Johnson, however, I include it. Unlike anyone other than Hayden White, Burke includes "irony" as yet another trope. I think it is appropriate since irony is the substitution of one word to mock another. It occurs, however, primarily for humor or sarcasm and, in this study, primarily in the use of personifications that mock or belittle claimed identities. I have not bothered to distinguish it from personification.

Chapter Two

1. Lobbies representing different economic sectors were also jealous of one another, and some sectors were separately honored by naming the World War I fleet of cargo vessels after them; e.g., the USS *American Banker, American Shipper, American Trader, American Farmer*, and such.

2. It was Mitchell, however, who "led and inspired" the economists who eventually established the U.S. national accounts. Mitchell's efforts to estimate na-

tional "wealth" was the first step in the United States toward a unified conception of economic activities (see Schumpeter 1954, 1166–67).

3. Not to be confused with the institutional approach of economists that made distinctions roughly similar to the categories of the *Tribune*'s Business and Financial pages.

4. Hoover was seeking the same voluntary cooperation on investment and production among business firms that he had obtained with nonprofits when he was head of the Red Cross. Henry Ford soon let him know that he was after profits and not about to cut or increase production.

5. The article was also published in the *Tribune*. Noyes was generally recognized as the most trusted journalist on economic news.

6. In 1938, Martin Marty (*Oh Yeah*, Viking Press, New York), filled a small book with similar newspaper balm.

7. The article was probably written by A. Noyes, a very respected journalist who wrote about economic activity. He was quoted by other journalists in both the *Times* and *Tribune*.

8. W. C Mitchell was highly respected institutional economist whose words were taken as support for this approach. Mitchell, however, may have had reservations since he had provided the most recent estimates of national income, a measure that would inform the National Income and Product Accounts. He also trained Simon Kuznets who, in turn, trained both Robert Nathan and Milton Gilbert who gave durable and newsworthy form to the National Accounts and the "economy" (see Perlman 1983, 135–50).

9. In 1931 rye grain was cheaper than sawdust, about 35 cents a bushel.

10. Both were financial and business reporters. For more detail on them and other early users of the concept see appendix 2.1.

11. This was the earliest mention of the "Great Depression." Only after the recovery in 1935 did I find a few references using the adjective *Great*. Following the 1935 recovery, however, the "Great Depression" became history only after it was over.

12. The statement is by Arthur Sears Henning and the first instance I was able to find of a reporter using the concept of the "economy" in the *Tribune*. See appendix 2.1 for his background.

13. Occasionally this usage occurred in the *Times*. Indeed, there was no agreed upon definition of unemployment in the early 1930s because some wanted to omit those who were "laid off" from those without prior or present employment (Duncan and Shelton 1978, 24).

14. Nor were there entries under "domestic economy," "national economy," or "economic systems." "Economic Systems" does occur much later but only after "the economy" was in widespread use.

15. This meaning had not made its way into the OED by 1990. I have not checked since then.

16. E. A. Johnson, "Economics and the Economy," *Journal of Political Economy* (June 1944).

17. Its ranking is only a little lower in Johansson and Hofland's 1989 study of 1961 British usage. (The Brown Corpus was compiled by Henry Kucera and W. Nelson Francis at Brown University, Providence, RI as a general corpus in the field of corpus linguistics.)

18. The dates were picked from a table of random numbers.

19. The counts given in table 2.1, however, refer only to those articles read in their entirety.

20. The word *macroeconomics* did not appear until the 1950s. Perlman (1983, 140) comments that "Macroeconomic" was another of those "words that were all but unknown" in the 1920s and 1930s.

21. I also read numerous biographies on newsmakers who were among the first to use the term.

22. All the italics here and hereafter are added by the author.

23. Up to this point "free enterprise" had been used to distinguish the American economic practice. The concept "capitalism" was hardly ever used in the articles. Much later it comes into occasional use to draw a contrast to the Soviet Union's communism.

24. Emmison (1985, 146) notes a similar pattern between 1930 and 1945 in England.

25. Here Keynes recognizes the continuing problem of conceiving of the economy as only that product which is measured by its sale in legal and documented markets. The older institutional economists would have included as well the product of housewives and the subsistence activities of households. In one of the meetings of the AEA, Edwin Sutherland invited them to consider including the costs and benefits of crime to various industries, particularly banking.

26. John Hendrick provides a brief description of the accounts in the *Encyclopedia of the Social Sciences*. For a splendid history of their development and their ramifications for practically all economic measurement, see Duncan and Shelton 1978.

27. The NRA eagle would decorate the masthead of the *Times* but not the *Tribune*.

28. Sloan's criticisms would become sufficiently newsworthy that FDR would invite him and some other business leaders to the White House in early 1938 to smooth over difficulties between business and government.

29. The concepts "net national product," and GDP and GNP were coming into use among economists (Duncan and Shelton 1978, 83–84). But I did not run across it in any of the 1930–39 news articles. Perlman remarks that the concept of macroeconomics was "a word then [1936] all but unknown" (1983, 140)

30. Ironically, Martin, a business economist, left in 1935 to work for the National Industrial Conference Board where as a "frequent critic of the Depart-

ment of Commerce figures" (Duncan and Shelton 1978, 80) he stirred up more attention to the national income and product accounts.

31. Apparently it was reviewed only in professional journals.

32. Which appears to have been virtually the same as his "The Means to Prosperity," which was published in the *Times* of London and the *New States-man and Nation* in 1933. Keynes does refer to the "economic machine" in *The General Theory* and, somewhere else to a "Robinson Crusoe economy," but I can no longer find the latter.

33. There was much exchange between the two groups, so their efforts were by no means independent (Perlman 1983, 140–44). See R. Parker 2005 for how Keynesian economics was imported into the Roosevelt administration.

34. The "Spark Plug Boys" gives some sense of the newsworthiness of economic research at the time. Richard Gilbert would go on to become the newsworthy chief economist in the Office of Price Administration during the war. His cousin, Milton, would head the group that completed Kuznets and Nathan's work on the national income and product accounts. Both were students of Kuznets.

Appendix 2.1 of this chapter rounds out the account of the early newsmakers who helped popularize the concept of "the economy."

35. At least those readers who wrote letters to the *Tribune*. See chapter 8.

36. Johnson's real skill was for media debates. Baruch had confided to FDR that Johnson was not a "first class man," but his gift for debate and invective saved FDR the trouble of similar rebuttals in the trench warfare over the "planned economy." Johnson supervised procurement in World War I and helped devise the Selective Service System. He also wrote novels and adventure stories. As the NRA lost favor among New Dealers, he was eased out to become a popular newspaper columnist ("Hugh Johnson Says") and eventually turned his invective on FDR.

37. The Hoover administration was otherwise rather secretive. Lamont went on to become industry spokesman for the Iron and Steel Institute, from which he then resigned in protest of NRA requirements. After that he disappeared from the *Times Index*.

38. Sloan was not cited nearly as often as Ford and Lamont in the *New York Times Index*, but when his comments were grouped with those of other businessmen, he was usually listed first. It was he that FDR asked to bring the businessmen's delegation to the White House and, afterward, it was Sloan who spoke for them.

39. McCormick took Henning's word for it that Dewey would defeat Truman and accordingly ran the famous headline in the 1948 election (Wendt 1979, 682–83).

40. Including many well known ones: e.g., Simon Kuznets, Milton Friedman, Alvin Hansen, Simeon Leland, O. M. W. Sprague, Joseph Schumpeter, Leo Wolman, and Albert Hart.

41. One of which included Edwin Sutherland speaking on the costs that white-collar crime imposed upon the economy.

42. Whipple was interviewed frequently by the *Tribune* as the president of a "typical middle-sized firm." He was a willing speaker and an eager user of federal statistics on the economy although adamantly opposed to government "interference."

Chapter Three

1. Bartolomeo de San Concordia, quoted in Yates (1966, 87). Concordia is paraphrasing St. Thomas Aquinas.

2. From Rudyard Kipling's "McAndrew's Hymn" (1893). Quoted in Asa Briggs's *The Power of Steam* (1982, 81). The self-regulating "machine" seems to have held a persistent fascination for westerners. From the Greeks' gods on stage to its use as a model for early physiologists (see Toulmin and Goodfield on "The Animal as Machine," 1962, 307–37), we seem to have found in it a semblance of ourselves.

3. Here I am obviously stretching Lakoff and Johnson's concept of a master metaphor to include all the tropic ingredients of a Burkeian dramatism (1980, 10–32).

4. These inconsistencies could be evaluated only with a much larger sample over long periods of time. One must record every mention of the "economy" (or appropriate pronoun) and at least the paragraph within which it occurs. I have done this for the economy, business, finance, and commerce in still other samples described later.

5. He refers to the economic machine but not to "the economy."

6. See chapter 8 below. See also Gamson's 1992 study of guided focus groups discussing some of the same topics, or Richardson's (1998, 220–50) study of TV viewers' restating economic news on television.

7. Between 60 and 70 percent of the terms come from the *New York Times*, which is about the same proportion of the total number of articles from that newspaper. The proportions are about the same for each narrative.

8. Mentions of the economy in either narrative are rare in the 1930s. Only three showed up in this sample.

9. "Balance" seems to be replacing the search for "objectivity" recorded by Schudson (1978).

10. Numbers in parentheses indicate phrases referred to later. Italics guide the reader to the more critical metaphors or phrases also referred to in the text.

11. It was the most analytical article that occurred in any of the samples. It makes use of conventional introductory economics but still relies upon figurative language to theorize his argument.

12. I have not included these figurative narratives because they wander off into an endless web that deserves separate attention.

13. I did find one figurative phrase—"reform economy"—that did not fit with either master metaphor. It occurred only in 1950 and then only once.

14. A partial exception is "finance." Finance was a fickle part of a natural world and could act like an ogre or be manipulated by malevolent personae. Finance shows its sometimes unwelcome self in the business dramatism.

15. Reviewers thought the "endless lists of words" too tedious for the reader so I have not included them. The reader can easily contrive his own dramatisms for finance, commerce, and such.

16. See Brewer (1980, 237) for some popular guidelines for constructing stories for children. The economy and business narrative generally fulfill these guidelines. In describing these narratives I have roughly followed Brewer's approach since he is also concerned with comprehension and memory. I do not try to systematically preserve the distinctions made by writers on literary style (e.g., Chatman 1971 and Culler 2000 [1975]), although I find them useful in a general way.

17. Remember there are over 1,400 front page articles for 1929 and over 400 for 1987. Of course, business or the economy may not appear as subject or object in that many of them.

18. In 1987 no separate language seems to have developed around the other Dow Jones averages (e.g., transportationals) or the other stock indices (e.g., NASDAQ, S&P). By the 1990s, as the other indices became more newsworthy, the language for the Dow Industrials was simply extended to them.

19. With rather simple reversals of some of these stages one can contrive the outline for all four of Frye's literary types: tragedy, irony, comedy, or romance.

20. The articles include all those referenced or appearing on the front page of the *Tribune* in each year (see the Methodological Appendix).

21. Even when reporting on both, the identities of the administration and Congress are almost always kept separate. In only two sample phrases (those marked by an *) were their identities fused.

22. Here one can see the advantage of going beyond a single master metaphor (Lakoff and Johnson 1980, 22–45) to reveal an entire dramatism. Dramatisms easily accommodate several metaphors, even seemingly contradictory ones.

Chapter Four

1. *Ad Herennium*, III, p. xxi, quoted in Yates (1966, 10).

2. Burke uses "master" trope to refer to those tropes that suggest all or most of the remaining figures of speech in a dramatism (that is, the tropes he lists in the introduction to *A Grammar of Motives*). At times, however, he uses one of

the tropes to characterize an entire dramatism. See White (1978, 1–23) and Lakoff and Johnson (1980) for similar variations in usage.

3. White (1978, 7–12) goes further, assigning the mastery of each trope to each stage of development identified by Piaget.

4. Which makes that only "newspapers of the record" with an appendix fall into easy access. This seems to be a declining practice among newspapers.

5. Many other "product men" (for example, "cotton men," "oil men") were mentioned in the 1929 *Tribune*, but I have limited the list to only those in the sample so as to remain in keeping with the parameters of the other findings.

6. Using Homeric society as an example, MacIntyre says "we cannot identify the Homeric virtues until we have first identified the key social roles in Homeric society and the requirements of each of them. The concept of *what anyone filling such-and-such a role ought to do* is prior to the concept of virtue; the latter concept has application only via the former" (1981, 184, emphasis in original). In practice MacIntyre shifts without distinction among roles, personae, and actual people as embodiments of the virtues.

7. Northrop Frye (1957, 186) also recognizes the literary necessity of embodied evil even in all literary genres.

8. As in factor analysis the author gets to name the dimensions in each contrast. My dimensions are simply generalized to a contrast among another persona. Further abstraction would lose the point.

9. Throughout much of the depression the *Tribune* continued to use the word "idle" to describe those who were "laid off." There was no personification of the unemployed in any of my 1929 samples.

10. Finance was an exception.

11. Norman and Harrison were scarcely mentioned in any other context. The Federal Reserve itself, however, was one of the "Ogres" in the 1929 stock market dramatism.

12. By 1987 Hirsch's cast of villains (1986) from the early stage of corporate takeovers had been replaced by the heroes in the Age of Aquarius. A study of *Tribune* articles on takeovers alone would have yielded only a few of the more colorful terms reported by Hirsch.

13. During the Pecora hearings after the 1929 crash, readers were reported to be shocked by the close financial relationship between lobbyist and political leaders. By 1987 lobbies seem to have regularized that exchange. Lobbies were just "lobbies."

14. News on takeovers, junk bonds, and other schemes in 1987 was separated from the remaining economic news until very late in 1987 when the insider scandal began.

15. The front page cartoon character "John Q. Public," which the *Tribune* used later to represent its own political constituency, had not appeared in 1929.

16. I acquired the habit of reading much of the business section although I coded only the front page articles.

17. The Republican "whip," although not referred to by that name in either sample. The term, however, was used frequently by columnists elsewhere.

Chapter Five

1. Quintilian, quoted in Yates (1966, 22).

2. Like phenomenologists, Burke argues that the reader must go beyond what is immediately available in viewed text to infer the larger "plot" within which it is embedded. Burke might argue that his generative principles are what guide our "intentionality" in textual materials.

3. Business and finance are combined here because their wordscapes coincide almost entirely although they have somewhat different narratives. There is some overlap among several of the dramatisms, but tracing them out would extend us way beyond reporting on the economy and, perhaps, as far as a secular Weltanschauung.

4. The *Indianapolis Star* and the *Herald-Times* in Bloomington, Indiana. I am speaking of that period before the *Herald-Times* totally abandoned anything other than local news.

5. Barry Schwartz 1981 argues that ranking by vertical position is universal owing to the relative stature of parents to that of their young children. However, if they do not learn it at home, they will certainly learn it from the media.

6. Cicero, from *De oratore*, quoted in Yates (1966, 4). Perhaps we could add imagery received by the ears to this quotation.

7. In references, drawn cartoons are almost always listed as "political cartoons." Listings to cartoons is taken to refer to the comics. I found no listing for "economic cartoons."

8. For a while I worked at Warner Brothers. It was remarkable how we could create an entirely new setting with ancient stock.

9. The word *get* suggests the reader's claim to some of the cartoon's meaning.

10. When cartoonists string together a series of panels the action and time always runs left to right as it would in text. Despite the "up and down" text, however, the Japanese do the same thing.

11. One might think that television would provide a more authentic visualization of the news, but the news on television is mostly "talking heads." Live television usually shows only the wreckage from some past event.

12. However, the 1929 *Tribune*'s front page "John Q. Public" was suited and a balding male.

13. This includes all personae, humans, animals, monsters, and objects. Heroes are big winners held up as exemplary models. Stymied personae are wor-

thies who have been frustrated by others. Knaves profit from the weakness of others but are not vicious. Dupes are personae who are done in by others. Villains are malicious. There were also mere Observers who only register a response (for example, alarm) to something else.

14. Only one cartoon recognized the ailing farmer, and he was soon to be rescued by Dr. Hoover (See fig. 5.11). None of the 1929 or 1930 letters to the *Tribune*'s "The Voice of the People" that are reported on in chapter 7 focused on the farm crisis and rural bank failures.

15. The statement is Carl Schorske's paraphrase of Langer in *Fin-de-siècle Vienna* (1981, 311).

16. I brought no talent to the studio. My father got me the job.

Chapter Six

1. In 1929 it was the "Finance" and "Commerce," section but for purposes of simplicity I will call both the business section.

2. The Industrials were always listed for market days but mentioned only after the crash. The *Tribune*'s industrial index and the DJIA are so highly correlated (.96) in 1929 that they can be used interchangeably.

3. See Maynard's *Bad News, Good News* (2003) to more fully appreciate the greater difficulty of dealing with bad news than good news. See also Thaler's "Confirmation Principle" (1987).

4. See Thaler (1987, 197–201).

5. Coolidge prosperity did not extent to farmers and farm communities. Farm families alone, however, made up almost a quarter of the population, and farm communities probably another 15 percent. There was little coverage of the farmers themselves although the failure of farm legislation got some coverage. See appendix 6.2.

6. The 1987 articles on the stock market mentioned some reports provided by private groups, but few of them made the front page.

7. Both Andrew Mellon who was secretary of the treasury and Robert Lamont, secretary of commerce, were prominent businessmen.

8. Scrutator had a daily column on the front page of the business section. I was unable to find out his name.

9. Dr. Friday had been "from" the University of Michigan for quite a while. According to Galbraith (1955, 60), he was an advisor to a Wall Street firm along with Irving Fisher who was at Yale but moonlighted on Wall Street.

10. Mitchell was head of the National City Bank in New York and a member of the New York Federal Reserve Board. He became a hero to stock market plungers when he advanced $25 million to traders in defiance of the board's policy. In almost all accounts of the crash Mitchell appears a buffoon or

opportunist who helped hype the 1929 bull market. Friedman and Schwartz's very detailed account (1963, 258–62) suggests that much of his posturing was an attempt to force the Federal Reserve Bank to take a more decisive stand than its "moral policy." However, he did not fare well in the Pecora hearing (see chapter 8).

11. I knew Fackler and asked him what he was up to. "Just trying to put an end to some unsettling rumors," he said. Fackler was a popular informant of the press and gave an early forecast. He was very aware of the distinction between "news" and "information" but recognized the need for both.

12. Chancellor (1999, 191–97) explores again the "new era" explanation of the 1929 crash.

13. Friedman and Schwartz (1963, 296) argue that the Federal Reserve's policy of "close synchronism produced much confidence within and without the System that the new monetary machinery offered a delicate yet effective means of smoothing economic fluctuations." Apparently bankers shared in this confidence as much as any "jazz age economists."

14. Fisher, Friday, and the banker Mitchell had been very close at hand during the bull market.

15. Privately Colonel McCormick was dissatisfied with Hoover and had telegraphed Arthur Sears Henning on March 4, "This man won't do" (Waldrop 1966, 27).

16. Farm news is discussed in greater detail in appendix 6.2.

17. The phrase "market break" was used only by the SEC. But everyone avoided the phrase "market failure."

18. The complete study also includes chronologies for October 6, and 14–16.

19. There is, however, some evidence in both years that journalists and their informants tended to attribute declines in the Dow to actions by the United States, other governments, "psychology," or celebrity forecasters. Rises in the Dow were more often attributed to fundamentals or the absence of bad news. See appendix 6.1.

Chapter Seven

1. In her recent work with Navaho and American children, Donna Eder finds that they strive mightily to discover the author's intentions (personal communication). Tompkins (1980, 201–32) includes a fascinating chapter on how the standards of appropriate literary criticism have changed as sociopolitical regimes have changed.

2. By 1987 there were separate sections for different suburbs, and the paper was being fragmented into sections aimed at taste, entertainment, and other consumer groups. There was less international news gathering and the national and

local news sections got smaller. The consumer sections had gotten larger. The political posture of the paper became more diffuse. ("Mainstream" it was said.) Still, in 1987 it was the sort of paper you could look to for "all the daily news." That could not be said of the current *Tribune*.

3. Nor do I have any of the editor's response to the 1987–88 letters. The editor of the earlier *Tribune* and *Herald* seems to have written each of his correspondents rather than only published their letters.

4. The sample includes all letters in October subsequent to the seventeenth so as to capture whatever readers might have made of the stock market crash directly afterward. Otherwise I took every eighth day in 1929–30 and 1987–88 so as to cycle evenly through the years.

5. Here I consulted the *Tribune*'s index as well as the detailed chronologies of the *World's Almanac*. Unlike Nord, I did not find any letters that were completely "off the wall." Perhaps the *Tribune* sorted them out.

6. Allowing women to serve on juries was a current issue but attracted only one letter.

7. The main problem is that the phrases are not repeated often enough to be sure they are widely used and that other phrases fit the same dramatism.

8. The writer seemed to want to make primitive monsters of the economists.

9. This does not mean that 1929–30 readers were more tolerant on moral issues, only that racial prejudice, homosexuality, and such were not at issue. A proposal that women serve on juries did draw two uncompromising letters in opposition.

10. References are in brackets.

Chapter Eight

1. Appendix 8.1 sorts Hirsch's collection of terms into the dramatisms that performed this transformation.

2. These seem rather tame innovations today but in the early 1920s the separation of ownership and management, corporate oligopolies, and the intrusion of government into the control of interest rates and the money supply were violations of "pure capitalism." There were many other innovations, particularly, in extending credit and marketing securities. Almost all of them are considered to be normal business practices today.

3. There were many other "innovations," prior to 1987: (1) the "efficient market theory," (2) the enlistment of Internet "day traders," (3) the valuation of firms and their CEOs on the basis of quarterly gains in stock value, and (4) the invention of "derivatives" for hedge funds. Chancellor (1999), Lewis (1989), and Lowenstein (2004) are good sources on how these "deviations" became "innovations" and the innovations became good business. MacKenzie and Millo 2003

provide an exquisitely detailed account of how hedging with derivatives was legitimated.

4. It is difficult to compare the cases because so much that was believed to be illegal turned out to be "only unethical."

5. See Adut (2005, 229–32) on the fortuitous happenings that often initiate scandals.

6. Hoover got even with him in his autobiography where he called him a "well intentioned well digger from South Dakota." Hoover was a mining engineer from Iowa.

7. By adding a new partner to the House of Morgan precisely on those dates the firm was enabled to revalue all its securities and declare a loss for the two subsequent years and pay no taxes.

8. D. Ritchie provides an account of the Pecora hearings in "The Pecora Wall Street Expose" in *Congress Investigates* (1975). Records of the hearings have served any number of subsequent publications.

9. This and the periods following roughly coincide with those in which the hearings were in session, usually five or fewer days a week.

10. Apparently, *syndicate* did not have the sinister connotations that it acquired later. Organized criminals may have found it attractive for reasons similar to those of the witnesses. Perhaps that is why Al Capone had already taken to calling his gang a Syndicate.

11. None of the witnesses seemed aware of Keynes's famous distinction between "investors" and "speculators" (1920, 138) but used the words as if either interchangeable or differing only in moral worth.

12. "New era thinking" was no more fully explained in the hearings than in all the previous coverage during 1929. It was usually referred to as "Coolidge Prosperity" during the hearings.

13. The *Tribune* had previously reasoned that the incoming Democrats would end any investigation started by Republicans.

14. Many of the witnesses seemed to frame the investigation as an inquiry into collective rather than individual malfeasance. Pecora certainly took that view in titling his book *Wall Street under Oath* (1939). The book was republished in 1968.

15. A few days later (June 6, 1933) Roosevelt sent a letter to Glass informing him that he would veto the Glass-Steagall bill if certain provisions in it were not dropped. The provisions were dropped.

16. Ironically, much of this legislation would be undone by the Reagan administration prior to 1987.

17. J. Morgan (the son, not J. P.) drew up a draft of this theory of fiduciary responsibility for the *Times*, arguing that the value of his firm's reputation was such that he would not dare neglect his responsibilities. Even after he testified that he knew little or nothing about what his partners were doing or how the ac-

countants drew up his tax returns, he was at a loss to understand why he was under investigation.

18. The number of articles is based on each paper's index. Reports extend back into the Carter administration although they increase noticeably in the Reagan administration.

19. The Florida land boom and bust in the late 1920s was also avoided in the Pecora hearings. Only F. L. Allen starts his book-long treatment of the 1929 crash with the Florida land boom (1931).

20.Including the mining of Nicaraguan waters, the E. F. Hutton admission to manipulating checking accounts, the Tower Commission Report that found Reagan confused and uninformed, and the Iran-Contra affair. None became an enduring scandal.

21. The 1929 crash did not lack for equally colorful characters who would have fitted into a similar city comedy. There was Ivan Kreuger, "the Match King"; Jesse Livermore, "the biggest bear on Wall Street"; and Charles Mitchell, a banker who defied the Federal Reserve to the applause of Wall Street. Only Mitchell was among those interviewed at the congressional hearings.

22. Chancellor (1999, 282) reports that two mathematically inclined economists carried out an analysis that showed that the 1987 crash was a chance occurrence with a probability of 10 to the 160!

23. The black-and-white photographs of crowds on Wall Street watching the stock prices crumble suggest to us that they had already grasped oncoming depression.

24. I used the index of each paper to locate the stories on the insiders. The *Times*'s coverage was more extensive, but the sample I examined was so similar in vocabulary that I saw no point in trying the reader's patience. The vocabulary from the *Tribune* was drawn from all indexed articles from early 1987 through 1988.

25. In an unpublished paper I find that reporting on organized and common crime frequently make the front page while corporate crime was reported primarily in the business section.

26. Which, to my regret, excluded Tom Wolfe's *Bonfire of the Vanities* (1987), a comedy of the Reagan era disguised as fiction.

27. That is, additional terms only turned up the same titles.

28. The online catalog is quite extensive and includes the holdings of eight different campuses. I used only those terms that seemed most effective in focusing on the crashes and crime waves: For 1929, "stock market crash or slump," "stock market/banking fraud," "Black Thursday," "Ferdinand Pecora," "Jesse Livermore," "Charles E. Mitchell," and "Ivar Kreuger." For 1987 I used "stock market crash or slump," "stock market/banking fraud," "insider trading," "Black Monday," "Gary Lynch (from SEC)," "Ivan Boesky," "Michael Milken." I stopped searching at the end of 2004.

29. All of them touch on both the crash and crime wave, although often very unequally. I want to thank Eric Hirschman for lending me his competence at computer searches and for his many other suggestions.

Chapter Nine

1. Life itself has no plot. To write about it you have to impose a plot. That is what the novelist, the journalist, and any other writer must do if the story is to meet Aristotle's standard of a tale that has a "probable or necessary sequence." Real life may be more or less scripted by norms and rules, but some things just happen.

2. War is probably almost as frequent (e.g., the war against poverty, cancer, and so on; everything but a war against war).

3. Analogies are sometimes said to be the main way that science has advanced. Most of the examples I have seen use analogies to explain advances in science to the lay public (for example, the big bang). Most often scientists themselves seem to work with idealized examples (for example, Einstein's railroad trains) rather than direct analogies.

4. I still have a textbook from Biology 101, titled *The Machine of the Body*. It was a good course.

5. This would seem to apply to Lakoff 1987 as well as Reid. My own view on the issue is that grounding is less a matter of universal experience than a kind of operational assignment that gives concepts an objective basis. In this view, grounded concepts refer to something "artificially bounded" rather than given by our senses or nature.

6. For a dramatic contrast see Peter Gay's (2001) rich account of journalists' and other writers' failure to counsel patience toward the end of the Weimar Republic.

7. I recently conducted a survey of the *American Prospect, Forbes, The Economist*, and the *Weekly Standard*. All use the machine metaphor, although for different purposes. What is "neo" about conservatism is an activism in economic policy.

8. See Kay Richardson's "Signs and Wonders: Interpreting the Economy through Television" (1998), for a particularly good example of how readers assign intentions to television news.

9. My recent survey of the *American Prospect, Forbes, The Economist*, and the *Weekly Standard*. As in note 7 above, all use the machine metaphor, although they do seem to have some vocabulary tests to sort out the faithful.

10. Certainly linguistic studies indicate a "conservative tendency" the larger and more diverse the speakers of a language. Small, isolated groups rapidly undergo language change.

11. I balk at this word because much of what we "retain" most easily is fiction or opinion. The sponge conceptualization of "information" in economics and elsewhere rescues the rational action approach from obvious limitations.

12. I have located no studies that evaluate the recall of rational versus irrational stories. Fairy tales and poems, however, are very memorable (see Baddeley 1990, 177–99).

13. Big ideas like the "information society" seem to impose this sort of compliance whatever their original aspirations. A computer in every house is now considered essential. But, has there been no improvement in school performance? I remember when television was supposed to revolutionize public education ("the best teachers in every living room," it was said). There was no improvement in student performance but everybody bought a television set.

14. Autonomy being the claim that culture is only an epiphenomenon or a dependent variable that has no further consequences.

Methodological Appendix

1. Especially since the 1929 bubble is sometimes said to be partially due to enlistment of midwesterners and other novices into the stock market (Burk, 1988, 47–65 and Cowing 1965).

2. WGN radio and television were long-standing acquisitions. From here on, 1987 becomes the anthropological present. By the time this reaches the reader, however, the *Daily News* will have been sold off by the *Tribune* and the Tribune Corporation will have acquired several other businesses.

3. Most of the books on the *Tribune* are also favorable or, at least, make the argument that much of the criticism of it is unjustified. Obviously the Hearst papers have come in for more critical attention. Still, it seems that only the "conservative" press has received much critical attention. The University of Chicago library catalog includes a massive number of entries on the *New York Times* but almost all of them are authored or published by the *New York Times* itself.

4. The *Sun Times* was resold in 1985 to a local group whose editorial policy has remained as conservative as Murdoch's.

5. Neither figure includes the nine articles in 1929 and one in 1987 that were referenced on the front page but could not be found in the interior of the paper.

6. However, reporting on farming is discussed briefly in an appendix (6.2) to chapter 6.

7. These figures are approximate and based on random samples (N = 55 in 1929 and N = 43 in 1987). Column inches are approximated from the estimated number of characters in each article because there are no extant copies of the 1929 *Tribune* and the microfilm level of reduction is unknown for that year.

8. *Tribune* journalists in 1929 may have had editorial encouragement to file

more stories. The *Tribune* was promoted on the basis of its volume (Wendt 1979, 85–86), and the number of pages in each 1929 weekday edition was blazoned under the masthead. A large, blocked-out square in the upper left-hand corner advertised, "Only 2 cents."

9. The secondary literature on the two crashes is discussed in chapter 8.

10. Coding every article appearing throughout the newspapers exceeded my personal resources, which was all that I relied upon.

11. I did not compare my coding of the sample articles in 1929 with that of anyone else because the difference in vocabularies, historic persons, and general awareness of contextual events seemed to require too much training of a research assistant. Subsequently, when coding the relatively simple and formulaic articles on the stock market in both the *Tribune* and the *New York Times*, I was able to check the coding against that of a research assistant. Agreement was generally in the area of 90 to 95 percent. Nonetheless, I read and coded all the articles and, where disagreements occurred, I made the choice.

12. She was not clairvoyant. Her intent was to encourage the use of the help wanted ads to estimate the demand for labor. Indeed, they subsequently came into wide use for this purpose.

13. There were women journalists writing for the 1929 *Tribune*, although they worked almost exclusively on "women's news": beauty, clubs, food, and so on (see Wendt 1979, 492).

14. Bendere asserted that 20 percent of those buying stocks were women, although "the better class of stock brokers" were refusing to sell to them. Galbraith (1955, 80–81) and Rees (1971, 22–25) continue the image of mass participation in the 1929 stock market but later on see it more as vicarious participation in a social climate of easy money and easy virtue. Sobel (1965, 252–54) downplays the role of small, uninformed investors.

15. The joke seems to have preceded the sensational suicides that Galbraith (1955, 133–37) says contributed to the myth of a suicide wave following the 1929 crash.

16. Niekirk did write a personal column for the Sunday magazine.

17. I read both of them regularly whether or not they fell into the sample.

Works Cited

This list of references does not include the books on stock crashes discussed in chapter 7 unless they had been cited elsewhere.

Abolafia, Mitchell Y. 2005. "Making Sense of Recession." In *The Economic Sociology of Capitalism*, ed. Victor Nee and Richard Swedberg, 204–26. Princeton, NJ: Princeton University Press.

Abolafia, Mitchell, and M. Kelduff. 1988. "Enacting Market Crisis: The Social Construction of a Speculative Bubble." *Administrative Science Quarterly* 33:177–93.

Adut, Ari. 2005. "A Theory of Scandals: Victorians, Homosexuality and the Fall of Oscar Wilde. *American Journal of Sociology* 111 (1):213–48.

Alexander, Jeffrey, and Philip Smith. 2001. "The Strong Program in Cultural Theory: Elements of a Structural Hermeneutics." In *Handbook of Sociological Theory*, ed. Jonathan Turner, 135–50. New York: Springer.

Allen, Frederick Lewis. 1931. *Only Yesterday: An Informal History of the 1920s*. New York: Harper.

———. 1935. *The Lords of Creation*. Chicago: University of Chicago, Quadrangle Books.

Alonso, William, and Paul Starr, eds. 1987. *The Politics of Numbers*. New York: Russell Sage Foundation.

Alverson, Hoyt. 1991. "Metaphor and Experience: Looking Over the Notion of Image Schema." In *Beyond Metaphor*, ed. James Fernandez, 94–117. Stanford, CA: Stanford University Press.

Ambrose, Stephen E. 1971. *Rise to Globalism: American Foreign Policy, 1938–1970*. Baltimore: Penguin Books.

Anderson, Benedict. 1983. *Imagined Communities*. London: Verso.

Arbel, Avner. 1989. *Crash: Ten Days in October—Will It Strike Again?* Chicago: Longman Financial Services, Chicago.

Babson, Roger. 1935. *Actions and Reactions: An Autobiography of Roger W. Babson.* New York: Harper.

Baddeley, Alan. 1976. *The Psychology of Memory.* New York: Basic Books.

———. 1990. *Human Memory: Theory and Practice.* Boston: Allyn and Bacon.

Bailey, Stephen K. 1950. *Congress Makes a Law.* New York: Columbia University Press.

Becker, Gary S. 1976. *The Economic Approach to Human Behavior.* Chicago: University of Chicago Press.

Becker, Gary S., and Guity Nashat Becker. 1997. *The Economics of Life.* New York: McGraw-Hill.

Beckner, Stephen K. 1996 *Back from the Brink: The Greenspan Years.* New York: Wiley.

Bennett, W. Lance, and Robert Entman, eds. 2001 *Mediated Politics.* Cambridge: Cambridge University Press.

Bierman, Harold, Jr. 1991. *The Great Myths of 1929 and the Lessons to Be Learned.* New York: Greenwood Press.

Bogart, Leo. 1989. *Press and Public.* Hillsdale, NJ: Erlbaum Associates.

———. 2000. *Commercial Culture: The Media System and the Public Interest.* New Brunswick, NJ: Transaction Publishers.

Booth, Wayne. 1961. *The Rhetoric of Fiction.* Chicago: University of Chicago Press.

Bose, Mihir. 1998. *The Crash: The Fundamental Flaws Which Caused the 1987–8 World Stock Market Slump and What They Mean for Future Financial Stability.* London: Bloomsbury.

Brewer, William F. 1980. "Literary Theory, Rhetoric, and Stylistics." In *Theoretical Issues in Reading Comprehension*, ed. R. Spiro, B. Bruce, and W. Brewer, chapter 9. Hillsdale, NJ: Lawrence Erlbaum Associates.

Brewer, William F., and Brandon J. Stone. 1975. "Acquisition of Spatial Anotonym Pairs." *Journal of Experimental Psychology* 19:299–307.

Brigante, John E. 1950. *The Feasibility Dispute: Determination of War Production Objectives for 1942 and 1943.* Washington, DC: Committee on Public Administration Causes.

Briggs, Asa. 1982. *The Power of Steam.* Chicago: University of Chicago Press.

Brooks, John. 1969. *Once in Golconda.* New York: Harper and Row.

Bruck, Connie. 1988. *The Predators' Ball.* New York: Simon and Schuster.

Bryant, Jennings, and Dolf Zillmann, eds. 1986. *Media Effects.* Hillsdale, NJ: Lawrence Erlbaum Associates.

Burk, James. 1988. *Values in the Marketplace.* New York: Walter de Gruyter.

Burke, Kenneth. 1945. *A Grammar of Motives.* New York: Prentice-Hall.

———. 1950. *A Rhetoric of Motives.* New York: Prentice-Hall.

Calavita, Kitty, Henry N. Pontell, and Robert H. Tillman. 1997. *Big Money Crime*. Berkeley: University of California Press.

Campagna, Anthony S. 1987. *U.S. National Economic Policy, 1917–1985*. Westport, CT: Praeger.

Carosso, Vincent. 1970. *Investment Banking in America*. Cambridge, MA: Harvard University Press.

Chancellor, Edward. 1999. *Devil Take the Hindmost: A History of Financial Speculation*. New York: Penguin.

Chartier, Roger. 1994. *The Order of Books*. Stanford, CA: Stanford University Press.

Chatman, Seymour. 1971. *Literary Style*. Oxford: Oxford University Press.

Chernow, Ron. 1991. *The House of Morgan*. New York: Simon and Schuster.

Churchill, Allen. 1957. *The Incredible Ivar Kreuger*. New York: Rinehart.

Colander, David C., and A. W. Coats. 1989. *The Spread of Economic Ideas*. Cambridge and New York: Cambridge University Press.

Converse, Philip. 1980. *American Social Attitudes*. Cambridge, MA: Harvard University Press.

Corner, John. "Meaning, Genre, and Context." In *Mass Media and Society*, ed. J. Curran and M. Gurvitch, 267–84. London: Edward Arnold.

Cowing, Cedric. 1965. *Populists, Plungers, and Progressives*. Princeton, NJ: Princeton University Press.

Culler, Jonathan. [1975] 2000. Literary Theory. New York: Oxford University Press.

Daft, R. L., and K. E. Weick. 1984. "Toward a Model of Organizations as Interpretive Systems. *Academy of Management Review* 9:284–95.

Darnton, Robert. 1982. "What Is the History of Books." *Daedalus* 111 (Summer):65–83.

——. 1984. *The Great Cat Massacre*. New York: Random House.

——. 1989. "First Steps toward a History of Reading." *Wilson Quarterly* 13:87–102.

DiMaggio, Paul. 1997. "Culture and Cognition." *Annual Review of Sociology* (Annual Reviews, Palo Alto, CA) 23:263–87.

Dornfeld, A. A. 1983. *Behind the Front Page: The Story of the City News Bureau of Chicago*. Chicago: Academy Chicago.

Duncan, Joseph, and William H. Shelton. 1978. *Revolution in United States Government Statistics, 1926–76*, Washington, DC: U.S. Department of Commerce.

Duncan, Otis Dudley. 1972. "Federal Statistics, Non-Federal Statisticians." *Statistical Association Proceedings of the Social Statistics Section* 151–53.

——. 1984. *Notes on Social Measurement: Historical and Critical*. New York: Russell Sage Foundation.

Emmison, Michael. 1985. "Class Images of the 'Economy,'" *Sociology* 19:19–38.

Entman, Robert M. 2004. *Projections of Power*. Chicago: University of Chicago Press.

Ettema, James S., and Charles Whitney. 1994. *Audiencemaking*. Thousand Oaks, CA: Sage Publications.

Farber, David. 2002. *Sloan Rules*. Chicago: University of Chicago Press.

Fernandez, James. 1986. *Persuasions and Performances*. Bloomington: Indiana University Press.

———. 1991. *Beyond Metaphor: The Theory of Tropes in Anthropology*. Stanford, CA: Stanford University Press.

Feron, Peter. 1979. *The Origins and Nature of the Great Slump, 1929–1932*. Atlantic Highlands, NJ: Humanities Press.

Finke, Roger. 2005. *The Churching of America*. New Brunswick, NJ: Rutgers University Press.

Finke, Ronald A. 1990. *Principles of Mental Imagery*. Cambridge, MA: MIT Press.

Fischel, Daniel. 1995. *Payback: The Conspiracy to Destroy Michael Milken and His Financial Revolution*. New York: HarperBusiness.

Fish, Stanley. 1980. *Is There a Text in This Class?* Cambridge, MA: Harvard University Press.

Fisher, Irving. 1930. *The Stock Market Crash—and After*. New York: Macmillan.

Fiss, Peer, and Paul M. Hirsch. 2005. "The Discourse of Globalization." *American Sociological Review* 70:29–52.

Flash, Edward S., Jr. 1965. *Economic Advice and Presidential Leadership*. New York: Columbia University Press.

Frantz, Douglas. 1987. *Levin and Co.: Wall Street's Insider Trading Scandal*. New York: Holt.

Friedman, Milton. 1975. *There's No Such Thing as a Free Lunch*. LaSalle, IL: Open Court.

Friedman, Milton, and A. J. Schwartz. 1963. *A Monetary History of the U.S., 1867–1960*. Princeton, NJ: Princeton University Press.

Frye, Northrop. 1957. *Anatomy of Criticism*. Princeton, NJ: Princeton University Press.

Galbraith, John Kenneth. 1955. *The Great Crash, 1929*. Boston: Houghton Mifflin.

Gamson, William. 1992. *Talking Politics*. New York and Cambridge: Cambridge University Press.

Garfinkel, Harold. 1967. *Studies in Ethnomethodology*. Englewood Cliffs, NJ: Prentice-Hall.

Gay, Peter. 2001. *Weimar Culture: The Outsider as Insider*. New York: Norton.

Geertz, Clifford. 1973. *The Interpretation of Cultures*. New York: Basic Books.

Glasser, Theodore, ed. 1999. *The Idea of Public Journalism*. New York: Guilford Press.

Goffman, Erving. 1967. *Interaction Ritual*. Chicago: Aldine.

———. 1974. *Frame Analysis*. Boston: Northwestern University Press.

Goronwy, Rees. 1971. *The Great Slump*. New York: Harper and Row.

Graber, Doris. 1984. *Processing the News*. New York: Longmans.

———. 2002. *Mass Media and American Politics,*. Washington, DC: CQ Press.

Gramsci, Antonio. 1980. *Hegemony and Revolution*. Berkeley: University of California Press.

Grant, James. 1992. *Money of the Mind: Borrowing and Lending in America from the Civil War to Michael Milken*. New York: Farrar Straus Giroux.

Griswold, Wendy. 1986. *Renaissance Revivals*. Chicago: University of Chicago Press.

Gusfield, Joseph R. 2000. *Performing Action*. New Brunswick, NJ: Transaction Publishers.

Hill, Christopher. 1972. *The World Turned Upside Down*. London: Pelican Books.

Hirsch, Paul. 1986. "From Ambushes to Golden Parachutes: Corporate Takeovers as an Instance of Cultural Framing and Institutional Integration." *American Journal of Sociology* 91:800–837.

Hirsch, Paul, and Michaela D. Soucey. 2006. "Organizational Restructuring and Its Consequences." *Annual Review of Sociology*, Palo Alto, CA, Annual Reviews, 171–89.

Hirsch, Paul, and Tracy A. Thompson. 1994. "The Stock Market as Audience." In *Audiencemaking*, ed. James S. Ettema. Thousand Oaks, CA: Sage Publications.

Jacobs, Mark D. 1990. *Screwing the System and Making It Work: Juvenile Justice in the No-Fault Society*. Chicago: University of Chicago Press.

———. 2005. "The Culture of Savings and Loan Scandal in the No-Fault Society." In *The Blackwell Companion to the Sociology of Culture*, ed. Mark D. Jacobs and N. Hanrahan, 364–89. Malden, MA: Blackwell.

James, Harold. 2001. *The End of Globalization: Lessons from the Great Depression*, Cambridge, MA: Harvard University Press.

Johansson, Stig, and Knut Hofland. 1989. *Frequency Analysis of English Vocabulary and Grammar*, vols. 1 and 2. Oxford: Clarendon.

Johnson, E. A. 1944. "Economics and the Economy." *Journal of Political Economy* 52 (June):160–63.

Johnstone, John, et al. 1972. "Professional Values of American Newsmen." *Public Opinion Quarterly* 36:522–40.

Keynes, John Maynard. 1920. *The Economic Consequences of the Peace*. New York: Harcourt Brace.

———. 1933. *The Means to Prosperity*. New York: Harcourt Brace.

———. 1936. *The General Theory of Employment, Interest, and Money*. London: Macmillan.

Kindleberger, Charles P. 1978 [rev. ed. 2000]. *Mania, Panics, and Crashes*. New York: Wiley.

———. 2000. *Mania, Panics, and Crashes*, rev. ed. New York: Wiley.

Klein, Maury. 2001. *Rainbow's End: The Crash of 1929*. New York: Oxford University Press.

Knight, Frank A. 1999. *Selected Essays*. Chicago: University of Chicago Press.

Kornbluth, Jesse. 1992. *Highly Confident: The Crime and Punishment of Michael Milken*. New York: Morrow.

Lakoff, George. 1987. *Women, Fire, and Dangerous Things*. Chicago: University of Chicago Press.

———. [1996] 2002. *Moral Politics*. Chicago: University of Chicago Press.

———. 2004. *Don't Think Like an Elephant*. White River, VT: Chelsea Green Publishing.

Lakoff, George, and Mark Johnson. 1980. *Metaphors We Live By*. Chicago: University of Chicago Press.

Lakoff, George, and Mark Turner. 1989. *More Than Cool Reason*. Chicago: University of Chicago Press.

Lakoff, Robin Talmach. 2000. *The Language War*. Berkeley: University of California Press.

Lang, Gladys, and Kurt Lang. 1983. *The Battle for Public Opinion*. New York: Columbia University Press.

Levine, Dennis. 1991. *Inside Out: An Insider's Account of Wall Street*. New York: G. P. Putnam's Sons.

Levitt, Arthur. 2002. *Take on the Street*. New York: Pantheon Books.

Lewis, Michael. 1989. *Liar's Poker*. New York: Penguin Books.

———. 2000. *The New New Thing*. New York: Penguin Books.

Lippman, Walter. [1927] 1993. *The Phantom Public*. New Brunswick, NJ: Transaction Publishers.

Lowenstein, Roger. 2004. *Origins of the Crash: The Great Bubble and Its Undoing*. New York: Penguin.

Lucie-Smith, Edward. 1981. *The Art of Caricature*. Ithaca, NY: Cornell University Press.

MacKenzie, Donald, and Yuval Millo. 2003. "Negotiating a Market, Performing Theory: The Historical Sociology of a Financial Derivatives Exchange." *American Journal of Sociology* 109:107–45

MacIntyre, Alasdair. 1981. *After Virtue*. Notre Dame, IN: University of Notre Dame Press.

Madrick, Jeffrey G. 1987. *Taking America: How We Got from the First Hostile Takeover to Megamergers, Corporate Raiding, and Scandal.* New York: Bantam Books.

May, Reuben Buford. 2001. *Talking at Trena's.* New York: New York University Press.

Mayer, Martin. 1992. *Stealing the Market.* New York: Basic Books.

———. 1993. *Nightmare on Wall Street: Solomon Brothers and the Corruption of the Market Place.* New York: Simon and Schuster.

Maynard, Douglas W. 2003. *Bad News, Good News: Conversational Order in Everyday Talk end Clinical Settings.* Chicago: University of Chicago Press.

McCloskey, Donald N. 1985. *The Rhetoric of Economics.* Madison: University of Wisconsin Press.

McKeon, Richard. 1987. *Rhetoric: Essays in Invention and Discovery.* Woodbridge, CT: Ox Bow Press.

McPhatter, William, ed. 1980. *The Business Beat.* Indianapolis: Bobbs-Merrill.

Mead, George Herbert. 1956. *The Social Psychology of George Herbert Mead,* ed. Anselm Strauss. Chicago: University of Chicago Press.

Melamed, Leo. 1996. *Escape to the Futures.* New York: John Wiley and Sons.

Merton, Robert K. 1968. *Social Theory and Social Structure.* New York: Free Press.

Metz, Tim. 1988. *Black Monday.* New York: W. W. Morrow.

Miller, Merton H. 1991. *Financial Innovations and Market Volatility.* Cambridge, MA: Blackwell.

Mills, C. Wright. 1940. "Situated Action and Vocabularies of Motives." *American Sociological Review* 5(6):904–13.

Morgenson, Gretchen. 2008. "Behind Insurer's Crisis, Blind Eye to a Web of Risk." *New York Times,* September 28.

Morley, David. 1981. "The Nationwide Audience: A Cultural Postscript." *Screen Education* 39:3–14.

———. 1992. *Television, Audiences, and Cultural Studies.* London: Routledge.

———. 1993. "Active Audience Theory." *Journal of Communication* 43:13–19.

Nee, Victor, and Richard Swedberg, eds. *The Economic Sociology of Capitalism.* Princeton, NJ: Princeton University Press.

Nelson, Robert H. 2001. *Economics as Religion.* University Park: Pennsylvania State University Press.

Noelle-Neumann, Elisabeth. 1984. *The Spiral of Silence.* Chicago: University of Chicago Press.

Nord, David Paul. 2001. *Communities of Journalism.* Urbana: University of Illinois Press.

Norman, Donald. 1988. *The Psychology of Everyday Things.* New York: Basic Books.

Norton, Hugh S. 1977. *The Employment Act and the Council of Economic Advisors*. Columbia: University of South Carolina Press.

Noyes, Alexander. 1938. *The Market Place*. Boston: Houghton Mifflin.

Ogburn, William Fielding. [1922] 1965. *Social Change*. New York: Dell.

Ortony, Andrew, ed. 1993. *Metaphor and Thought*. Cambridge and New York: Cambridge University Press.

Paivio, Allan. 1990. *Images in Mind*. New York: Harvester Wheatsheaf, 1991.

Park, Robert E. 1967. *On Social Control and Collective Behavior*. Chicago: University of Chicago Press.

Parker, Richard. 2005. *John Kenneth Galbraith*. New York: Farrar, Straus and Giroux.

Parry, Milman. 1987. *The Making of Homeric Verse*. New York: Oxford University Press.

Pecora, Ferdinand. 1939. *Wall Street under Oath*. New York: Simon and Schuster.

Perlman, Mark. 1987. "Political Purpose and the National Accounts." In *The Politics of Numbers*, ed. William Alonso and Paul Starr, 133–52. New York: Russell Sage Foundation.

Perrow, Charles. 1984. *Normal Accidents: Living with High Risk Technologies*. New York: Basic Books.

Platt, Harlan D. 1994. *The First Junk Bond: A Story of Corporate Boom and Bust*. Armonk, NY: M. E. Sharpe.

Ponnuru, Ramesh. 2007. "The Home Front." *National Review*, February 12, 17–26.

Propp, Vladimir. 1968. *Theory and History of Folklore*. Minneapolis: University of Minneapolis Press.

Radway, Janice. 1984. "Interpretive Communities and Variable Literacies: The Function of Romance Reading." *Daedalus* 113:49–73.

Reid, Thomas. 1997. *An Inquiry into the Human Mind*, ed. Derek Brookes. University Park: Pennsylvania State University Press.

Richardson, Kay. 1997. "Signs and Wonders: Interpreting the Economy through Television." In *Approaches to Media Discourse*, ed. Allan Bell and Peter Garrett, 220–50. Malden, MA: Blackwell.

Ritchie, D. 1975. "The Pecora Wall Street Expose." In *Congress Investigates*, ed. A. Schlesinger and R. Burns, vol. 4, 2555–732. New York: Chelsea House.

———. 1977. "The Legislative Impact of the Pecora Investigations." *Capital Studies* (Fall):87–101.

Roosevelt, Franklin. 1933, *Looking Forward*. New York: John Day.

Rosch, Eleanor. 1973. "On the Internal Structure of Perceptual and Semantic Categories." In *Cognitive Development and the Acquisition of Language*, ed. T. E. Moore, 112–43. New York: Academic Press.

———. 1975. "Universal and Cultural Specifics in Human Categorization." In

Cross Cultural Perspectives on Learning, ed. R. Brislin, S. Bochner, and W. Lonner. New York: Halsted Press.

Rosch, Eleanor, and Barbara B. Lloyd, eds. 1978. *Cognition and Categorization.* Hillsdale, NJ: Erlbaum Associates.

Rosch, Eleanor, and Carolyn B. Mervis. 1975. "Family Resemblances: Studies in the Internal Structure of Categories." *Cognitive Psychology* 7:573–605.

Rosch, Eleanor, and Carolyn B. Mervis. 1977. "Children's Sorting: A Reconceptualization Based on the Nature of Abstraction in Natural Categories." In *Readings in Child Development,* ed. Russell Smart and Mollie Smart, 140–48. New York: Macmillan.

Rosch, Eleanor, et al. 1976. "Basic Objects in Natural Categories." *Cognitive Psychology* 8:382–439.

Rosmarin, Adena. 1985. *The Power of Genre.* Minneapolis: University of Minnesota Press.

Rothschild, Emma. 2001. *Economic Sentiments.* Cambridge, MA: Harvard University Press.

Rothschild, John. 1991. *Going for Broke: How Robert Champeau Bankrupted the Retail Industry, Jolted the Junk Bond Market, and Brought the Booming Eighties to a Crashing End.* New York: Simon and Schuster.

Sahlins, Marshall. 1978. *Culture and Practical Reason.* Chicago: University of Chicago Press.

Sarnoff, Paul. 1967. *Jesse Livermore: Speculator King.* Palisades Park, NJ: Investor's Press.

Schegloff, Emanuel. 1987. "Between Macro and Micro: Context and Other Connections." In *The Micro-Macro Link,* ed. J. Alexander, R. M. B. Geisen, and N. Smelser. Berkeley: University of California Press.

Schlesinger, Arthur, ed. 1975. *Congress Investigates.* New York: Chelsea House.

Schorske, Carl. 1981. *Fin-de-siècle Vienna.* New York: Random House.

Schudson, Michael. 1978. *Discovering the News: A Social History of American Newspapers.* New York: Basic Books.

———. 1989. "Perspectives from Media Studies on the Efficacy of Symbols: How Culture Works." *Theory and Society* 18:153–80.

———. 1995. *The Power of News.* Cambridge, MA: Harvard University Press.

———. 1998. *The Good Citizen.* Cambridge, MA: Harvard University Press.

Schumpeter, Joseph A. 1942. *Capitalism, Socialism, and Democracy.* New York: Harper.

———. 1954. *History of Economic Analysis.* New York: Oxford University Press.

———. [1939] 1964. *Business Cycles: A Theoretical, Historical, and Statistical Analysis of the Capitalist Process.* New York: McGraw-Hill.

Schwartz, Barry. 1981. *Vertical Classification.* Chicago: University of Chicago Press.

Seligman, Joel. 2000. *The Transformation of Wall Street*, 3rd. ed. New York: Aspen Publishers.

Simon, Herbert. 1974. "How Big Is a Chunk." *Science* 183:482–88.

Smith, Philip. 2005. *Why War?* Chicago: University of Chicago Press.

Snow, David, E. Burke Rochford Jr., Steven K. Worden, and Richard D. Benford. 1986. *American Sociological Review* 51:464–81.

Sobel, Robert. 1965. *The Big Board: A History of the New York Stock Market.* New York: Free Press.

———. 1968. *The Great Bull Market: Wall Street in the 1920s.* New York: Norton.

———. 1977. *Inside Wall Street.* New York: Norton.

———. 1988. *Panic on Wall Street: A Classic History of America's Financial Disasters with a New Exploration of the Crash of 1987*, rev. ed. New York: Dutton.

———. 1991. *The Life and Times of Dillon Read.* New York: Dutton.

———. 1993. *Dangerous Dreamers: The Financial Innovations from Charles Merrill to Michael Milken.* New York: John Wiley.

———. 1998. *Coolidge: An American Enigma.* Washington, DC: Regnery.

Somers, Margaret R. 1992. "Narrativity, Narrative Identity, and Social Action." *Social Science History* 16:591–630.

Somers, Margaret R., and Fred Block. 2005. "Two Hundred Years of Welfare Debate." *American Sociological Review* 70:260–87.

Soros, George. 1998. *The Crisis of Global Capitalism.* New York: Public Affairs.

———. 2002. *On Globalization.* New York: Public Affairs.

———. 2008. *The New Paradigm for Financial Markets.* New York: Public Affairs.

Sparling, Earl. 1930. *Mystery Men of Wall Street.* New York: Greenberg.

Steffens, Lincoln. 1931. *The Autobiography of Lincoln Steffen.* New York: Harcourt, Brace.

Stein, Benjamin. 1992. *A License to Steal: The Untold Story of Michael Milken and the Conspiracy to Bilk the Nation.* New York: Simon and Schuster.

Stevens, Mark. 1987. *The Insiders: The Truth beyond the Scandal Rocking Wall Street.* New York: Putnam.

Stewart, James. 1991. *Den of Thieves.* New York: Simon and Schuster.

Stiglitz, Joseph. 2002. *Globalization and Its Discontents.* New York: Norton.

Stillman, Richard J. 1986. *Dow Jones Industrial Averages.* Homewood, IL: Dow Jones and Irwin.

Suttles, Gerald. 1968. *The Social Order of the Slum.* Chicago: University of Chicago Press.

———. 1990. *The Man-Made City.* Chicago: University of Chicago Press.

Swidler, Ann. 1986. "Culture in Action: Symbols and Strategies." *American Sociological Review* 51:23–86.

———. 2001. *Talk of Love: How Culture Matters*. Chicago: University of Chicago Press.

Taylor, Mark C. 2004. *Confidence Games*. Chicago: University of Chicago Press.

Thaler, R. 1987. "The January Effect." *Economic Perspectives* 1:197–201.

Thornton, Brian. 1998. "Gospel of Fearlessness or 'Outright Lies': A Historical Examination of Magazine Letters to the Editor." *American Journalism* 15 (Spring):37–57.

Tompkins, Jane P., ed. 1980. *Reader Response Criticism*. Baltimore: Johns Hopkins University Press.

Toulmin, Stephen. 1990. *Cosmopolis*. Chicago: University of Chicago Press.

———. 2001. *Return to Reason*. Cambridge, MA: Harvard University Press.

Toulmin, Stephen, and June Goodfield. 1962. *The Architecture of Matter*. Chicago: University of Chicago Press.

———. 1965. *The Discovery of Time* New York: Harper and Row.

Tuchman, Gaye. 1978. *Making News*. New York: Free Press.

Unger, Rudolph M. 1991. *The Chicago Tribune News Staff: 1929s–1960s*. Unpublished manuscript.

U.S. Securities and Exchange Commission. February 1988. *The October 1987 Market Break*. Washington, DC: U.S. Government Printing Office.

Wagner-Pacifici, Robin Erica. *The Art of Surrender: Decomposing Sovereignty at Conflict's End*. Chicago: University of Chicago Press, 2005.

Waldrop, Frank. 1966. *McCormick of Chicago*. Westport, CT: Greenwood Press.

Walter, Ingo. 1990. *The Secret Money Market: Inside the Dark World of Tax Evasion, Financial Fraud, Insider Trading, Money Laundering, and Capital Flight*. New York: Harper and Row.

Wason, P. C. 1968. "Reasoning about a Rule." *Quarterly Journal of Experimental Psychology* 20:273–81.

Weick, Karl. 1995. *Sensemaking in Organizations*. Thousand Oaks, CA: Sage Publications.

Wendt, Lloyd. 1979. *Chicago Tribune: The Rise of a Great American Newspaper*. Chicago: Rand McNally.

White, Eugene Nelson. 1990. *Crashes and Panics*. Homewood, IL: Dow Jones-Irwin.

White, Hayden. 1978. *Tropics of Discourse*. Baltimore: Johns Hopkins University Press.

White, William Allen. 1938. *A Puritan in Babylon*. Gloucester, MA: Patterson Smith.

Wood, Christopher. 1989. *Boom and Bust*. New York: Atheneum.

Woodward, Bob. 2000. *Maestro: Greenspan's Fed and the American Boom*. New York: Simon and Schuster.

Yates, Frances A. 1966 *The Art of Memory* Chicago: University of Chicago Press.

Index

Abolafia, Mitch, 8
academy, construction of language and, 12
Adams, R. L., 124
agency. *See* scene and agency, journalists'
    use of
Age of Aquarius, 180
Aggarual, Reena, 125
agriculture: cartoons and, 107–8, 220n14;
    Coolidge prosperity and, 220n5; farm
    news and, 17–18, 134–35, 141–42, 199,
    200; farm relief and, 127, 128; "Radical
    Republicans" and, 120; tariffs and, 124
A.I.G., xv
Alexander, Jeffrey, 194–95, 196
Allais, Maurice, xiii
Allen, F. L., 178, 198, 224n19
American Economic Association, 24, 31,
    39–40, 214n25
American Economic Congress, 28
American Prospect, 225n7
American Sociological Association, viii
analogies, limitations of, 188, 225n3
AP (Associated Press). *See* Associated
    Press (AP)
Archimedean point, 73, 81
Aristotle, 47, 48–49
Arndt, Michael, 208
Art of Memory, The (Yates), 73–74, 111
Associated Press (AP), 97
Ayres, Leonard, 23, 32

Babson, Roger, 126, 131, 140, 142
Baddeley, Alan, 74, 111
Bad News, Good News (Maynard), 220n3

balance, versus objectivity, 216n9
banking, shadow system of, xiii–xv
Bank of England, 218n13
Baruch, Bernard, 39, 215n36
Bateson, Gregory, 7
Becker, Howard, 14
Bellow, Saul, 148
Bendere, Edward, 204, 227n14
Bezanson, Anne, 124, 204, 227n12
Binder, Alan, 125
Birch, David, 124–25
Black, John D., 124
Block, Fred, 211n1
Boesky, Ivan, 169, 170, 174
Bogan, Jim, 101
Bonfire of the Vanities (Wolfe), 224n26
boosterism, economic crisis of 2008 and, x
Brewer, William F., 217n16
Bridgeman, P. T., 12
Brooks, John, 198
Brown Corpus, 214n17
Bruck, Connie, 178
Brush, M. C., 158–59
Buffet, Warren, ix, xvi
Burk, James, 168, 198
Burke, Kenneth: dramatisms and, 12–15,
    46, 111, 212nn14–15, 216n3; Erving
    Goffman and, 212n13; influence of,
    212n13; on intentionality, 219n2; pen-
    tad of, ix; on scene and agency, 88, 89;
    tropes and, 45–46, 72–73, 111, 212n15,
    217–18n2
Bush, George H. W., 170
business and government, 32–33, 77

business cycle, 18–23, 116, 118–26
Business Cycles (Schumpeter), 178
business owners, glamorization of, 117–18
Business Week, xii–xiii

Calavita, Kitty, xiii
Calvin, John, 193
capitalism: agriculture and, 135; as concept, 214n23; "Cowboy Capitalism" and, 131; violations of pure version of, 222n2
Capone, Al, 223n10
Caraway, Thaddeus, 128
Carter, Jimmy, 125
cartoons: forms of, 100–101, 219n7; gestalt and, 88, 110; inanimate objects in, 105, 110; in Japan, 219n11; movie-making and, 219n8; as narrative, 100–101; in 1929 versus 1987, 102–5, 107–10; party line and, 99–100; personae and, 101–5, 219–20n13; purpose of, 99; readers' understanding of, 100, 219n9; reusable stock and, 112; sequence of text and action in, 101, 219n11
casuistries, 13, 212n11
CEOs (chief executive officers), glamorization of, 117–18
Cermak, Anton, 148
Chancellor, Edward, 131, 179, 224n22
charity, newspaper readers' attitude toward, 142
Chernow, Ron, 129
Chicago Daily News, 199
Chicago Daily Tribune. See *Chicago Tribune*
Chicago Futures Exchange, 209
Chicago Herald, 137–38
Chicago Sun Times, 199, 226n4
Chicago Tribune: academic economists in, 123–24; article credits in, 205–7; books about, 226n3; business cycle and, 19, 20–22, 115; business section of, 17–18, 213n3, 220n1; canon of corruption and, 176; cartoons in, 99–100, 110; as *Chicago Daily Tribune*, 197; circulation of, 197; commercial press era and, 138, 221–22n2; conservative bias of, 122, 198–99; continuity of rhetoric and, 6–7; "Dewey defeats Truman" and, 215n39; distribution of journalistic attention in,

208; economic policy as romance in, 86; economists and, 126; *economy* as word in, 23–24, 205, 213n12; Arthur Sears Henning and, 39; heroes of capitalism in, 77; history of, 197–200; industrial index of, 116–17, 202, 220n2; insider scandal in, 171–72, 224n24; journalists at, 205–8, 226–27n8; letters to the editor in, 137–38; on National Industrial Recovery Act (NIRA), 18; on New Deal, 22; after 1929 crash, 122, 127–28; after 1987 crash, 129; Pecora hearings in, 159; on political parties and investigations, 223n13; price of, 226–27n8; John Q. Public in, 218n15, 219n12; reputation of, 198–99; seasonal business reporting and, 122–23; size of, 226–27n8; as source for study, 3; support for Hoover's policies in, 84; unemployment in, 76, 218n9; weekly business news cycle in, 116–18; wire services and, 97, 200, 206–8; women journalists at, 227n13; wordscapes in, 165. *See also* "Voice of the People" (*Chicago Tribune*); *specific topics of coverage*
chief executive officers. *See* CEOs (chief executive officers), glamorization of
Chomsky, Noam, 49
church, construction of language and, 12–13
Churchill, Winston, 200
circulation figures, 197
Clague, Ewan, 41
Clinton, Bill, 129
Coats, A. W., 45
cognition: culture and, x–xi; morality and, viii
Colander, David C., 45
Collins, Dorothy, 208
commodity prices, 213n9
communism, 214n23
Communities of Journalism (Nord), 137
Congress: economic expertise and, 35, 37; economic policy narratives and, 65–69, 83; national income and, 30; after 1987 crash, 170; as ogre, 79; Pecora hearings and, 156; Reagan administration and, 85–86; trade negotiations and, 121–22; in "Voice of the People," 144; whip in, 85, 219n17; wordscapes and, 95–97

contract, industrial and social, 6
Coolidge, Calvin: on business, 58; Coolidge prosperity and, 82, 127, 134–35, 155, 162, 220n5, 223n12; as defender of normalcy, 86; as hero of economic policy romance, 86; natural narrative of business and, 84; policies of, 127; Ronald Reagan and, 69; as sheltered from controversy, 83; as Silent Cal, 35
corporations: buy outs and, 125, 142, 145; Corporate America dramatism and, 75; invention of, 39; merger mania and, 174–75, 180; takeovers and, 153–55, 168, 170, 174–75, 179–80, 218n12; valuation of firms and CEOs and, 222–23n3
corruption: canon of, 176–79, 181–83; individual versus systemic, xiii; no-fault society and, x
Cosmopolis, 5
"Cowboy Capitalism" (Reagan), 131
Cowing, Cedric, 198
Crawford, Arthur, 207, 208
crime: books on, 181–83; versus ethics violations, 223n4; as fuel for purifying flames, 179; as innovation, 153–55; insider trading and, 171–72; in 1929 versus 1987, 169; syndicates and, 223n10; varying coverage of by type, 171–72, 224n25; Wall Street crime waves and, 168–69
crowd control, as role of business press, viii
cultural objects, durability of, 193
culture: autonomy of, 194–95, 226n14; causation and, 195–96; cognition and, x–xi; dramatisms and, 190–96
culture, sociology of, viii–ix

Darnton, Robert, 137
Darwin, Charles, 71
defense spending, 126
de Lama, George, 208
Democratic Party, 84
depression. see Great Depression
derivatives, ix, xiii–xiv, 178–79, 222–23n3
Dewey, Thomas, 215n39
dictionary, 12–13
DiMaggio, Paul, 111, 192
dollar narrative, 70
Dow Jones Industrial Average: business news cycle and, 116–17; Chicago Tribune's industrial index and, 220n2; dollar narrative and, 70; economic crisis of 2008 and, ix–x; measurement of movement in, 131–32; narrative of in 1987, 63–64, 217n18; reasons for stock market changes and, 221n19; research methodology and, 202; word analysis and, 63–64
dramatisms: agency and, 57; big ideas and, 193; Kenneth Burke and, 13–15, 46; business and government, 217n14; of business in 1929, 74–76, 90–91; crime as innovation and, 154; cultural studies and, 190–96; daily news and, 74; definition of, 13, 212n12; economy as machine and, 46, 51, 76–78; foreign policy narratives and, 69; frame analysis and, 12; genre and, 193–94; grounding of, 196; of Paul Hirsch, 179–80; insider scandal and, 171, 172, 174; master metaphors and, 216n3, 217n22; medical, 51; memory and, 72–74, 176; news as thermostat and, 190–91; persistence of, 196; power of, 188–89; problematic nature of, 190–91; readers as coauthors and, 136; resonation and, 194; system failure and, 176; tropes and, 47, 217–18n2; "Voice of the People" and, 143–46; wordscapes and, 97, 219n3. See also stories; specific dramatisms
Dun and Bradstreet, 122
Duncan, Otis Dudley, 117
Durkheim, Émile, 82–83

economic collapse, maps of reality and, ix
Economic Consequences of the Peace (Keynes), 31
economic crisis of 1929: academic economists on, 123–24, 126, 131; aftermath of, 6, 154; authorities on economy during, 35–36, 37; blame for, 122, 204, 209, 227n14; business cycle and, 18–21, 115; business news cycle and, 117; in canon of corruption, 177–78, 179, 181–83; cartoons and, 102–5, 107–10; colorful characters and, 224n21; congressional and presidential narratives of, 66–68; dramatisms and, 15, 74–76, 90–91; Florida land boom and, 224n19; front page economic news preceding, 82; innovation

economic crisis of 1929 (*continued*)
and, 155; insider trading and, 171–72;
Marshallian economics and, 16; master narrative of, 47; as national cleansing, 179; Pecora hearings and, 81, 162,
218n13; personae in, 77, 78–80, 82–84;
photographic record of, 224n23; presidential and economic wordscape and,
95–97; presidential response to, 127–
28; press's contribution to, 141, vii; reasons for stock market changes and,
132–34; seasonal business news and,
118–20, 122–23; stock market narrative
and, 61–62; stock market wordscape
and, 94–95; suggested solutions for,
141–42; suicide wave following, 227n15;
vocabulary of business and, 58–59;
"Voice of the People" and, 139–46. *See
also* Great Depression; Marshallian
economics
economic crisis of 1987: academic economists on, 123, 124–26, 131; aftermath of, 6, 154; authorities on economy during, 36–37; business cycle and,
115; business news cycle and, 117; in
canon of corruption, 182–83; cartoons
and, 102–5, 107–10; causes of, 170–71;
as comedy, 168–69, 174–75, 179; congressional and presidential narratives
of, 66–68; corporate takeovers and,
218n12; crime wave and, 168–69; economic indicator narrative and, 70; economic machine dramatism and, 76–
78; economic machine wordscape and,
92–94; innovation and, 155; insider
scandal and, 81, 169–75, 218n14; master narrative of, 46–47, 53; merger mania and, 174; personae in, 77, 80–82,
85–86, 172; "predisposition to believe"
and, 130; presidential and economic
wordscape and, 96–97; presidential response to, 128–29; press's contribution
to, vii; probability of, 224n22; reasons
for stock market changes and, 132–34,
221n19; seasonal business news and,
118–23; stock market narrative and, 61–
62; stock market wordscape and, 94–95;
suggested solutions for, 142–43; "Voice
of the People" and, 139–46; *Wall Street
Journal* analysis of, 129–30

economic crisis of 2008, ix–xi, xvi
economic indicator narrative, 70
economic policy, 65–70, 217n1
economics: efficient market theory and,
222–23n3; institutional, 17; *macroeconomics* as word and, 214n20; popular, 139–43; post-1929 revolution in, 16;
post-Keynesian, 155; readers' lack of familiarity with, 45; religion and, 211n1;
unified conception of, 212–13n2. *See
also* Keynesian economics; Marshallian
economics; Reaganomics
"Economic Scene" (Silk), 55–57, 216n11
Economist, 30, 225n7
economists: as academic experts, 123–26,
131; on chance in 1987 crash, 224n22;
influence of on business, 32; jazz age,
75, 79–80, 84, 126, 221n13; as monsters,
222n8
economy: bubbles in, 131, 226n1; as casino, xi, xii–xiii; definition of, 23–24,
26–27, 29–30, 38, 213n15; early users
of concept of, 38–41; as engine, 5; entitlement and, 37–38; as expert knowledge, 35–37; figurative grounding of,
xi–xii; freight haulage as measure of,
76; graphic visualization of, 35–36;
grounding of, 5, 16–41; as information system, xvi; as machine, xii, xvi,
46–58, 215n32; meaning of, viii; medical emergency narrative and, 50–52; as
national, 40; natural recovery of, 32;
as natural system, xvi, 4–5; planned,
28–29, 33–34, 39, 60, 215n36; "Robinson Crusoe," 215n32; scope of, 27, 30,
46, 214n25; as sick, xii; social contract
and, 37–38; soundness of, 129; as spectral, xiii; standardization of references
to, 29–35; temporal shifts and, 54–55;
as thrift, 23–24, 25; as unified and national, 16; virus metaphor and, xiv–xv;
vocabulary for, 45; as word, 24–29, 34–
35, 40–41, 205; word *economic* and, 24–
25; world, 29
Eder, Donna, 221n1
Edie, Lionel, 23, 32, 124
Edward Scott Beck award, 39
Eisenhower, Dwight D., 6
Emmison, Mike, 30–31, 214n24
Entman, Robert, 9

ethics, innovation and, 155
Europe, as compared to United States, 82
European Union, 189
evil, literary embodiment of, 218n7
experts: academic economists as, 123–26; businesspeople as, 115, 123; definition of, 209; economy as expert and, 35–37, 40; as personae, 77–78, 80–81, 85; research methodology and, 203; in "Voice of the People," 146

Fackler, Walter, 125, 221n11
farms. *See* agriculture
Federal Reserve: close synchronism policy of, 221n13; economic crisis of 1929 and, 122; economic crisis of 1987 and, 77; Index of Industrial Activity of, 122; jazz age economists and, 126; Charles Mitchell and, 220–21n10, 224n21; monetary policy and, 129–30, 155; as ogre, 218n11; ridicule of, 208; Scrutator on, 206; stock market and, 80, 132
Fels, Rendigs, 178
Fernandez, James, 73, 81
fiduciary responsibility, 168, 223–24n17
figurative language: analogies and, 188; behavior and, 153–54; change making and, 10–11; death of, 212n9; dramatisms and, 14; figurative ground and, xi–xii; necessity of, 192; in 1929 versus 1987, 169; as only descriptive, 169; sources for, 11, 12–13; unification of, 97; in "Voice of the People," 143–46, 150–52
finance: natural narrative of business and, 217n14; personification of, 77, 78, 218n10
financial instruments: moral ambiguity and, 178; undecipherable, xiii–xiv
Fischel, Daniel, 178
Fish, Stanley, 136
Fisher, Irving: bull market and, 221n14; in canon of corruption, 178; David Friday and, 220n9; on reflation, 21; on remedies for Great Depression, 22; in weeks before 1929 crash, 124
Forbes, 225n7
Ford, Edsel, 157–58
Ford, Henry: as business owner, 117; cartoons and, 109; as commentator on economy, 39; as national hero, 35; in

New York Times Index, 215n38; after 1929 crash, 128; optimism of, 119; profit-seeking of, 213n4
foreign policy and international trade: economic policy narratives and, 68–70, 82–86; front page coverage of, 121; as issue important to readers, 147; seasonal reporting and, 120; stock market and, 132; trade deficit and, 126. *See also* tariffs
Forrest, John, 40
frame analysis: experience and emotion and, 10–11; frames in transition and, 8–9; literal versus figurative language and, 12; media studies and, 9–13; methodology and, 7–9; persistence of frames and, 193; scene and agency and, 89; stock market narratives and, 65; vocabulary and, 11–13
Frame Analysis (Goffman), 7, 193
Francis, W. Nelson, 23
Franklin, Benjamin, 193
free enterprise, 40, 214n23
Freeman, James, 129
Friday, David: background of, 220n9; bull market and, 221n14; on credit and investments, 124; on natural recovery, 23, 32; as promoter of stocks, 126
Friedman, Milton, 71, 215n40, 220–21n10, 221n13
Frye, Northrop, 86, 175, 195, 217n19, 218n7

Galbraith, John Kenneth: in canon of corruption, 178; on *Chicago Tribune*, 198; on David Friday, 220n9; on *New York Times*, 197; on stock market crash, 125, 200, 227n14; on suicide wave, 227n15
gambling dramatism, 160–68
Garfinkel, Harold, 149
Garner, John Nance, 22
Gay, Peter, 225n6
GDP (Gross Domestic Product). *See* Gross Domestic Product (GDP)
Geertz, Clifford, ix, viii
General Theory of Employment, Interest, and Money (Keynes), 30–31, 215nn31–32
Germany, 225n6
Gilbert, Milton, 213n8, 215n34
Gilbert, Richard, 33, 215n34

Glaser, Dan, 212n13
Glass, Carter, 167, 168
Glass-Steagall Act, 168, 223n15
globalization, 6–7, 189, 211n2
GNP (Gross National Product). *See* Gross
    National Product (GNP)
Goffman, Erving, 7, 14, 65, 193, 212n13
Goforth, Wayne, 73, 74
Grammar of Motives, A (Burke), 217–18n2
Gray, William, 156
Great Crash, The (Galbraith), 178, 200
Great Depression: business cycle and, 21–
    23; corruption and, xiii; earliest men-
    tion of, 213n11; U.S. accounts system
    and, 31; word *depression* and, 128, 142,
    171. *See also* economic crisis of 1929
Greenspan, Alan, 6
Griswold, Wendy, 168, 170, 174, 175
Gross Domestic Product (GDP), 214n29
Gross National Product (GNP), 38, 214n29
grounding: of dramatisms, 196; of econ-
    omy, 5; in experience, 188, 225n5; figu-
    rative ground and, xi–xii; resonation
    and, 194; word usage and, 13
Gruber, William, 206
Gusfield, Joe, 212n13

Hansen, Alvin, 215n40
Harris, William, 126
Harrison, George, 77, 218n11
Hart, Albert, 215n40
Harvard School of Scientific Manage-
    ment, 155
Harvey, Fred, 20, 21, 206–7, 209
Haufbrauer, Gary, 126
Hearst newspapers, 226n3
Hendrick, John, 214n26
Henning, Arthur Sears: background of, 39,
    207; blame for 1929 crash and, 128; on
    business and government, 32–33; con-
    cept of economy and, 213n12; "Dewey
    defeats Truman" and, 215n39; on eco-
    nomic recovery, 22; journalistic focus
    of, 208
Herald-Times (Bloomington), 219n4
Herbie films, 49
Hermann, J. W., 142
Herrlinger, David, 129
Hirsch, Paul, 153–54, 174, 179–80, 218n12
Hirschman, Eric, 225n29

history: mnemonic effect and, 74; newspa-
    pers of the record and, 218n4
Homeric society, virtue and, 218n6
Hoover, Herbert: assurances by, 131; buy-
    at-home pleas of, 21; cabinet of, 39; car-
    toons and, 100, 104, 106, 109, 220n14;
    foreign relations and, 69; as hero, 104;
    "Hoover prosperity" and, 82, 97, 109,
    127–28, 155; hopes of, 169; journalists
    and, 35; Robert McCormick and, 84,
    221n15; moratorium on foreign debts
    and, 26; natural narrative of business
    and, 84; after 1929 crash, 127–28; on
    Peter Norbeck, 223n6; Pecora hear-
    ings and, 156; planned economy and,
    28–29; popularity of, 128; on prosper-
    ity, 16; "prosperity pow wows" and, 19,
    60, 128, 141, 143; readers' mirroring of,
    141; reelection hopes of, 156; remedies
    for depression and, 18, 213n4; secretive
    administration of, 215n37; as sheltered
    from controversy, 83; on soundness of
    economy, 129; as Superman, 144
House of Morgan, 165, 167, 223n7
housing market, xv
"How to Avoid a Slump" (Keynes), 31,
    215n32
Human Memory (Baddeley), 111
Hume, David, 71
Hutton, E. F., 224n20

ideology, popular: analogies and, 188; big
    ideas and, 193; dramatisms and, 190–
    96; problematic, 191; readers of news
    and, 189–90; stories and, 187–88
images, memory and, 72
income, national. *See* National Income and
    Product Accounts
income tax, 22
Indianapolis Star, 219n4
Indiana University, 177
individualism, no-fault society and, x
inflation, as virus, xiv
information: retention of, 192, 226n11;
    sponge concept and, 111, 226n11; tech-
    nology and, 226n13
innovation, 155, 222–23nn2–3
insider trading, 156, 168, 170–75, 224n18
institutional language, 194
International Harvester, 18

international trade. *See* foreign policy and international trade; tariffs
Internet, 222–23n3, xvi
Interpretation of Cultures, The (Geertz), viii
Iran-Contra affair, 224n20
Iron and Steel Institute, 215n37
irony, 14, 212n9, 212n15

James, Harold, 211n2
James, William, 7
Jazz Economists, 75, 79, 80, 84
Jenks, Jeremiah, 124
jobless. *See* unemployment
Johnson, Hugh, 28, 38–39, 215n36
Johnson, Mark, 212n15, 216n3
journalism: changing informants for, 4; conversation among journalists and, 201; first draft of history and, 175–76; incoherence of, 3; patience and, 189, 225n6; personification and, 73; political versus commercial press and, 138–39; readers and, 189–90, 191; unsourced articles and, 123. *See also* news, consumers of
judges, construction of language and, 12
junk bonds, 178–79

Kahn, Otto, 160, 162
Keynes, John Maynard: concept of economy and, 38, 39; economic crisis of 1929 and, 15; on economic machine, 48, 215n32; on economy as casino, xiii; *economy* as word and, xi, 27; general theory of employment and, 30–31; on investors versus speculators, 223n11; on money supply, 22; newsworthiness of, 31; on scope of economy, 214n25
Keynesian economics: dramatisms and, 15; economic regulation and, 16; machine narrative and, 54, 191, 194; 1987 economic machine wordscape and, 93; popular ideology and, 189
Kindleberger, Charles P., 178, 179
King, Martin Luther, Jr., 41
King, Wilford, 22
Klein, Julius, 127–28
Kornbluth, Jesse, 178
Kreuger, Ivan, 224n21
Krock, Arthur, 167–68

Kucera, Henry, 23
Kuznets, Simon, 29–30, 31, 213n8, 215n34, 215n40

Lakoff, George: on artificial words, 211n4; on figurative language, 10–11; grounding in experience and, 225n5; on master metaphors, 216n3; master tropes and, 212nn14–15; on personification, 72, 212n15
Lamont, Charles, 203
Lamont, Robert: background of, 39, 215n37, 220n7; concept of economy and, 38; *economy* as word and, 25–26; in *New York Times Index*, 215nn37–38; stock market crash of 1929, and, 18–19, 127–28
Lamont, Thomas, 118
Landon, Alf, 32
Langer, Susanne, 110
language. *See* figurative language; institutional language; linguistic studies; natural language
Lawson, William, 207
Legge, Alexander, 18, 135
Leland, Simeon, 215n40
Leontief, Wassily, 36
Levine, Dennis, 169, 170
Levy, Frank, 125
Lewis, Michael, 178, xiii
Liar's Poker (Lewis), 178, xiii
limited liability, vii
linguistic studies, 225n10
Lippmann, Walter, 187, 188, 190–91
Livermore, Jesse, 224n21
lobbyists, 83–84, 203, 212n1, 218n13
Locher, Dick, 99, 103, 104, 112
Locke, John, 10, 71
Los Angeles Times, xiii, 197
Lynch, Gary, 174

machine narrative of economy: active mode of, 53–54; anthropomorphism and, 49; biology and, 225n4; cartoons and, 108–9; communicability of, 49–50; globalization and, 189; Greek cycle and, 68; impersonal forces and, 209; Keynesian economics and, 54, 189, 191, 194; longtime fascination with, 216n2; versus medical emergency narrative,

machine narrative of economy (*continued*)
50–52, 54, 57–58; versus natural narrative of business, 60; 1987 personae and,
76–78; persistence of, 191; popular ideology and, 188; seasonal reporting and,
119; word analysis and, 46–49, 52–57,
216nn7–8; wordscape of, 92–94
MacIntyre, Alasdaire, 76, 218n6
MacNeley (cartoonist), 99, 104
macroeconomics, as word, 214n29
magic, innovations as, 155
Malthus, Thomas, 71
market fundamentalism, 6, 211n1
Marshall, George, 38
Marshall, Ray, 125
Marshallian economics: 1987 economic
machine wordscape and, 93; economic
crisis of 1929 and, 15, 16, 20; invisible
hand and, 58; natural narrative of busi-
ness and, 60, 84
Marshall Plan, 38
Martin, Robert, 30, 214–15n30
Marx, Karl, 187
Match King, 224n21
Mather, O. A. "Cotton," 21, 206, 207, 208
Mayer, Martin, 178
Maynard, Douglas, 8, 220n3
McCormick, Robert: *Chicago Tribune* and,
198; Henning, Arthur Sears, and, 39,
128, 207, 215n38; on Hoover's suitability,
221n15; Smoot-Hawley Tariff and, 84
McCutcheon, John T., 99
McKean, Erin, 212n10
Mead, George Herbert, 76, 154
Meade, James, 31, 39
"Means to Prosperity, The" (Keynes),
215n32
media studies, 9–13
medical narrative: cartoons and, 109; versus machine narrative, 50–52, 54, 57–
58; versus natural narrative of business,
60; 1987 personae and, 76; popular ideology and, 188; word analysis and, 51–
52, 54, 55–57, 216n7
Mellon, Andrew, 18, 122, 128, 220n7
Mellon fight, 67, 68
memory: dramatisms and, 72–74, 176; images and, 72; psychological theory and,
111; schemata and, 111, 192, 196; social,
193, 194; virtual worlds and, 110

metaphor: dead, 12; definition and mission
of, 3; dramatisms and, 217n22; frame
analysis and, 10–11; master, 179, 216n3,
217n13, 217n22; as master trope, 14;
metaphorical machines and, 187–88
methodology: autonomy of culture and,
194–95; canon of corruption and, 177,
224–25nn26–29; choice of sources and
events and, 4, 40, 197–98, 199; coding
system and, 201–5, 227nn10–11; Dow
Jones movement and, 131–32; durability of cultural objects and, 193; factor analysis and, 218n8; frame analysis
and, 7–9; front page focus and, 82, 199–
201, 219n16, 226n5; genre and, 195; insider scandal and, 224n24; length of articles and, 200, 226n7; of media studies,
9; number of articles and, 217n17; reviewers' distaste for, 217n15; Suttles as
sociologist and, ix, vii–viii, xii; "Voice
of the People" and, 138–39, 222n7,
222nn4–5; word *economy* and, 205;
word usage analysis and, 23–24, 216n4
metonyms, 3, 10–11, 14, 212n9
metrics, norms and, 117
Mexico, as compared to United States, 82
Milken, Michael, 37, 168, 169, 170, 178–79
Miller, Merton, 125, 178–79
Mills, C. Wright, 14, 195
Mind, Self, and Society (Mead), 76
Mitchell, Charles, 124, 220–21n10, 221n14,
224n21
Mitchell, Wesley C., 17, 19, 212–13n2,
213n8
Moley, "Professor," 22
monetary policy, 129–30, 155, 222n2
morality: cognition and, viii; versus efficiency, 81; innovation and, 155, 178;
insider scandal and, 174; personifica-
tion and, 73, 75–76; prescriptive stories
and, 187
Morgan, J. P., Jr., 157, 167, 223–24n17
Morgenson, Gretchen, xv
Morley, David, 137
motives, vocabularies of, 195–96
Murdoch, Rupert, 199, 226n4

narratives: alternative, 47; cartoons and,
100–101; dramatisms as, 13–14, 15;
fairy tales and, 65; literary types and,

217n19; news as first draft of history
and, 175–76; news stories and, 72; for
organized crime, 97; rhetorical function of, 70–71; romance and, 86–87,
127; scene and agency and, 89; *Star
Trek* and, 62; tennis match versus historical novel, 68; us versus them, 69;
wordscapes and, 90–99. *See also* dramatisms; stories; *specific narratives*
NASDAQ, 117, 217n18
Nathan, Robert, 29–30, 31, 38, 39, 213n8
National Accounts. *See* National Income
and Product Accounts
National Conference Board, 21
National Income and Product Accounts,
27, 29–35, 213n8, 214n26, 215n34
National Industrial Conference Board,
214–15n30
National Industrial Recovery Act (NIRA),
18, 22
National Recovery Act (NRA), 28–29, 39,
214n27, 215nn36–37
National Resource Committee, 35
natural language, 188
natural narrative of business, 58–60; *Chicago Tribune*'s conservative position
and, 122; determinism in 1929 and, 189;
finance and, 217n14; Greek cycle and,
68; Hoover economic policies and, 84;
persistence of, 191; seasonal reporting
and, 119
Nebraska Sheep Growers Association, 73
Nelson, Robert, 211n1
neoconservatism, 189, 191, 225n7
net national product, 214n29
New Deal, 6, 22, 28
news, consumers of: belief and doubt
among, 136; as interpretive communities, 137–38
New Statesman, 30
New York Daily News, 197, 198, 226n2
New York Times: analysis of reporting of,
xii; Associated Press and, 97; books
about, 226n3; on business cycle, 18–20,
21, 22; business section of, 17; circulation of, 197; concept of economy in, 30;
Depression-era austerity at, 23; economic problems as virus in, xiv–xv;
economy as casino in, xiii; *economy* as
word in, 23–24, 205; John Kenneth Gal-

braith and, 200; influence of, 197; insider scandal and, 171, 224n24; masthead of, 214n27; on National Industrial
Recovery Act (NIRA), 18; Pecora
hearings in, 159; signs of 2008 eco-
nomic crisis and, x; as source for study,
4; unemployment in, 213n13. *See also
specific topics of coverage*
New York Times Index: economy in, 23,
213n14; vocabulary changes in, 41
Nicaragua, 224n20
Niekirk, William, 206, 208, 227n16
Nixon, Richard M., 41
Noelle-Neumann, Elisabeth, 136
no-fault society, economic crisis of 2008
and, x
Norbeck, Peter, 156, 223n6
Nord, David, 137, 138, 139, 222n6
Norman, Montague, 77, 218n11
Norton, L. J., 124
Norton, Mary, 203
Noyes, Alexander D., 18, 21, 24, 178, 213n5

Obama, Barack, xiv
objectivity, 12, 216n9
October 1987 Market Break, The (SEC),
130
Ogburn, William, xii
Organization for Economic Cooperation
and Development, 208
Orr, Carey, 99
Outsiders (Burke), 212n13
Oxford English Corpus (ed. McKean),
212n10
Oxford English Dictionary, 213n15

Parson, Talcott, 195
patriotism, 40
Pecora, Ferdinand, 156–58, 160–62, 165–
68, 176, 223n14
Pecora hearings: aims of, 156–57; blame for
1929 crash and, 171; collective versus
individual malfeasance and, 223n14;
economy as casino and, xiii; Florida land boom and, 224n19; gambling
narrative and, 160–62; lobbyists and,
218n13; Mitchell, Charles, and, 220–
21n10; "new era thinking" and, 223n12;
news coverage of, 141; personae in, 81,
162–64; results of, 168; Franklin

Pecora hearings (*continued*)
  Roosevelt and, 167–68; system failure
  and, 156–59; web of influence and, 165–
  66; wordscape of, 164–65
Perlman, Mark, 214n20, 214n29
personae: in canon of corruption, 179; cartoons and, 100, 101–5, 219–20n13; corporate takeovers and, 153–54; merger
  mania and, 180; in 1929 business narrative, 74–76; in 1929 international economic policy narrative, 82–84; in 1929
  stock market narrative, 78–80; in 1987
  economic machine dramatism, 76–78;
  in 1987 international economic policy
  narrative, 85–86; in 1987 stock market
  narrative, 80–82; in 1987 Wall Street
  scandal, 172–73, 174; in Pecora hearings, 162–64; reasons for stock market
  changes and, 132–34; in "Voice of the
  People," 144–45, 148, 150–51
personification: "dead," 212n9; economic
  crisis of 1987 and, 76–78; frame analysis and, 10–11; moral space and, 73;
  product men and, 218n5; as trope, 72–
  73, 212n15; of unemployed, 78, 218n9.
  See also personae
Petty, Tom, 207, 208
Phantom Public, The (Lippmann), 187
Piaget, Jean, 111
political cartoons. *See* cartoons
politicians, construction of language
  and, 12
Pontell, Henry, xiii
Ponzi schemes, xiv
Poor Richard's Almanac (Franklin), 193
positivism, 194–96
Povich, Elaine, 208
Pratt, Ruth, 204
Prechter, Bob, 129
Predator's Ball (Bruck), 178
Presentation of Self in Everyday Life
  (Goffman), 212n13
presidency: business cycle and, 127–29;
  economic expertise and, 35, 37; eco-
  nomic policy narratives and, 65–70; imperial, 86; personification of, 82; wordscapes and, 95–97
propaganda, boomerang effect and, 136
Propp, Vladimir, 49, 65
prosperity: agriculture and, 135; cartoons

and, 108–9; Herbert Hoover on, 16;
  presidents and, 127; theory of permanent, 123; as word, 25
Protestant Ethic, 193
Public, John Q., cartoons of, 102, 218n15,
  219n12
public versus private realms, x

"Radical Republicans," 83–84, 104, 120,
  122, 140
Raskob, John, 159
Ratajczak, D., 124
rational action theory, 195–96
Reader's Guide to Periodical Literature,
  economy in, 23
Reagan, Nancy, 104
Reagan, Ronald: admission of ignorance
  by, 128, 131; adviser resignations and,
  125; aftermath of 1987 crash and, 6;
  cartoons and, 100–101, 104, 106, 109;
  "come home America" and, 85, 86; as
  confused and uninformed, 224n20; on
  currency values, 126; deification of,
  104; Depression-era legislation and,
  223n16; foreign relations and, 69, 85–
  86; as the Gipper, 71, 85; as Great Communicator, 69; as hero of economic
  policy romance, 86; on inflation, xiv; insider scandal and, 127; monetary policy of, 129; after 1987 crash, 128–29,
  170, 176; "Reagan Revolution" and, 87;
  slogans for, 149; on soundness of economy, 129. *See also* Reaganomics
Reaganomics: in 1987 wordscape, 96, 97;
  satisfaction with, 82; slogans for, 127;
  stock market crash and, 125; as Voodoo
  economics, 155
Rees, Goronwy, 227n14
reform economy, master metaphor and, 60
regulation, social, 187–96
Reid, Thomas, 188, 211n4, 225n5
religion, 191, 211n1
Republican Party, 82, 84, 140. *See also*
  "Radical Republicans"
resonation, 194
retirement accounts, innovations with, 155
Reynolds, George, 20, 21
rhetoric, 4–6
Riordan, James, 204
risk management, xiv

Rockefeller, John D., 128
Rockefeller, Percy, 159
Romer, Paul, 125
Roosevelt, Franklin: business leaders and, 214n28, 215n38; continuing debates over policies of, 189, 191; criticisms of New Deal and, 22; Glass-Steagall Act and, 168, 223n15; Hugh Johnson and, 215n36; journalistic courtesy and, 84; National Industrial Recovery Act and, 18; Pecora hearings and, 167–68; as Reagan's hero, 6; social contract and, 6
Roosevelt administration: concept of economy and, 38–39; planned economy and, 34, 60
Rubin, Robert, 129
rule of law, no-fault society and, x

Sahlins, Marshall, xi
S&P, 217n18
Sarbanes-Oxley Act, 169
savings and loan scandal, 170
SCB (Survey of Current Business). See Survey of Current Business (SCB)
scene and agency, journalists' use of, 88–89
schemata: memory and, 111, 192, 196; visual art and, 192–93
Schudson, Michael: on consumers of news, 136; frame analysis and, 8–9, 10–11, 13; on objectivity, 216n9; on social memory, 193, 194
Schultz, Charles, 23
Schumpeter, Joseph, 178, 215n40
Schwab, Charles, 128
Schwartz, A. J., 220–21n10
Schwartz, Barry, 219n5
science, construction of language and, 12–13
Scott, James, 125–26
"Scrutator," 17, 124, 206, 207, 220n8
seasonal reporting, 118–23, 131
SEC (Securities and Exchange Commission): on aftermath of 1987 crash, 6; blame for 1987 crash and, 170; as first line of defense, 173, 174; on "market break," 130, 221n17; personae in 1987 stock market and, 80; Wall Street Journal and, 129–30
Securities Act, 168
Securities and Exchange Commission

(SEC). See SEC (Securities and Exchange Commission)
Securities Exchange Act, 168
Selective Service System, 215n36
Silk, Leonard, 55–57, 216n11
Simon, Herbert, 111
Sloan, Alfred P.: background of, 39; on business and government, 32–33; businessmen's delegation to White House and, 215n38; as business owner, 117; concept of economy and, 38; economy as word and, 26; as inventor of modern corporation, 39; as national hero, 35; in New York Times Index, 215n38; optimism of, 119; on planned economy, 29, 214n28
Smith, Adam: daily vocabulary and, 71; economic machine wordscape and, 93, 196; invisible hand and, 58, 188; natural narrative of business and, 60, 84
Smith, Philip, 194–95
Smoot, Reed, 203
Smoot-Hawley Tariff, 82, 83, 84, 120
Snow, David, 211n6
Sobel, Robert, 178, 197–98, 227n14
socialism, workplace, 6–7
social movements, 11, 211n6
Social Order of the Slum (Suttles), vii–ix
social regulation. See regulation, social
social science, popular ideology and, 187–88
sociology of culture, viii–ix
Somers, Margaret, 211n1
Soros, George, x, xvi, 6, 129, 211n2
source domain, 10, 11, 211n4
Soviet Union, 214n23
"Spark Plug Boys," 33, 215n34
speculation: Hoover administration and, 128; spectral economy and, xiv; stock market in 1929 and, 78
Sprague, O. M. W., 215n40
Sprinkel, Beryl, 125
Star Trek, 62
statistics, as backward looking, 125
Stewart, Charles, 124
Stigler, George, 126
stock market: bulls and bears in, 81, 156, 162; business news cycle and, 117, 118; cartoons and, 105; computer trading and, 125; currency values and, 126;

stock market (*continued*)
front page coverage and, 121, 220n6;
gambling and, 160–62; "glamour" or
"household" stocks and, 132; Internet
day trading and, 222–23n3; manic public and, 162–64; narratives of, 60–63,
64–65, 79, 217n18; before 1987 crash,
129–30; personae in, 78–82, 132–34;
profit taking and, 117; reasons given for
changes in, 132–34, 221n19; seasonal
reporting and, 120; valuation of firms
and CEOs and, 222–23n3; valuation of
stocks and, 129; word analysis and, 61–
62; wordscapes of, 93–94. *See also* Dow
Jones Industrial Average
Stone, Richard, 31, 39
stories: dramatisms as, 13, 15; plot and,
225n1; popular ideology and, 187; rational versus irrational, 226n12. *See also*
dramatisms; narratives
Structure of the American Economy, The,
35–36
suicide, 204, 227n15
Summers, Lawrence, 125
Survey of Current Business (*SCB*), 30,
31, 36
Sutherland, Edwin, 214n25, 216n41
Suttles, Gerald, ix, vii–ix, xii, 3
Swidler, Ann, 8, 190–93
synecdoche, as master trope, 14

tariffs, 82, 97, 120–21, 124, 141–42
tax cuts, 155
Taylor, Mark, xii, xiii–xiv
television, authenticity and, 101
Thaler, R., 134
*Theory of Employment, Interest, and
Money* (Keynes), 48
Time Magazine, 30
Times Index. See New York Times Index
Tompkins, Jane P., 221n1
Tower Commission Report, 224n20
Tribune Corporation, 226n2
tropes: cartoons and, 100; commonality of,
45; dramatism and, 47, 217–18n2; mas-
ter, 14, 212nn14–15; mastery of, 218n3;
movement of subjects and, 73; personi-
fication as, 72–73; resonation and, 194;
scene and agency and, 89
Truman, Harry S., 6, 215n39

Uncle Sam, cartoons and, 104, 106
unemployment: definition of, 213n13; "idle
workers" and, 22, 76, 77, 218n9; jobless as persona and, 78; in "Voice of the
People," 143
University of Michigan, 119
USA Today, 197

virtue, 76, 218n6
visual art, 192–93
vocabulary: Associated Press's standardization of, 97; in canon of corruption,
179; entry into corpus by, 212n10; established and novel use of, 11–12; formalization of, 13; genre versus metaphor
and, 179; insider scandal and, 173–74,
224n24; mnemonic value of, 155; of motives, 195–96; natural language versus artificial words and, 211n4; Pecora
hearings and, 158, 160–62; persistence
of, 191–92; problematic ideology and,
191; in "Voice of the People," 150–52;
war and, 225n2
"Voice of the People" (*Chicago Tribune*):
interpretive communities and, 148–49;
issues important to readers in, 146–48,
149, 222n9; methodology and, 138–39;
personae in, 144–45, 148, 150–51; popular economics and, 139–43; readers'
dramatism of 1929 crash and, 143–46;
repeated vocabulary in, 150–52; women
on juries in, 222n6
Volcker, Paul, ix, xvi
Volstead Act, 21
Von Zukerstein, Ivan, 142

Wall Street: crime on, 154; Federal Re-
serve and, 208; as persona, 172–73, 174;
photographs of crowds and, 224n23.
See also insider trading
Wall Street Journal, 129–30, 197
Wall Street under Oath (Pecora), 223n14
Warner Brothers, 112, 219n8
War Production Board, 31, 215n33
Warva, Francis, 204
Washington Post, 197
Weber, Max, 193
Weekly Standard, 225n7
Weick, Karl, 8
Welch, Jack, 37

Weltanschauung, 5, 219n3
Wendt, Lloyd, 208
Wetmore, Frank, 20–21
WGN radio and television, 226n2
Whipple, Jacobs, 40, 216n42
White, E. N., 178, 179
White, Hayden, 111, 212nn14–15, 218n3
White, William Allen, 178
Whitney, George, 158, 162
Whitney, Richard, 158, 162, 168
Why War (Smith), 195
Wider, Pat, 207
Wittgenstein, Ludwig, 7
Wolfe, Tom, 224n26
Wolman, Leo, 215n40
women: blame for 1929 crash and, 204,
    227n14; as journalists at *Chicago Tri-
    bune*, 227n13; jury service and, 222n6,

222n9; research methodology and,
    203–4
wordscapes: of business and finance, 90–
    91, 219n3; construction of, 98, 219n5; of
    economic machine, 92–94; gestalt and,
    88, 110; individuals' reaction to eco-
    nomic crises and, vii; as landscapes, 89,
    98; of 1987 Wall Street scandal, 172–73,
    174–75; of Pecora hearings, 164–65; of
    presidency and Congress, 95–97; pur-
    pose of, 90, 98–99; of stock market,
    93–95
worldview, ideology and rhetoric and, 5
World War I, reparations payments and,
    59–60, 82

Yates, Francis, 73–74, 111
Young, F. Walt, 141